INSIDE THEIR HEADS
PSYCHOLOGICAL PROFILES
OF FAMOUS PEOPLE

Richard D. Ryder

ryelands

First published in Great Britain in 2015

British Library Cataloguing-in-Publication Data
A CIP record for this title is available from the British Library

ISBN 987 1 906551 42 1

RYELANDS
An imprint of Halsgrove
Halsgrove House
Ryelands Business Park
Bagley Road, Wellington
Somerset TA21 9PZ
T: 01823 653777
F: 01823 665294
email: sales@halsgrove.com

Part of the Halsgrove group of companies.
Information on all Halsgrove titles is available at: www.halsgrove.com

Printed by Short Run Press Ltd, Exeter

CONTENTS

THE AUTHOR

Dr Richard D. Ryder worked for many years as a clinical psychologist and psychotherapist in Oxford, and was Mellon Professor at Tulane University. He studied Experimental Psychology at Cambridge University, Social Psychology at Columbia University (New York), Clinical Psychology at Edinburgh University, and Advanced Psychotherapeutic Skills at the Tavistock Clinic. His Ph.D. is from Cambridge University. He is also an ethicist. His previous books include *Nelson, Hitler and Diana* (Imprint Academic 2009), and *Speciesism, Painism and Happiness* (Imprint Academic 2011).

INTRODUCTION

Psychobiography is an exciting new field. Trying to discover the secrets of the mind is like a search for hidden treasure. In this book I examine the lives of twenty celebrities of the past so as to unearth their often deeply concealed reasons for doing what they did. I use the same techniques as I have used as a psychologist with patients.

I want to emphasise that I am not trying to produce potted biographies or abbreviated versions of what has already been published. I am providing additional (psychological) comment. So I am supplying a great deal that is entirely new. My novel interpretations of my subjects' personalities and motivations throughout this book are completely my own. They are original. So where they are wrong, this is not the fault of the excellent biographers who have supplied such huge quantities of basic data for analysis.

Some readers may be disturbed by the open and direct way in which I deal with intimate subjects such as sex. In as much as such issues can impinge importantly upon personality formation and the behaviour of my subjects, I have had to do so, just as I would in psychotherapy. My subjects are dead and so cannot be embarrassed.

The psychotherapist is very much like a detective in trying to put together all the available clues into a coherent theory. In each case there are many possible explanations for a subject's behaviour and each one needs to be tested and, if disproved, discarded. This is a central feature in the process of psychotherapy.

In recent years there has been an upsurge of public interest in history and in the psychologies of its leading characters. So it is high time that a psychologist became involved.

I have selected my subjects more or less at random, when very good biographies have become available, and not because they offer some striking abnormalities of behaviour. I have tried in every case to keep an open mind and to allow the evidence to speak for itself. Two questions are addressed in all cases. First, how were our famous subjects' personalities created and, secondly, how did their personalities affect their actions? I feel I have made some fascinating discoveries.

(Note: References in the book are usually to page numbers together with the initials of the author.)

ACKNOWLEDGEMENTS

I would first like to thank Dr Robert Oxlade who has not only helped me with psychiatric insights, but persuaded me to take up psychobiography in the first place. Dr Michael Hession, too, has encouraged me to break new ground. Professors Joao and Hugh Denman have also assisted me immensely. I also thank several distinguished historians for their encouragement, including Dr Alison Weir, Dr Ian Mortimer and Professor Margaret MacMillan. I am grateful to Dr Malcolm Warner for medical information.

My main debt however, must be to the great biographers who have discovered and recorded so much about the lives of the subjects of this book. They have ploughed the field, turning up many thousands of fascinating nuggets of information for me to seize upon. It has been a joint archaeological endeavour. They have done the excavations while I have merely made some interpretations. I feel a deep debt of gratitude and respect to them for their expertise. I am grateful also to Simon Butler of Halsgrove for his creative support.

Finally, I must thank my colleague Barbara Gardner who has typed and edited my often shambolic offerings. Without her there would have been utter chaos.

1

THOMAS HARDY (1840 – 1928)

Novelist and Poet

Thomas was born, apparently lifeless, at eight o'clock on the morning of 2 June 1840 in the hamlet of Higher Bockhampton near Dorchester in the county of Dorset. He was so weak that his survival remained doubtful for days. Thomas's mother, Jemima, had wanted to call her first child Christopher, but family tradition prevailed and, like his father and grandfather before him, the child was christened 'Thomas'. His father was a tall, strong, fine-looking and kindly man who had inherited the small family building business when his father had died in 1837. On Sundays Thomas (senior) played the violin in the local church at Stinsford, and it was here, probably in 1835, that he met his future wife Jemima. In the summer of 1839 she had become pregnant and, under pressure from his brother-in-law, Thomas reluctantly married her on 21 December of that year. Our subject, Thomas, was born five months later.

The family home was a thatched cob cottage, almost surrounded by heath and woodland, at the end of a line of cottages inhabited mostly by other working people. The hamlet lacked shops, village green or church, but within two miles there were large houses and the county town of Dorchester itself.

Jemima Hand (the writer's mother) had been born in the north of the county in 1813, in the village of Melbury Osmond, the fifth child in a family of seven, her mother Betty Swetman, from well-established yeoman stock. Like her daughter, Betty too had become pregnant out of wedlock and been married in a hurry and against her father's wishes to the handsome George Hand, the sometime servant of the village clergyman. The new family proved an unhappy one and George took to drink. Often he was out of work and sometimes violent. Betty tried to escape her hardships by reading sophisticated works by Addison, Steele, Milton, Richardson and Fielding. She wore pretty clothes and, following Culpepper, dispensed herbal remedies to the sick of the village. Betty felt hard done by, repeating the phrase – "I should not have been poor if right had took its place" (5). This reflected her feeling that she had been forced to marry beneath her class, thereby losing both the respect of her father and his material support. Betty also missed the care of her mother Maria who had died two years before her daughter's unfortunate pregnancy. Betty had thus lost simultaneously her social standing and the hope of any inheritance from her father's estate. So when her father and husband died in the same year, Betty found herself alone with her seven children and no income. She received some help from the Poor Law Overseers of the parish but this was both meagre and reluctant.

We can see that the childhood years of the writer's mother, Jemima Hand, were thus filled with the sort of hardships eventually to be found in so many of Hardy's novels. The writer's grandfather George Hand was not only violent, impecunious and drunken, he also had another woman. He died when Jemima was nine, and his widow Betty buried him beside his mistress, as Bathsheba buried Troy in Fanny's grave in *Far from the Madding Crowd*.

Jemima would often allude to the poverty and bleakness of her childhood to her son Thomas, telling him she had suffered "some very distressful experiences of which she could never speak… without pain". We can only speculate as to what these were, but Claire Tomalin has suggested that one may have been when she had stolen a book. Jemima merely told her son that she had once seen a "child whipped at the cart-tail round Yeovil for stealing a book from a stall". Was this in fact Jemima herself? Clearly, her childhood had been one of extreme and barefoot deprivation. Furthermore, all this was in the context of her mother's feeling that these hardships were ill-deserved. If Betty had not fallen pregnant, if George had not drunk, if old Swetman had not rejected his pregnant daughter, then none of this would have happened. Instead, Betty would have enjoyed the status due to the daughter of a small respectable landowning farmer. Her father, after all, had rented fifty acres of land and her mother had come from a family involved in publishing.

Jemima was the fifth of Betty's seven children. Such middle children often feel at a disadvantage. They see their eldest siblings given responsibilities and almost adult status, while the youngest receive most of the parental attention. So, for Jemima, her mother's belief that providence had cast her down may have struck home with special intensity. Life was unfair. Indeed, a strange vision, inscribed by Thomas in his personal notebook for 30 October 1870, records "Mother's notion, and also mine: that a figure stands in our van with an arm uplifted, to knock us back from any pleasant prospect we indulge in as probable." Here, surely, is the figure of Fate, familiar in all of Hardy's novels. Some external force, so mother and son believed, stood in their way, dashing their hopes and destroying their happiness. For Jemima, fate was, perhaps, also an excuse to help her reduce her own guilt for becoming, so unwisely, pregnant.

When Jemima reached the age of thirteen there was a sudden and miraculous change in her fortunes. She took a job in service with a member of the Fox-Strangways family, whose head, the Earl of Ilchester, lived at Melbury House. She would continue to work for members of this literate and enlightened family for the next thirteen years until her marriage, and this experience of living among the Whig elite transformed her outlook on life. It was a rags to riches experience. All the drabness and desperation she had known as a destitute child were suddenly replaced by magnificent houses and scholarly minds. Her employers not only read books, they also wrote them. Furthermore, Jemima visited London with her employers and this opened her eyes to the fascinations of the metropolis; she quickly decided to make her life there. This was the ambition that was then thwarted by her own unwanted pregnancy and forced marriage in 1839. Instead, she would have to live her long life in an overcrowded mud cottage in the middle of nowhere, surrounded by neighbours she found to be "rustic and quaint" (1). Jemima was described as the most talented of Betty's children and she inherited from her mother not only her love of books but her determination to rise again in society. After her marriage, she forbade the speaking of Dorset dialect inside her home. Jemima was, said Thomas, a progressive woman and ambitious for her son (6).

Jemima's husband's family, however, had also been fortunate in the quality of their local gentry. In what was generally a fiercely conservative and unkindly county, the Hardys had been beholden to a liberal and intelligent family, the Pitts of Kingston Maurward. Indeed the Pitts and the Fox-Strangways were among the few great families of Dorset of that time who had been sympathetic to the political and social reforms of the period. Dorset, in the first part of the nineteenth century, had been noted for its low agricultural wages, extreme poverty and resistance to reform. It was a place of misery. The Corn Laws had driven up the price of bread, rioters were destroying farm machinery, anti-Catholic feeling was still marked by demonstrations, and criminals were still being hanged in public. Earlier, it had been the county of some of Judge Jeffreys' most vicious Assizes, Lord Eldon's Ultra Conservative politics and, later, the harsh suppression of the Tolpuddle martyrs. All these savageries were well remembered by generations of Dorset's oppressed working classes. Dorset was also a county through which bands of slaves and convicts had been driven to ports along the south coast, and where the moorland gibbets had often carried bodies of executed felons. For Betty Hand the psychological escape from such horrors had been through her books, and her daughter Jemima had followed her example. Jemima however had gone further and had planned to escape the deprivations of Dorset altogether by running a gentleman's club in London. When this ambition was nipped in the bud by her unintended pregnancy and reluctant marriage to Thomas Hardy (the builder), the only good result had been the arrival of her baby Thomas. Jemima determined that he should lead an entirely different kind of life from the remainder of the Hardy family, one more fitting for a boy from her mother's educated background. He was too frail to be a builder, she decided. If she could not herself escape from her existence, then he would be trained to do so on her behalf. Sitting on his mother's knee little Thomas listened to her stories of hardship and read the books she urged him to read. The message he unconsciously absorbed was that books were the means to escape and success. They had been his mother's and his grandmother's only source of joy and so, by going a step further, not only by reading books but actually by *writing* them, he could also help his mother and grandmother to be happy. I believe that the unspoken instruction he received from his mother was simply this: fulfil my frustrated ambition for me – write books, make money, go to wonderful London, climb up the social ladder and become a gentleman! This is precisely what little Thomas eventually did.

It is clear that Thomas's most influential relationships as a young child were with his mother and his two grandmothers, Betty and Mary. Both grannies were treasuries of family history and sources of affection for him. The three women, however, had all suffered extreme hardships: Betty, as we have seen, had endured violence from her husband and the ostracism of her father that had led to her poverty; Mary (who shared the cottage at Bockhampton with them) had lost both her parents in childhood; and Jemima, as a child, had been hungry, barefoot, and, perhaps, whipped. None cared to talk too openly about these experiences yet, as a child, Thomas shared these secret memories with them.

After Jemima's illness in about 1846, and the loss of her mother Betty in 1847, she became acutely unhappy and her marriage ran into overt difficulties. Jemima reacted by travelling to Hatfield in 1848 to visit her sister Martha, taking the eight year old Thomas with her as her chosen companion. Jemima clung to him possessively, and he responded with devoted loyalty, developing a lasting sense of responsibility towards her. Thomas later recalled that the two of them felt "united against the world" (7) at this time.

Thomas' Personality.

As a child Thomas was quite a solitary boy, avoiding the company of other children in the lane. His parents were protective of him and he was special in their eyes. In 1844, the Pitts sold Kingston Maurward house and its estate. The new owners who moved in were Francis and Julia Martin, and in 1848 Thomas was sent to the school in Lower Bockhampton where Julia Martin (a childless wife) had become heavily involved. Little Thomas became her favourite and she sat him on her knee. Although she was thirty years his senior, and so about the same age as his mother, this experience was for Thomas an erotic one. Then it was that Jemima, jealous of Thomas' infatuation, removed him to another school and took him away to visit her sister in London. Julia vindictively retaliated by causing Thomas Hardy (senior) to lose his regular work at Kingston Maurward. After a few years, however, the Martins sold up and left Dorset. Years later, in 1862, Thomas tried to renew the relationship with Julia in London but found a woman, now in her fifties, with whom he no longer felt at ease. I believe that the failure of this impossible love affair upset him far more than has been realised and was probably the reason why he returned prematurely to Dorset in 1867, much to his mother's disappointment, apparently angry and miserable, and set about writing his first novel, the title at least of which, *The Poor Man and the Lady,* was clearly relevant. The novel was, however, rejected by several London publishers on account of its outspoken attacks upon powerful institutions. The following year came his first published book, *Desperate Remedies*; a tale of social climbers aspiring to become aristocracy. While still living at home with his parents and siblings he then published *Under the Greenwood Tree* (1872), *A Pair of Blue Eyes* (1873) and *Far from the Madding Crowd* (1874). The latter was his first great success and allowed him finally to leave home (at the age of thirty-four) and to marry Emma Gifford in the same year, against his mother's wishes. Eleven novels followed in the years 1876 to 1895, ending with *Jude the Obscure* in 1895, each succeeding novel taking on ever darker shades of tragedy. Hardy's novels see the whole of creation as groaning in pain, controlled by some indifferent power of Fate. There are no human villains in his greatest novels – just weak and selfish people and missed opportunities. Even Fate itself is not malicious, merely 'purblind'. Hardy was always obsessed with the past – in particular the past as experienced by both his grandmothers and his mother. Indeed, it is these experiences that form the emotional substance of his books:

We two kept house, the Past and I,
The Past and I,
Through all my tasks it hovered nigh,
Leaving me never alone…
The Ghost of the Past

In the middle years it seems that Thomas was occasionally depressed. His jottings in his notebook in the early 1870s sometimes reveal a preoccupation with "manhood's glooms" (9), yet he also described himself as quite often feeling "ecstatic". One must conclude that he was cyclothymic; that is to say his mood went up and down more or less spontaneously, without ever being so extreme as to cause him, or anyone else, real difficulties. Perhaps creative artists are often like this: the stream of their creativity swelling as their mood rises and then being checked for quality as the mood descends again. Such periods of mild depression would help to account for the feeling in Hardy's novels that life is ultimately pointless and painful. Whether these dark moods were caused by his mother's constant tales of hardship or whether they merely ensured that Thomas took these stories to heart, illustrates a perennial problem. Does depressed mood cause the ideas of gloom or do the ideas of gloom cause the depressed mood? Both, it seems, can happen. Anyway, he returned from London feeling "socialistic, not to say revolutionary" (10) and *The Poor Man and the Lady*'s political message is an attack on the callousness of the middle and upper classes and their indifference to the poor (11). As Claire Tomalin observes, *The Poor Man and the Lady* was a dry-run for *Jude* (12). The obsession with social class continues in *Ethelburta* (1876) but, in general, Thomas subsequently manages to subdue his criticisms of the ruling classes, gradually putting the blame for the miseries of the world upon the superhuman force of Fate or Destiny. Why did he do this? Was it because he knew he stood a better chance of having his books published and acclaimed if he did so? Partly, perhaps. Or was it because, on reflection, he could see that some of the upper classes (for example, the Pitts and the Fox-Strangways of Dorset) had *not* always been guilty of callousness or indifference? On the contrary, they had sometimes thrown themselves into politics on the side of the poor and underprivileged.

Thomas was not only, of course, interested in love relationships between rich and poor, upper class and lower, but also between old and young. The love between a poor teenage boy and a twenty-eight year old married and titled woman is dealt with in *Two on a Tower* (1882) and, again, harks back to his love for Julia. Again, it is the older woman who seduces the boy in this clearly erotic story. Rarely were Thomas' women, real or imagined, of the same age or class as himself. His attraction to Emma, his first wife, is a case in point. She came from impoverished gentry and was a defiant, almost tomboyish, redhead; an outdoor girl who rode horses astride and not side-saddle. Emma saw in him an ambitious young man who, like her, was part rebel and part someone who was determined to succeed in conventional terms. His second wife, Florence, was nearly forty years younger than him and a fan of the now famous author. He saw in her the physical attractions of youth, and she was awed by his celebrity. Both wives had their own literary ambitions and both died unfulfilled. In fact Thomas could, more happily, have lived the life of a bohemian batchelor, although he lacked the confidence to do this. There were always two sides to Thomas – would-be lover and would-be respectable gentleman. He was fascinated by women, recognising their rights to equality with men, their sexuality and the frequent unhappiness of their lives. Thomas was not really a man for marrying, however, remaining wedded throughout his life to his mother and her memories.

By middle age, Thomas had indeed done all that his three kinswomen had wanted him to do. He had written books, made money, lived in London and returned to Dorset as a wealthy man. One of his favourite photographs of himself was taken by Hermann Lea in 1903 – heavy stockings, tweed jacket, plus fours, wing collar and book in hand: all bespoke the uniform of the educated country gentleman. His transformation appeared to be complete.

Commentators have remarked that it is not easy to connect the man, Thomas Hardy, with his books. He appeared quiet, conventional, shy and contented, while his novels are full of scandal, tragedy and malign forces. Claire Tomalin remarks that "neither Hardy nor anyone else has explained where his black view of life came from (13)" and goes on to suggest it may have been caused by unusual sensitivity and his loss of Christian belief. There is certainly an extraordinary sensitivity in Hardy which, I believe, is often to be found in pampered children, where any sort of loss can precipitate depression. But I do not feel this is the reason for the tragedy in his novels. There are two additional factors of huge psychological importance that help to explain Hardy's apparent pessimism. The first is his mild cyclothymia which meant that when his mood was spontaneously low (there does not have to be any obvious external cause for this) then he inevitably became preoccupied with gloomy thoughts. This happens to all or most people who are depressed. Gloomy thoughts are themselves signs of a depressed mood. The second and far more important reason is that, as a child, Hardy was the focus of his mother's attentions and this forceful woman pumped little Thomas full of stories of her own very real hardships and childhood tragedies. His two grandmothers added their own concentrated infusions of misery: of orphanhood, paternal rejection and marital violence, in a Dorset environment already characterised by exceptional poverty, cruelty and injustice. So, for the first eight years of his life Thomas may have heard little else but tales of woe from these three intelligent, powerful and highly frustrated women. They extolled books to him and told him, in effect, to go out into the world and do what their genders and their marriages prevented them from doing – that is to say, write books and become rich and famous.

Thomas saw the 'cause of things' as 'neither moral nor immoral' (letter, 20 December 1920) and was often surprised or hurt when people commented adversely on the blackness of his novels; and on the constant pain, set-backs and frustrations of sexual desire which they contain. He hated, in particular, any accusation that he was piling on the agonies gratuitously or that, as his life appeared so successful and secure, that he was painting an artificial picture. The real reason for Thomas' surprise at such criticisms of his work is that these miserable experiences were indeed *not* his own. They were his mother's and grandmothers' experiences! He never admitted to this, of course, either because he felt this would damage his credibility as an author or because he simply was unaware, as people truly can be, of how much of his thinking had been unconsciously incorporated from them.

Undoubtedly, Thomas felt a great obligation towards his mother and guilt that he had twice disobeyed her wishes: first by returning from a liberating career in London to live again in the wilds of Dorset, and secondly, by marrying, contrary to her criticism of matrimony in general. For her, marriage had meant almost total frustration. The relationship between his wife (Emma) and his mother (and indeed with his sisters) remained dysfunctional for decades, with Thomas subtly siding, and increasingly so, with his family and against Emma. Underlying all his guilt was the primal guilt that he had thwarted his mother's career by being born at all.

Thomas always stoutly denied that his novels were autobiographical and, in a sense, we can now see that this was true. They came from his "imagination" – that is to say from all the moans and groans he had absorbed from his mother and grandmothers in infancy and childhood. It also explains why, increasingly, he did not want to share the creative process with Emma. It was with his mother, or the representation of his mother inside his head, that he shared the process. Yet Thomas seems to have been unaware of how much his novels were being written by his mother. The clue is in how he described the writing process – "I simply let it come" he said. Without fully realising it, he was his mother's amanuensis. Of course, he did not repeat her stories in detail. In the books, genders are changed from real life and so are locations; he reclothed her tales in new disguises. But the great bleak themes of rejection, poverty, pride, romantic disillusionment, death, dangerous passion, frustration, ambition, class, pregnancy and destitution are endlessly retold. Basically, Thomas was unconsciously doing what his mother had wanted him to do, but this was on two levels: first, he was venting her anger about her own life through the content of his novels, thereby expressing or releasing her pent-up feelings cathartically; but, secondly, he was also providing vicariously, the solution to all these problems. He was making money, writing books, becoming famous, escaping from Dorset, meeting great people in London, and climbing the class ladder on his mother's behalf.

Then, in old age, it was as if he began to sense that what he had been writing for all these years had come from his mother and not from himself. While visitors came and went, offering him acclaim and respect, paying court to him at Max Gate, he kept aloof, wrapped up in himself, secretly encoding his true feelings in his poetry. His fierce dog Wessex expressed some of Thomas's secret contempt for the sycophants who surrounded him, by biting them. In later years Thomas began to worry how he had become "false to myself, my simple self that was, and is not now" (15). In consequence, he turned increasingly to poetry and, after *Jude* in 1895, he wrote no more novels. They had all been written, in a sense, to meet his mother's unspoken wishes. His poetry, on the other hand, is more truly about himself. After his mother died in 1904 Hardy felt a sense of release and the output of poetry increased, as it also did when Emma died eight years later in 1912.

Conclusions

Thomas Hardy is one of the clearest examples of a child acting out and fulfilling the frustrated ambitions of a parent. In this case it was his mother's (Jemima's) fantasies and frustrations that provided the child with his main motivation in life. She had wanted to better herself in London and been frustrated by an unwanted pregnancy – that is to say with the arrival of Thomas himself. She told him he was special and delicate, and he believed it. Jemima totally dominated Thomas's life, not dying until he was sixty-four. Her great escape had been books and so, like her, Thomas read books and then wrote them, as offerings and propitiations to her for having ruined her life by being born. Thomas's social achievements became his mother's vicarious channel of escape.

As we have seen, Jemima's life repeated in many ways that of her own mother, Betty, who had fallen down the social ladder because she, too, had become pregnant out of wedlock and been forced to marry beneath her class. She, too, had read books as an escape from her miseries. Betty had died in 1847, when Thomas was seven, and he remembered her well.

Thomas Hardy is of interest as a subject because he not only became an author and a social success in order to gratify his mother's (and his grandmothers') fantasies, but he filled his novels with *their* experiences and *their* longings, *their* anger against the cruelty of the church, employers, work houses, snobs, prudes and the middle classes, the horrors of *their* poverty, and *their* experiences of the tyranny of the class system itself. Thomas could hardly climb the social ladder by overtly attacking the upper classes so he disguised some of his anger, only totally revealing it in his first and last novels (*The Poor Man and the Lady* and *Jude the Obscure*.) Instead, he attributed the blame to the more acceptable and anonymous figure of Fate, that was used, partly as an excuse, by his mother.

INSIDE THEIR HEADS

Nearly all of Thomas Hardy's writings are about Dorset country people. Yet he lived much of his life in London among the rich and the famous. He dined at great houses, meeting statesmen and royalty. Why did he bother? He hardly used such experiences in his books. The answer is that living the life of a gentleman in town was itself fulfilling what his mother and grandmothers had wanted him to do. Like book-writing, neither activity was an end in itself; both were to satisfy the unspoken demands of his kinswomen. So Thomas lived in two worlds; in his own words "vibrating at a swing between the artificial gaieties of a London season and the quaintness of a primitive rustic life (2)." Note the similar words used here as by his mother when she described her own contrasting experiences of life with the intellectual Fox-Strangways and in Bockhampton. Thomas, as rustic and celebrity-watcher, was repeating Jemima's own double experience of the world. He was generally a cheerful, friendly and happy man. Almost his only regrets were for his lost or unfulfilled loves – for cousin Tryphena (who died in 1890), for Emma (his first wife), for Julia Martin and for some of his other old flames, and for the many beautiful women he had met and wished were his. Thomas' own frustrations were more romantic and sexual than his mother's.

So, in his novels, Hardy deals with Fate and the tragedies and travails experienced by his mother and grandmothers. The books seldom reveal much about the author himself, and the characters they contain appear rather as silhouettes. In his poetry, however, Hardy speaks for himself, Fate is absent, and people are portrayed in greater detail, sometimes bathed in emotions that are absent in the novels. The novels are often set in a Dorset reminiscent of a previous generation – further evidence that they are, in reality, about his female forebears' experiences and not his own. He was a poet by conviction but a novelist by proxy. Thomas had so incorporated his mother's and grandmother's memories and fantasies into his own thinking that he was sometimes uncertain as to where the boundary lay between himself and them. The sexual content of his writings was mostly his own, although even here, too, he may have been sometimes reflecting his mother's frustrations. Like many writers, Hardy was highly sexed. He wrote of himself at the end of his life (*Winter Words*, 1928):

Quite young-
A brisk-eyed youth, and highly strung:
One whose desires
And inner fires
Moved him as wires.

And you may have met one stiff and old,

If not in years; of manner cold;
Who seemed as stone,
And never had known
Of mirth and moan.

He concludes, after describing other contrasting characteristics:-

All these specimens of man,
So various in their pith and plan,
Curious to say
Were one *man. Yea*
I was all they. (3)

No wonder Hardy kept himself under wraps until the very end. His own auto-biography (*Life* by Florence Hardy) still paints a picture of the calm, sophisti-cated gentleman that his mother wanted him to be. Half-consciously he had kept up this pretence all his life, but in later years, after his mother at long last was dead, he yearned to drop the mask:-

Let there be truth at last...
Nothing needs disguise
Further in any wise... (4)

So, what was there underneath his disguise? People found Thomas quiet and shy. As we have seen, he hid his thoughts behind a façade of polite gentility. Outwardly he appeared conventional, yet inside he teemed with a resentment of privilege, fierce compassion for underdogs (animals as well as humans), and strong sexual feelings for women both young and old. Class status was of huge importance in the nineteenth century – and especially to Jemima and her mother Betty. Thomas was, of course, both rural and urban, and neither. He did not quite fit any of the usual categories. Born a countryman, he had lived some years in London and then returned to Dorset to design his own middle class house, Max Gate, up on the hill on the edge of the county's capital town. It be-came a sort of play-set where he could act the part of a gentleman before the audience of the world, and his own family down in the valley. He had climbed the social ladder, attaining the trappings of gentility, but had by-passed the usual conventions of class by becoming a celebrity. (Dickens had done this before him.) To become a famous writer was not exactly a way to the top of the social tree, but it was a good way around it. Yet by doing this he was creating a status that did no more than express the aspirations felt by his mother and her mother.

Neither woman, despite poverty, had ever been resigned to their apparently lowly status, nor accepted their full responsibility for their out-of-wedlock pregnancies that had forced them down the ladder. They had always felt that they had fallen down the social scale unfairly. They had been knocked back by that strange and visionary figure ahead of them.

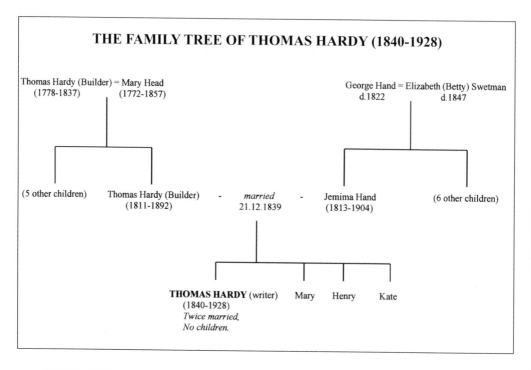

THE FAMILY TREE OF THOMAS HARDY (1840-1928)

Thomas Hardy (Builder) = Mary Head
(1778-1837)   (1772-1857)

George Hand = Elizabeth (Betty) Swetman
d.1822   d.1847

(5 other children)   Thomas Hardy (Builder)   -   *married*   -   Jemima Hand   (6 other children)
(1811-1892)   21.12.1839   (1813-1904)

THOMAS HARDY (writer)   Mary   Henry   Kate
(1840-1928)
Twice married,
No children.

SOURCES

Margaret Drabble: (Editor) *The Genius of Thomas Hardy,* Weidenfeld & Nicholson, London, 1976

Robert Gittings: *The Young Thomas Hardy,* 1975

Ben Harwood: *The Life and Works of Thomas Hardy,* Inspiring Places, 2010

Michael Millgate: *Thomas Hardy : A Biography Revisited,* 2004

Ralph Pite: *Thomas Hardy : The Guarded Life,* Yale University Press, London, 2007

R.A. Scott-James: *Thomas Hardy (1840 – 1928),* pub. For the British Council by Longman's, London, 1951

Claire Tomalin: *Thomas Hardy : The Time Torn Man,* Penguin, London, 2006

2

JANE AUSTEN (1775 – 1817)

Novelist

Unlike Charles Dickens with his insecure childhood driving him to condemn and to entertain, or Thomas Hardy becoming the mouthpiece for his mother's and grandmothers' discontents, Jane Austen appears to be very straight forward. Born in the hamlet of Steventon in Hampshire in 1775, of a tough-minded rector and his equally hard-working wife, Jane grew up in a large, active and ambitious family, the seventh of eight children. The forty-two years of Jane's life, outwardly at least, were to remain singularly uneventful. Relationships within the Austen family were generally harmonious and mutually supportive. Indeed, one could say that Jane's needs for affection, admiration, friendship and attachment were all satisfied within the folds of her close-knit family. The only emotional basics she lacked were the pleasures of sex and parenthood.

Six out of Jane's siblings were brothers with whom she was on affectionate and friendly terms, while her older sister Cassandra became her lifelong confidante. Jane always looked up to and admired Cassandra. As maternally deprived children sometimes do, they turned to each other for love, security and understanding. Two of her brothers gained scholarships to Oxford, one (George) was mentally handicapped, another was adopted by rich relations and two went into the Navy, both eventually becoming Admirals. Not content with scratching a living as a rector, Jane's father also managed a large farm and, with his wife, ran a small boarding school for boys based at the rectory where the family lived. It is hardly surprising that neither parent, hard up and heavily occupied as they were, had much time to develop close or emotional relationships with their many children. Indeed, Mrs Austen, who produced almost a baby a year for the first ten years of her marriage, resorted to the not unheard of expediency of placing each of her babies to be cared for by nurses in the village, from the age of a few weeks until they were a year or eighteen months of age. They were, in this regard, treated almost as orphaned farm animals. But this system seemed to work: none of the children (other than George) grew up to be obviously disordered, and most led lives of achievement. It does suggest, however, that Mrs Austen was not supremely motherly.

So, is there anything of significance to be said by a psychologist about Jane Austen, in addressing such questions as to why Jane became a novelist, why she was so good at it, and on the relationship between her art and her life?

As with nearly all writers, there is in Jane Austen's family the presence of a literary, or would-be literary, parent. In Jane's case it was her mother who, in the few moments of spare time she had, would occasionally pen a witty verse, sometimes acerbic, always well crafted. Indeed, the whole family was partial to puns and word games and Jane's oldest teenage brother, James, would regularly put on the production of plays around Christmas time, for which he would write clever prologues and epilogues in verse. As a young man he founded and edited a journal called *The Loiterer.* In his memorial verse to Jane he wrote:-

> *Though quick and keen her mental eye*
> *Poor Nature's foibles to descry*
> *And seemed forever on the watch,*
> *Some traits of ridicule to catch,*
> *Yet not a word she ever pen'd*
> *Which hurt the feelings of a friend...*

Jane would write stories to amuse her broadminded and cultivated family, reading them aloud. Her main motive was to make her family laugh. As one of the youngest in the family, she had become the family comic, and eventually she overtook her brother James as the family's principal writer. Her parents and her brothers encouraged and constructively criticised her work. Her most admiring sibling in this respect was probably her youngest brother Charles. It was the suave and witty Henry, however, who would eventually act on her behalf in dealing with her publishers.

What role, then, did Jane's father take in encouraging his daughter's literary career? First and foremost he provided his precious daughter with a library of some five hundred books, many of which she devoured avidly. Jane particularly enjoyed tales of turbulent romance where, as in the stories about Charlotte Smith's hero, Frederic Delamere, women were abducted and men behaved badly. Jane's *First Impressions* of 1797 (eventually to be rewritten as *Pride and Prejudice*) so impressed her father that he tried, unsuccessfully, to get it published, even offering to put up money for this venture. We can deduce from a note in his own hand that he approved of Jane's literary efforts and regarded them as breaking new ground.

Sadly, we know terribly little of the quality of the relationships between Jane and her parents, other than that these were positive but restrained. Mr and Mrs Austen come across as pioneers of the British 'no-nonsense' culture that was to dominate the country throughout the nineteenth and the first half of the twentieth centuries. The Austen family's attitude to life was a blend of Puritan work ethic with the rationality of the Enlightenment. Although literary and even intellectual on occasions, they valued the down-to-earth, unsentimental and practical approach to life. The emphasis was on sense rather than sensibility. The boys joined the Navy and the Army, and one became a hunting parson. There was a tough-mindedness about all of them that would become more common among the upper classes as the new century advanced. Perhaps some of this hard-headedness was encouraged by the nation's response to the threats of Napoleonic invasion and social revolution. If the 1780s had been soft and decadent, the early 1800s had to be hard and strong as British men fought the French in a score of bloody battles by land and sea.

Some of this brusqueness rubbed off on Jane. As a child she had grown up surrounded by boys – not only her brothers but the upper class boys being educated by her parents. By all accounts she enjoyed the rough and tumble of boys' games. She was never exactly masculine in outlook but grew up feeling at home with men and knowing all about boys' interests and attitudes. As a child she was clearly drawn to boys' jokes and to their fascinations with vehicles, accidents, drunkeness, physical deformities, ugliness, mantraps and violence. One must only wonder about sex. Was Jane also caught up in the usual bawdiness of boyhood? She probably saw more of boys' bodies than most girls of her era and must, surely, have heard more of their earthy humour. There was certainly nothing prim about Jane Austen.

An important motive in the lives of our forebears has always been that of social status or class. Every society in every era has had its own beliefs about class, and its own criteria for determining class. In the early twenty-first century, we live at a time when social class in Britain happens to be less of an obsession than it has been at almost any other time since the end of the Middle Ages. Other criteria such as wealth and celebrity appear, temporarily at least, to have obscured class. Perhaps for this reason biographers have often underestimated the importance of social class in their attempts to understand their nineteenth century subjects. Class carries its own subculture and thus much of our behaviour can be explained in this way as conformity, or otherwise, to class norms. Great authors are not immune from the effects of class although a few may have pretended to be. Writers can come from any class, of course, and can be egalitarians just as well as snobs. One feature of class, however, that has affected several great authors, is having a parent who feels himself or herself to have lost social standing. Take Thomas Hardy's mother and grandmother, for example. Although both would have appeared to an outsider to be living almost peasant-like existences in early nineteenth century Dorset, both considered their origins to be considerably above the rural working class of which they appeared to be members. Not only is the idea of fallen class status featured in some of Hardy's novels (such as *Tess of The D'Urbevilles)*, I believe that it fashioned the whole of his life (1). We see a similar situation affecting Charles Dickens, whose extraordinary father spoke and behaved as though he was a member of the aristocracy when in fact he was merely a clerk in the Navy Office.

In the case of Jane Austen, both parents came from impoverished upper class backgrounds. Jane's mother's family, the Leighs, had numerous titled connections and Jane's father, similarly, could look back to ancestors who had been wealthy gentry in the reign of Charles II. Jane's father had, however, lost both his parents before he was six, and been cared for by an aunt in Tonbridge and a book-selling uncle in London. At sixteen he gained a scholarship to Oxford where he worked hard and did well, becoming a college Chaplain and Proctor, meeting and marrying the Master of Balliol's niece, Cassandra Leigh, in 1764, and acquiring the rectorship of Steventon through the kindness of a cousin.

So Jane grew up in a large bookish family which had little or no inherited wealth but which still believed itself to be gentry. They owned no land, and had little money, but they had good breeding and, more importantly in terms of survival, they were intelligent, ambitious, well-educated and hard working. From the eighteenth century onwards the English had become obsessed with the nuances of class and these, surely, became of particular importance among those, such as the Austens, who felt their class status was being threatened. Jane herself may not have been a snob but her novels reveal her fascination with these class differences as well as with the relationships between class and wealth, and, indeed, between the proprieties of class and deeper moral virtues. Unlike Hardy she did not, in her life, ape the manners of classes superior to her own nor did she, like Dickens, attack in her novels the cruelties of working class poverty. She was, however, always concerned with the underdog, making friends throughout her short life with various intelligent servants, and trying to help them. We can conclude that class, and the real or imagined loss of class status, were potent influences in Austen's background, as in the background of some other writers.

There were often a dozen or so young people living at the Steventon Rectory and none stood out above the others as special parental favourites. Mr and Mrs Austen, remarkably, were to all the children both their teachers and their friends, creating a cheerful, ambitious, word-filled and humorous family culture. Jane, as seventh out of eight siblings, must have sometimes felt just one of a crowd. But her facility with the written word allowed her eventually to establish her own identity. She shared with the rest of the family their tendency to observe their human environment, deriving great amusement from the foibles and failings of outsiders. Jane, and her family, found other people funny. Together they laughed at the outside world, thereby enhancing the cohesion of their own family. Social life for upper middle class families in Hampshire at the time was a round of parties that usually included dancing. Such "balls" took place not only in the large country houses but also in the Assembly Rooms in Basingstoke. Jane loved dancing and clearly hoped she would one day meet a dancing partner whom she would marry. Although she met several with whom she began to fall in love, none of these relationships actually led to matrimony. Jane was neither beautiful nor wealthy, so her options were restricted and, by their late twenties, both Jane and her beloved sister Cassandra, had accepted spinsterhood. Although Cassandra was only three years older than her, Jane occasionally looked to her older sister for the warmth and attention that their mother did not lavish upon them. For these two girls at least the Austen family itself became a substitute for matrimony. The two spinsters were constantly in demand as companions for the sick and dying, carers of children, advisors on family problems and as houseguests. Their needs for passion and parenthood were never to be satisfied, but in all other ways their constant interactions with some thirty relatives kept them materially supported and emotionally occupied throughout their lives.

Much of Jane's energy was deployed into writing. She noted not only the quirks of other people but began to reflect upon their underlying motives. Her novels often have a cynical, or at least a satirical, tone. She did not model her characters exactly upon her acquaintances or friends, and the lives she portrays in her novels are largely from her imagination. In an age when the etiquette associated with snobbery was an issue of considerable attention, it is interesting to note that Jane's characters are often of a class a little lower than her own. She was, in other words, often looking down upon and gently mocking the attitudes and values of the provincial middle classes as they aspired to climb the social ladder. On the other hand she could equally be critical of the pretentions of London 'society'. Either way, one feels, she preferred the utter rationality and humour of the Austen family to the absurdities and affectations of wider society.

Until the last few months of her life Jane was, in fact, dependent financially upon the male members of her family. In her novels her heroines are concerned about matrimony often for financial reasons. Love is also important for most of them, but love without liquidity is out of the question as a solution to life's difficulties. Jane's own favourite fictional heroine appears to have been Elizabeth Bennett from her novel '*Pride and Prejudice*' – a tough young woman whose honest and principled approach to life is finally rewarded by marriage to a fabulously wealthy and upright man of a class above her own. Although her greatest novels are much about courtship and marriage, Jane herself never married, her need for financial support being satisfied by her father and, later, by her brothers.

We know that Jane had begun producing writings in her middle teens. These caricatured the sentimental fiction of the late eighteenth century and parodied the sort of over-emotional behaviour that the Austen family deprecated. During the 1790s she produced prototypes for both *Pride and Prejudice* (not published until 1813) and *Sense and Sensibility* (published eventually in 1811) as well as some elegantly expressed and daring works such as *Lesley Castle* (probably written in 1793) and *Lady Susan* (possibly written in 1794) which reveal an often forgotten dramatic side to Jane Austen – their themes including adultery by a young mother who abandons her baby, and a female sexual predator who uses her charm to manipulate and abuse. After this, Jane backed away from such extremes in her writings. Claire Tomalin suggests: "She decided to censor that part of her imagination that interested itself in women's wickedness, and particularly sexual wickedness."(2). Jane surely harboured strong feelings of irritation towards those she considered to be stupid, pompous or prejudiced against women and, however restrained her novels subsequently became, there is always, under their surface, the smouldering of suppressed passion and her muted ridicule of the fools she sometimes found around her. The subtlety and control of her adult writings paralleled that of the general restraint she maintained in her own personal life.

When her father retired suddenly to Bath in 1801, handing over the rectory at Steventon to his eldest son, Jane's writing output dwindled sharply. It slowed further when her father died four years later. Maybe she had been, after all, writing primarily for *his* entertainment, and perhaps to reassure him that the well born Austens had not come down in the world. For several years she was fairly silent. Only in Chawton in 1811 did Jane begin to write busily again, with *Mansfield Park* (published 1814), *Emma* (published 1816) and *Persuasion* (begun in 1815 and published posthumously in 1818). In all her novels there is the feeling that for Jane the real world is that of her family, and that she is looking down upon the society of Basingstoke and its environs with slight amusement and condescension.

Paula Byrne's penetrations of Jane Austen's private life have confirmed these general observations and thrown light on her more intimate thoughts and devotions. Jane was a serious Anglican but wanted to keep her religion private. She certainly did not want her novels to become 'dramatised sermons'. Her two principle interests in religion were her own salvation in heaven and the central Christian ethic of love: two prayers in her own handwriting stress her concern for "the discomfort of our fellow creatures", mentioning especially orphans, widows, captives and prisoners. (PB 198/199) Slaves too were on her list. Perhaps the hidden motive for religion was her love for her father, himself an unobtrusive Tory Anglican rector who never forced his religion upon anyone, always taking a broadminded and tolerant approach. Jane disliked intensively the fervour of the contemporary Evangelicals. When she tried to work out her own religious position, in writing to her niece Fanny on courtship matters in 1814, she quite quickly discovered her own inconsistencies on the subject: "I am feeling differently every moment" she confessed. Ultimately, she was entirely Anglican, like her father. Together they took a very English position, quietly and reasonably respecting kindness, decency and moderation. They were not shocked by adultery or sexual passion, but sought to express their religion through good works among the poor and in support of the abolition of the slave-trade. Jane always stressed the importance of "fortitude" and "exertion". There had to be control and self-discipline. Her family's whole culture was Christian, and it embraced the forgiveness of sinners, a certain amount of irreverence and, above all, wit and good humour. In her final illness Jane told her friend Anne Sharp of her gratitude to God for having her family around her, and for being "blessed in the tenderness of such a family". (PB.209) Her family was everything to her.

Jane's attitude towards sex has remained rather a mystery. Surrounded by so many boys in her childhood (six brothers and up to eight boy pupils at their parents' school), the subject must have come up. Girls, just as much as boys, are naturally interested in the subject from an early age. Their own bodies and those of others are inevitably fascinating. It seems likely that Jane always shared a bed with her older sister Cassandra and, possibly the bath tub also. In a relatively small house how could two adults, two girls and a dozen boys not, deliberately or inadvertently, be exposed to each other? The distribution and usage of chamber pots, for example, must have been a problem, and the sound effects of bodily functions must have been frequent reminders of the usually more hidden sides of ordinary human behaviour. Urination, defecation and masturbation must all have been detectable, it could not have been otherwise. These things may be concealed in a modern household, with one or two children in separate beds in a house with two or more lavatories and modern plumbing, but not in the Steventon Rectory with up to a dozen persons, mostly teenage boys, crowded under the same roof, and without a proper bathroom! I point this out to help dispel the continuing misperception of Jane as being a prim little vestal. She wasn't. Perhaps it all became too much of a difficulty and was one of the reasons why the Austens eventually sent away their two daughters, aged ten and seven, to boarding school in Oxford and Reading, for three years. There is no suggestion of open sexual experiences among the children at Steventon, or of serious romantic entanglements, but one pupil at least, John Wallop, (Lord Lymington), went on to become a notorious sexual delinquent never, however, losing entirely his friendship with Jane.

Early nineteenth century upper class families might sometimes have had ten or twelve children under one roof but they often lived in far larger houses than a Rectory. Furthermore, at Steventon, the ratio of boys to girls was around ten to one, and most of the boys were not blood relations. It was an unusual situation for Cassandra and Jane to grow up in, and I would like to know far more about it. Jane, it seems, adjusted by taking (to an extent) the tom-boy route, identifying with the boys and joining in their rough and tumbles, protected, no doubt, by her beloved brothers. I doubt whether these experiences were responsible for Jane's eventual choice of spinsterhood, but they may well have removed any illusions about young men. She could see through them to their basic natures, unduped by later good manners or chivalrous pretentions. Such unromantic attitudes were very much encouraged by Jane's down to earth parents who opposed sentimentality of all sorts, whether in literature or life. Despite her extreme closeness to her sister, however, there are no suggestions that Jane's inclinations were at all lesbian. She had several good maternalistic female friendships, usually with older women, but these do not appear to have been either romantic or erotic in quality. Furthermore, she loved her father and her brothers dearly, and clearly showed an interest in several of her male dancing partners. It is highly unlikely that she ever had sexual experiences with other people, although not impossible.

Upper class Regency girls did sometimes get pregnant before marriage, as a mistress of one of the Leigh in-laws had done, and incest and homosexuality also occurred. Her own Aunt Phila (Jane's father's sister) and her cousin Eliza (probably fathered by the great Warren Hastings) both led extremely colourful and flirtatious lives and were admired by their young relative Jane Austen. Jane certainly knew about such sexual adventures and even made some naughty sexual jokes, the most famous of which is the pun she puts into the mouth of her anti-heroine, Mary Crawford, in *Mansfield Park*, who says to her sister:

> *Certainly, my home at my uncle's brought me acquainted with a circle of admirals. Of Rears, and Vices, I saw enough. Now, do not be suspecting me of a pun, I entreat.* (JB 243).

The last sentence demonstrates that Jane's pun was quite deliberate and that she did not want her readers to miss it. With two naval brothers (who both became admirals) it was probably a family joke she had used before. Admiral Francis Austen recalled it forty years later.

Jane also made bad taste jokes about death, and usually aimed at men:

> *Mr Waller is dead, I see: - I cannot grieve about it nor, perhaps, can his Widow very much.* (JB 97)

Then there was the one about:

> *Mrs Holder being dead! Poor woman, she has done the only thing in the world she could possibly do, to make one cease to abuse her.*

The most infamous is her comment (addressed to Cassandra as usual) about Mrs Hall's miscarriage:

> *Owing to a fright. – I suppose she happened unawares to look at her husband.*

These latter jokes reveal Jane's undoubted cattiness. She could not help but feel superior to most other people. Again, it was her sense of the family's specialness. In terms of wit, intellect and social class, the family really were a cut above most of the outside world that she encountered. We can see that Jane's life was gripped in a conflict between her natural cattiness and her Christian kindness. Her novels reveal this tension. One of her great motivations, of course, remained her desire to make her family laugh, and the raw material for her jokes was, quite simply, other people.

Why didn't Jane marry? First, as I have said, she was neither a beauty nor an heiress, although her wit did attract some suitors. But she was not going to be naively swept off her feet by first-love or silly infatuation. She was not going to marry unless she was in love, but nor would she make an unsuitable union into poverty. Money mattered to her. And where could she find her match in wit and cynicism? She could not fall for any mental inferior. She already had the closest possible friendship with her sister Cassandra to whom she could reveal not only her good thoughts but also some of her bad ones. Cassandra had given up and settled romantically for spinsterhood after the death of her fiancée. For Jane, her writing continued to be, I suspect, an unconscious link with her dead father and, in later years, the publication of books became a surrogate form of parenthood for her. She admitted this. She would not have wanted to give this up in order to become a housewife. Both sisters could do without sexual satisfaction and both were, I think, genuinely afraid of pregnancy and childbirth. (Several of their acquaintances had died in labour). Above all they had their amazing family which satisfied most of their needs for affection, amusement, admiration, attachment and self-fulfilment. Jane's motives for becoming a novelist were to achieve success, of course, but also to please her family. At first it was her father whom she had wished to impress and then, after his death, it was Henry and her beloved sister Cassandra who became her special audiences.

So what, in summary, can we say of Jane Austen? She was always a shy, witty and kind person who wanted to be a writer from the age of twelve. She was fascinated by people around her and found them to be hilariously funny, retailing her observations to her family. After an adolescent flirtation with writing stories of a Gothic persuasion, Jane aimed at writing books that were "natural" and "true to life". True to her family's culture, she rejected the standard "sentimental" and hysterical heroines of the eighteenth century in favour of witty, spirited and feisty women who influenced their own lives. No doubt such characters were based, to an extent, upon her own Aunt Phila (who went to India to find a man and became the mistress of Warren Hastings) and Phila's flirtatious daughter Eliza who married Jane's closest brother Henry after her French aristocratic husband was guillotined. In adulthood, Jane would often stay with them in London. It is likely that her exciting sister-in-law influenced her considerably, and it is unsurprising that some of Jane's female characters went further than mere flirtation in being cast as irreverent, spirited, seductive and even amoral.

Appreciation of Jane's position within her family is crucial if we are to understand her. She loved all of her siblings and they loved her. Except for her handicapped and absent brother George, all her siblings were cultivated, well-adjusted and successful people. After her brothers found jobs they were often away from home and it was Jane's prolific letter writing that helped to hold the family together. Her older sister Cassandra became a kind of surrogate mother for her, while her capable and hard working real mother remained an emotional blank. We don't know enough about this relationship, but it seems to have been weaker than Jane's relationships to the others. Did her mother take against

Jane, perhaps because of Jane's very good relationship with her father? Or was the mother lacking in maternal feelings generally? Jane's father was a remarkable man and, as we have seen, worked extremely hard to keep his large family affluent. One senses that Jane was his favourite child. He gave her her writing desk, allowed her to read any book in his library including some racy novels by Fielding and Richardson, and encouraged her early writings. With Jane he enjoyed a highly verbal, witty and affectionate relationship and this is reflected in her novels where the truly loving males are often depicted as paternal or fraternal figures. As we have noted, after her father's death Jane became less productive for several years, although continuing to revise and polish her as yet unpublished books. She was a perfectionist. The retitled *"Sense and Sensibility"* echoed one of the great dichotomies within her own life, between reason and feeling (or even, in Freudian terms, ego and id). This dichotomy hints at the general suppression of Jane's wilder feelings. It is the most important of Jane's underlying psychological subjects: the fundamental divide between the exponents of sense and those of sensibility, between obsessives and hysteroids, between head and heart, sensitisers and repressors, between slow considered responses and instant cognitive bias. It seems this was an issue for the whole Austen family, whose culture very much encouraged the side of common sense. They believed in reason and not hysteria, denial, or sentimentality. Pride, prejudice and first impressions are all to be treated with suspicion. (*Pride and Prejudice* had earlier been titled *First Impressions*.)

The lack of maternal love is central to Jane's own case and may have forced Jane to develop a dependence upon her whole family from which she never escaped or wanted to escape. She was not, however, a 'Stay at home', as previously imagined. On the contrary, she was a constant traveller from Bath to Southampton, to Kent, to Devon and Dorset for the seaside holidays, and to the excitements of London where, if she had the money, she would indulge in mad shopping sprees for the latest clothes. By the standards of her day, Jane was quite a widely experienced woman of the world, travel on the Continent being virtually impossible, of course, during the Napoleonic era.

Although drawn to older women for friendship, probably to make up for her mother's emotional absence, Jane got along famously with her brothers and had no illusions about men in general. She liked them, yet we don't really know if she ever yearned for them sexually. Her fear of the potentially fatal consequences of pregnancy could have been a powerful reason why she continued to burrow into the bosom of her family. Besides, she had seen her mother's writing talents frustrated by the continuous production of children. Jane said, understandably, that she did not want to "marry without affection" and that she was "rejoicing in her own freedom". But these reasons for her failure to marry sound just a little incomplete. She had a reasonable supply of suitors, so was there actually some sexual antipathy towards men that might, two hundred years later, in more liberal times, have led her to become a lesbian? We shall never know.

Another point that is sometimes still missed is that her pride in her family was so important that it moulded her whole outlook. Class was of supreme importance in Regency times and the Austens were not middle class but on the edges of aristocracy. Although somewhat impoverished, her parents had worked extremely hard to maintain the family's social position. They had even arranged for one of their sons, Edward, to be adopted by wealthy relatives. He later had to change his surname, but never lost touch with his siblings, indeed he supported the three Austen women by offering them the house at Chawton where Jane finally completed her novels, before her untimely death in 1817. So why did Jane write so often about "the middling classes of society"? This was completely new for a novelist at the time. I think the answer is that she needed to look *down* upon them slightly so that she could laugh at them. By laughing at them, and by sharing these jokes with her family, she was unconsciously asserting and reinforcing her own family's precarious sense of cohesion and superiority. It was also what her beloved father had wanted to do – although orphaned and impecunious, he had dedicated his life to maintaining his family's social standing. Jane, his loving daughter, helped him to do this.

Of course the whole issue of comedy itself raises questions. Why *did* Jane want to be the family comic? Just to get attention? Why *did* she find other people so amusing? I think this again reflects her commitment to her own family and to its attitudes and values. People who did not conform to her family's way of life were, almost by definition, funny. Wit is quite often hostile. Satire and ridicule are ways of asserting the superiority of the satirist. By doing this Jane not only boosted her own self-esteem but, again, that of the whole family. She was saying to her father, through her stories: "look at these funny middle-class people, they are not like us!" This was confirming her father's deep need to preserve (without obvious snobbery) his pride in the Austen family. By persevering as a writer Jane was continuing her fond relationship with her deceased father. If I am right, this may also help to explain why Jane wanted anonymity as an author, right up to a few months before her death. She feared her books might be rejected. When, finally, they were successful, she relished her fame.

Jane's books and her life seem to become increasingly fascinating as the years go by. Being able to discern in her stories human beings just like ourselves, beneath the taffetas and silks of Georgian England, adds to their charm. What more can a psychologist say on Jane Austen's behalf? She was, in so many ways, the product simply of her successful family's exceptional genes and culture. Highly intelligent, slightly frustrated, extremely observant, she found her talent, perfected it and wrote half a dozen of the most elegant novels ever written in the English language.

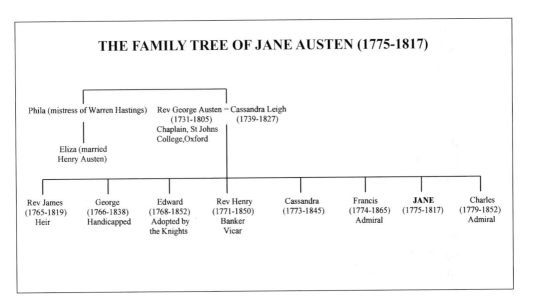

THE FAMILY TREE OF JANE AUSTEN (1775-1817)

Phila (mistress of Warren Hastings)

Rev George Austen = Cassandra Leigh
(1731-1805)   (1739-1827)
Chaplain, St Johns
College, Oxford

Eliza (married
Henry Austen)

Rev James	George	Edward	Rev Henry	Cassandra	Francis	JANE	Charles
(1765-1819)	(1766-1838)	(1768-1852)	(1771-1850)	(1773-1845)	(1774-1865)	(1775-1817)	(1779-1852)
Heir	Handicapped	Adopted by the Knights	Banker Vicar		Admiral		Admiral

SOURCES

Paula Byrne. *The Real Jane Austen: A Life in Small Things*, William Collins. 2013.
Caroline Sanderson. *Jane Austen*, The History Press, 2014.
Claire Tomalin. *Jane Austen: A Life*, New York, Alfred A Knopf. 1997.

3

CHARLES DICKENS (1812 – 1870)

Author and Actor

One of the strangest things about the life of Charles Dickens is the 'absence' of his mother. She certainly existed, of course, and lived, often within a few miles of Charles, and died when he was aged fifty-one. Yet Charles left surprisingly few records of her, despite the fact that the relationship between a son and his mother is usually one of the most formative of all relationships. Was the absence of record an indication that Charles was an exception to this rule or was it quite the opposite?

Charles was born on the outskirts of Portsmouth in 1812, the first son of John Dickens (aged 27), clerk in the Naval Pay Office, and his wife Elizabeth (aged 23). They already had a daughter Fanny, aged nearly 2. Elizabeth was one of the ten children of Charles Barrow who had been obliged to leave England suddenly in 1810 for defrauding the Navy Pay Office. She has been described as a "slim, energetic young woman" who, according to her own account, spent the evening before Charles' birth at a dance, as if trying to ward off her imminent adult status as a parent (CT 7). Her portrait shows rather pinched and asymmetrical features, but whether or not she was as unimpressive as the picture suggests, she certainly had a lot to put up with as the growing Dickens family, hounded for debt, moved from house to house. She was a model for the garrulous Mrs Nickleby, whose confused babbling was based, according to Charles, upon his mother's conversation (CT 95). Later, she was described by an ac-

quaintance as an agreeable and matter of fact person who did indeed love dancing, although Charles disapproved of this habit. She may also have inspired,
to a degree, Mrs Micawber who forgets that David Copperfield (often seen as
Charles himself) is a child, addressing him as an adult and expecting him to
show adult competence and independence. An early biographer describes Elizabeth as "a cheerful soul, fond of joining in the amusements of young people"
(PA 6). Both of Charles' parents have a feckless and immature quality.

Charles' father, John Dickens, a model for Mr Micawber, seems to have seen
himself as something of a gentleman. He spoke in a florid manner and perpet-
ually spent far beyond his means. One reason for this behaviour is suggested
by Claire Tomalin who implies that John's real father may have been his
mother's employer, Lord Crewe, in whose household John remained, with his
mother, until he was twenty-one. If John even half believed this, it may have
been the origin of his affectations of grandeur and his constant need to spend
more than he could afford on books, wines and other gentlemanly extravagances.
John had certainly been favoured by the Crewe connection and had grown up
among the eloquent Whig aristocracy of the turn of the century (CT 4).

The chronology of events in childhood is of supreme importance. Charles,
as the first son, will have been his parents' principal object of attention from
his birth on 7 February 1812 until the birth of his brother Alfred Allen Dickens
on 28 March 1814. So baby Charles was only two and a bit when his brother
was born, when there may have been a complete change in parental attitude.
From being made to feel the centre of his parents' universe, the little Charles
may, literally overnight, have found himself suddenly demoted and left to fend
for himself. Most parents do not allow such a sudden change to happen, but
others can focus only on one child at a time. To accentuate this, the new baby,
Alfred, was sickly and after six months, died. We do not know exactly how
the parents reacted to this bereavement, only that Elizabeth herself was also reported to be ill and that a nurse cared for Fanny and Charles. Furthermore,
debts were mounting and the family began moving from house to house, partly
to avoid their debtors. They moved when Charles was five months old, and
again shortly after the baby Alfred's death when Charles was two and a half,
this time to live in London. A general picture emerges of a father psychologically denying his financial problems and of a mother stressed by bereavement
and the repeated changes of abode. Maybe, for the first time, Elizabeth was
realising that she had married, not a prosperous gentleman, but an incorrigibly
optimistic fraud.

Infants cannot understand such situations in adult terms but only in terms of
overall emotion. Baby Charles would have felt the family insecurity at this
time and the loss of his mother's former cosseting. He may, as Peter Ackroyd

has suggested (PA 12), also have felt jealous anger towards his usurping brother Alfred and even some guilt when Alfred died. Maybe these were the infantile experiences that lay behind Charles' coolness towards his mother in adult life - a mother who had lavished love upon him for his first two years and then suddenly withdrawn it. The reasons for this withdrawal of care – the preoccupation with her sick baby and her own bereavement and depression – being beyond the comprehension of the infant Charles, who simply construed her neglect as wilful rejection.

Only a year later, in April 1816, another baby was born. This was Charles' younger sister Letitia. At the end of the year the family moved yet again, this time to Chatham. Charles was only five but could just about read, his mother having given him (and presumably his older sister Fanny) daily lessons. In describing these, Charles used almost exactly the words used by David Copperfield – "I faintly remember her teaching me the alphabet, and when I look upon the fat black letters in the primer, the puzzling novelty of their shapes and the easy good nature of O and S, always seem to present themselves before me as they used to do." (CT 10). Do we detect here the origin of Charles' love of letters and words, associated as it may have been with the rare and much prized attention of his mother?

Charles' mother had come from a family of ten where she, herself, had probably experienced only rationed quantities of parental love. Instead, she had enjoyed the special support of at least two of her brothers and one of her sisters, and these members of the Barrow family continued to support the Dickens family throughout Charles' early life. But was their help for their dependent sister Elizabeth one reason why she prematurely expected her eldest son to do likewise for her? She had experienced her two oldest brothers helping her childhood family and so, naively, may have expected Charles to do the same before he was of an age to do so. Charles still yearned to be cared for and yet he found both of his parents expecting his "adult" support! Is this why Charles felt anger towards them? Matters were not made better by his father's continued financial incompetence and by the arrival of three more babies into the family: Frederick in 1820, another Alfred in 1822 and Augustus in 1827. As more and more emotional demands were made on Elizabeth, less love and care were available for Charles. She reacted to this stress by regression, preferring to "join in the amusements of young people" as if she was still a child herself.

Peter Ackroyd has pointed out how there is a sorrowfulness and coldness at the heart of Dickens' novels, all of which are concerned with family life and its failings (PA 5). They express a longing for greater love and stability which was what Charles himself yearned for. David Copperfield (to an extent a portrait of Charles) actually identifies himself with a baby at breast, and the narrator in

Master Humphrey's Clock was "happy to nestle in her breast – happy to weep when she did – happy in not knowing why". These could be references to the infant Charles' yearning to be cuddled by his childish mother.

It is interesting that most of Charles' younger sibling rivals for his mother's love, were boys. There had been two Alfreds, Frederick and Augustus. In adulthood Charles formed better relations with his sisters Fanny and Letitia than with his brothers. When it came to his own children, Charles was never at ease with his own sons, only with his two surviving daughters, Mamie and Katey. Indeed, of his seven sons, five were sent abroad. He did not really want them. Out of a sense of duty, of course, he appropriately provided for them in material terms, but he treated them with firm discipline and grew further apart from them as they matured. He wanted no more rivals.

The chronology remains important. Charles, as a little boy, seems to have enjoyed his home in Chatham where the family lived from 1817 till 1822 when, under pressure from creditors, they moved back again to London. Things went from middling to far worse when, in February 1824, Charles' father was finally arrested for debt and committed to the Marshalsea prison. Charles, aged twelve, now found himself the man of the family, living in a cold house in Gower Street and expected to be responsible for the welfare of his mother and four siblings. On the well-meaning advice of Elizabeth Dickens' brother-in-law, Charles was found a job in a factory on the Thames near Charing Cross, at six shillings a week. The work involved covering and labelling pots of blacking. On the face of it, this seems a reasonable expediency, considering the family's desperate situation, yet Charles construed it as humiliation. To make matters worse in his eyes, his parents had openly condoned the arrangement and Charles interpreted this as a straightforward parental put-down. Charles had already formed a view of himself as being someone exceptional, destined for a remarkable career. Thus, to find himself working in dilapidated premises alongside working-class boys of his own age was, for Charles, deeply shameful. The other workers called him "the young gentleman" and this underlines the importance of class for Charles. He had, to this extent, adopted his father's view of himself as a gentleman fallen on hard times –

No words can express the secret agony of my soul as I sank into this companionship... the sense I had of being utterly neglected and hopeless; of the shame I felt in my position ... my whole nature was penetrated with grief and humiliation. (JF Chap 2).

These events meant a disruption of Charles' meagre formal education (although not to his emotional education) as he clearly experienced awful feelings of shame and insecurity. Towards both his parents, and particularly his mother, he now felt increased anger. As he saw it, his parents had sent him out to slave for the family, and he felt misused by them.

In some ways both John and Elizabeth Dickens had the character of fraudsters. The father, like many a confidence trickster, half believing in his own hard luck stories and grandiose self-image, while the mother, more manipulative, was out to squeeze what she could from others, rather as her own father had done. In later years, once Charles was successful, his father would constantly pester him for money. Yet there was a comic quality about his father's behaviour, and a warmth, that caused Charles repeatedly to forgive him. For his mother, however, Charles reserved a cool disdain. She had reversed the roles of parent and child, forcing him to behave as a grown up and denying him maternal love when he was still a child.

Yet, of course, there was much in this painful experience that was to benefit Charles as a writer. The exploitation of children became one of the central themes of his novels. So also did cruelty, shame and rejection. Furthermore, the insecurity that the young Charles experienced in the blacking factory gave him the determination to succeed and make money, a determination so strong that throughout his life people would remark upon his prodigious levels of energy, agitation and cheerfulness. He was, as so many creative achievers seem to be, clearly hypomanic. He also became a bit of a 'control freak'. As an adult he always loved a party, blotting out all his negative feelings with songs, theatricals, alcohol and good company. Yet he always remained in charge. For the young Charles the theatre became an antidote to depression and, as a young man, he nearly became an actor, partly because, as an actor, he would find himself to be the centre of attention. Although it was his career as a writer that he chose to develop, he would, increasingly, crave to act out his own dramas upon the stage and, by the time he was forty-five he probably spent as much time acting as writing. Indeed, he had, by the end of his life, become a highly accomplished and extremely well paid performer.

As a young man Charles became incredibly hard working, mysteriously walking the streets of London at night, hurriedly dashing off instalments of his novels, throwing lavish parties, hobnobbing with artists and writers, and rushing off on hectic trips to the Continent, sometimes for no clearly defined purpose. He also toured America.

There is one aspect of Charles' life that has been overlooked by most biographers, and that is Charles' strong sexuality. Almost everyone has sexual preferences and tends to look for certain psychological and physical characteristics in their sexual partners. For Charles it was young and subordinate girls that he fell for, and it is very striking how Charles liked to surround himself with pretty young women. First it was the three Hogarth girls, then the young prostitutes he cared for in London, and finally the Ternan women. He ended his days with his two daughters Mamie and Katey, his young housekeeper Georgina Hogarth and his even younger mistress Nelly. These women were all between fifteen and twenty seven years younger than himself and they clearly adored him. At the time of his death in 1870 he was writing *The Mystery of Edwin Drood* – a story that not only questions the reality of youthful romantic love but portrays the obsession for teenage girls of two middle-aged men. I strongly suspect that Charles was a regular womaniser and had accompanied several of his more bohemian friends – such as William Macready the actor, Daniel Maclise the painter and Wilkie Collins the author, on visits to the brothels of London, Rome and Paris. He would have gone to great lengths of course to conceal this side of his life, but Charles was nothing if not a master of disguise and secrecy. (Is this why Wilkie Collins, the great pioneer of a franker view of sex, never wrote the expected biography of Charles? Only the boringly conventional John Forster was groomed for this privilege.) Charles would burn most of his private letters and, in many ways, he was more of a Regency buck than a mid-Victorian moraliser so, as the middle class puritanical mores of the 1850s caught up with him, he would go to greater and greater lengths to conceal his sensuality. The opportunities were certainly there, however. The streets of every city in Europe at that time offered clubs, houses of ill-repute and ladies of the night. The almost constant travelling abroad, the long enigmatic nocturnal walks and the seeking out of unconventional company were constant features of Charles' life from his twenties onwards. Studiously, he tended to avoid the overt mentioning of sex in his novels, and its absence is striking, even for the times. Instead, he dressed up his erotic fantasies and relationships in the socially acceptable romantic language of his day. His novels certainly reveal his knowledge of the demi-monde, although his portrayal of fallen women has been described as curiously clichéd. Innocent and saintly young females are also a feature of his work.

I believe that two important events in his life can only be understood if seen as manifestations of Charles' intense sex drive: his reaction to the death of Mary Hogarth (his wife Catherine's younger and prettier sister) and the later rejection of his wife. In 1837 the newly married Charles clearly fell in love with Mary and for a number of weeks Mary cohabited with the young couple. Indeed, as her unhappy sister Catherine lay pregnant at home, Charles and the seventeen year old Mary had a good time together, going out to entertainments in London. One night Charles took both sisters, Catherine and Mary, to the theatre. They returned home for supper and a drink, and retired to bed at around one o'clock in the morning. According to Charles, he then heard a cry from Mary's bedroom and went in there to find that she was ill. At three o'clock that afternoon she died in his arms. His reaction was one of extreme and dramatic grief. Catherine, on the other hand "became so calm and cheerful that I wonder to see her" he said. Charles, distraught, even postponed the next instalments of *Pickwick* and *Oliver Twist*, and announced that he wanted, when he died, to be buried in Mary's grave. He wrote her epitaph, describing Mary as "young, beautiful and good" and throughout his life continued to describe her as a paragon of virtue. Not only did Charles show himself to be insensitive to his wife's feelings on this score, but he went out of his way to assure the world that Mary was free of any fault. I have to confess that all this seems to me to suggest that Charles was trying to deny his own guilt. Had he started a sexual relationship with Mary or was it just in his mind? Had he been in her bedroom that night *before* she was suddenly taken ill, had he touched her or kissed her? Had she suffered a miscarriage or attempted an abortion? We shall never know.

Within a relatively short time, however, Charles found a substitute for Mary in his wife's still younger sister Georgina (1827–1917) who, aged fifteen, and against her parents' wishes, moved into his household in 1842. She was to stay there, playing the role of his housekeeper at least, until the end of Charles' life. Again, whether or not there was an overtly sexual component to this relationship is unknown.

Another clue to Charles' obsession with sexually available young girls was his decision in 1846 to establish a hostel in Lime Grove for young prostitutes, which he curiously named Urania Cottage. Did he have sex with any of its inmates? It would have been so easy to do so. He interviewed all the girls applying for entry, was obsessively involved in every detail of their management, and clearly felt affection for them. He kept in touch with some of them for years. Young women inspired him: they were his muses – just as Urania herself is a muse in Greek mythology. It was rather taken for granted by the Greeks that young and beautiful women (there were nine of them in their mythology) could inspire a male artist. The mood that accompanies sexual attraction seems to promote creativity.

Charles' closest collaborator in his work with the young prostitutes, Baroness Burdett-Coutts, broke off their relationship around 1858. Had she suddenly realised the extent to which Charles' life was being driven by his libido or was she, too, romantically involved? Was her reaction that of the jilted lover rather than the shocked spinster? Although outwardly very conventional, this extremely rich woman would end up marrying a man no less than 37 years younger than herself – perhaps itself a sign of secret eroticism on her part – as such toyboyism often is. Was she a surreptitious 'player' too?

In August 1857, Charles met the Ternan family of actresses – a mother and her three daughters, and the following year he separated from his wife Catherine, announcing that they were "not made for each other". She was now forty-two and had grown fat and physically unattractive. It was as simple as that. Charles always had an eye for pretty teenagers and he was now in love with the youngest of the Ternan sisters, Nelly. He was forty-five and she was eighteen. She was to continue as his mistress until he died in 1870. Maybe her mother and her sisters had also slept with him, in return for the financial support they so desperately needed.

Nelly was not an entirely naïve victim. After Charles' death she would move to Oxford claiming to be fourteen years younger than she was, associating with the students, and marrying one of them, twelve years her junior, in 1876. I am not saying she was a fortune hunter or a 'cougar', but she could clearly look after herself, and knew what she wanted.

One of the rather charming features of the last twelve years of Charles' life is that he spent them surrounded by his little coterie of young women – Georgina (fifteen years younger than him), his daughters Mamie (twenty-six years younger) and Katey (twenty-seven years younger), and his mistress Nelly (also twenty seven years younger). All four women knew each other well and remained friends for the remainder of their lives. Working in theatres all over the country, the ageing star also made friends with quite a few other young actresses in the last ten years of his life, and helped several financially. Was there a pay-off? He also enjoyed hypnotising young ladies – a fascinating party trick that epitomised the power he liked to have over them.

If I was forced to guess whether Charles had had many sexual relationships with young women during his lifetime, I would have to guess in the affirmative. Most of these would have been casual affairs with prostitutes and actresses. But to say they were superficial relationships and therefore unimportant for him would be to miss the point. Charles was, I suspect, driven by an overwhelming sex drive that was central to his existence. It was the strongest drive in his life. The indirect evidence for this is the record of his extraordinary and mysterious nocturnal hyper-activity, his exceptional secrecy, his love of parties surrounded by adulating young women, his gruelling reading tours, his eternal restlessness and his fondness for foreign travel, especially to France where he found the bohemian way of life so liberating. This is probably where he took his teenage mistress Nelly for her confinement. Much of Charles' energy would have been spent in concealing his sex life from the world generally, as well as from his family and most of his friends. Only a few were in the know. Those who are not overwhelmingly driven by sexual desires (and there are many such people) can find it difficult to understand and forgive those who are. Yet sexual cravings can be just as compelling as any drug addiction. Charles was a man of paradoxes – kind but occasionally cruel, long suffering but impatient, jocund and depressed, selfless and selfish. Perhaps his cruelty towards his wife was fuelled by the anger and revenge he had felt for his unloving mother. Katey, his most perceptive child, probably revealed some inkling of his secret life and of her approval of it, when she said, strangely, of her father, long after his death – "he was not a good man, but he was not a fast man, but he was wonderful!… I loved him for his faults". (CT 415). He had substituted a clique of pretty young women for the youthful, almost infantile, mother who had let him down. To say that Charles was primarily a heterosexual paedophile, and that his writing and acting were largely means of seduction and procurement, would be absurd, probably inaccurate and offensive. I am not saying that. But in a society that is still recovering from the Jimmy Saville revelations we can begin to see how, for some celebrities and public performers, their celebrity is partly a means to this end. Their overwhelming drive is their infatuation, physical as well as mental, with young people. For centuries great men and some famous women too, have shown their predilection for youthful bodies and youthful company. From Julius Caesar to Oscar Wilde there have been many examples of older men and women worshipping the puberty of others. As the age of puberty has dropped, society has failed to make the appropriate moral and legal adjustments. In Dickens' day, young girls in London averagely started puberty (menarche) at seventeen and a half years of age, while sometimes marrying or losing their virginities far younger. It is just possible that Charles Dickens was caught in such a predicament. If so, at the time when Victorian middle-class prudery began to grip the nation, how was he to satisfy his overwhelming cravings? All this is, of course, mere speculation. If I was professionally counselling Charles today, however, this is one of the hypotheses I would want to research with him.

Conclusions

Ironically, John Dickens always impressed upon Charles that the boy could be successful and famous if he worked hard, and Charles went along with this. When Charles was a child, John had showed obvious pride in his son, and passed on to him his own feeling that he was out of the ordinary. The unspoken message from his father was 'Charles, your duty is to regain the family's specialness and affluence that (through no fault of my own) I have been forced to relinquish'. A secondary message was – 'and as eldest son it is your duty to look after your parents'. With his mother, Charles had a far more bitter relationship. As a baby he had, no doubt, briefly been the apple of her eye and the centre of her attention. When other births and deaths of siblings ensued, and as John's financial incompetence became apparent to her, Elizabeth, depressed, anxious and immature, grew to regard Charles primarily as a potential source of income for herself. So she tried to turn him, prematurely, into an adult.

Charles, still yearning for maternal love, saw this attitude as maternal rejection. When, at twelve, he was sent to work in the run down blacking factory, he construed this as the final insult from his mother, and he never forgave her. Yet his fascination with teenage girls may have been unconsciously connected with his longing for the love of his childlike mother.

Driven to succeed and earn the family's money, Charles chose the medium of words, perhaps as these were associated unconsciously with his mother's teaching, but also, perhaps, because of his father's eccentric grandiloquence. He yearned still to be the centre of attention and, rather exaggeratedly wrote, disguised as fiction, about his own unhappy childhood experiences – of poverty, loss of love, squalor, idiosyncracy, incompetence and cruelty. He pedalled also the antidotes to his personal misery – comedy, theatricality, conviviality, kindness and happy endings. Privately, however, his greatest solace was, I suspect, the company of much younger women.

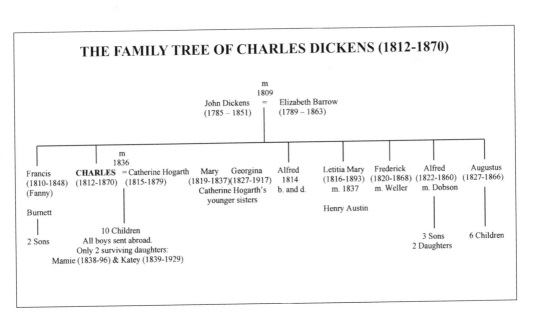

SOURCES

Peter Ackroyd: *Dickens: A Biography*, London, Sinclair Stevenson, 1990.

John Forster: *The Life of Charles Dickens*, London, Chapman and Hall, 1872-74.

Claire Tomalin: *Charles Dickens: A Life*, London, Penguin Books, 2011.

4

AGATHA CHRISTIE (1890 - 1976)

Writer

The case of Agatha Christie is, surely, an example of where the psychologist can be of little use. There was nothing mysterious about Agatha Christie. She was a perfectly normal and straightforward English woman who took up writing as a needed source of income, and stuck to it professionally over the course of nearly sixty years. Perhaps the only possible questions are why did she select the genre of the detective story, rather than some other genre, and why was she so good at it?

Agatha's actual autobiography, published in 1977, just after her death, is remarkably bright and breezy. She is not one to dwell on the darker side of things. Nevertheless it is a fascinating tale of an interesting life. She depicts her childhood as occasionally lonely but, more often, as surrounded by eccentric and bustling late Victorian adults. She was very fond of the animals and the servants, particularly her nanny (Nursie – 'a firm realist') and the family's cook (the 'majestic' Jane) who never, in forty years of employment, ever displayed any emotion. Servants were usually happy, Agatha remarks, because they were 'appreciated as experts; far from being slaves they were more frequently tyrants'.

Agatha describes her father as an easy-going and lazy man with nothing much to do except laugh good-naturedly, while her mother was an "enigmatic and arresting personality" with startlingly original ideas. Agatha partly attributes her parents' happy marriage to their age difference of around eleven years, and cites several other happy couples with even greater differences in age. (She was herself many years older than her second husband). Both her brother and her much older sister, Madge (later to be called Punkie) were on good terms with their parents, and Punkie emerges as a huge influence over the little Agatha. (AC 106) We are told that Punkie was the clever one in the family, and that she was always witty and entertaining and for ever telling stories. Punkie would pretend they had an older sister who was mad and lived in a cave, and she would take on the identity of this sister, speaking in an 'oily' and frightening voice. (AC 54) Agatha used to feel indescribable terror on these occasions, but enjoyed it. She asks 'why did I *like* being frightened?' and concludes that one needs to 'prove yourself to yourself…you want to be frightened a little – but not too much'. Agatha's first written story was about the noble Lady Madge (good) and the bloody Lady Agatha (bad), but Punkie (Madge) wanted to be the bad one – "she thought it would be much more fun to be wicked". So they shared together a girlish ghoulishness and a sense of melodrama. It was when she was a few years older (about ten) that Agatha began to notice that Punkie had an extraordinary fascination for men, having 'a great deal of sexual magnetism.' Agatha dedicated one of her most successful books, *The Murder of Roger Ackroyd*, to her sister: 'To Punkie, who likes an orthodox detective story, murder, inquest, and suspicion, falling on everyone in turn!'

Agatha is rather scathing about herself as a child. She had, she says, no ambition at all, other than to make a happy marriage and thus to find contentment. She did not feel she was particularly good at anything. It was the dynamic Punkie who got her to start writing, betting her she could not write a detective story. We can see that Punkie was both a model and a rival for Agatha. But, more than this, she was also responsible for cultivating two important traits in her sister that would characterise her writing – Agatha's love of setting and solving puzzles, and her fascination with being slightly frightened. In a sense Punkie was Agatha's muse. Perhaps Agatha was acting out a part of Punkie's life for her – a part that Punkie never had time to develop. Much of what Agatha did was done to impress Punkie.

Agatha's first husband was a real catch. Tall, handsome, brave and witty, he was almost immediately cast into the cauldron of the Great War where he was repeatedly decorated for bravery and mentioned in dispatches. Yet Agatha does not really seem to have understood what this meant for him in psychological terms. She had noticed that, on leave from the front, Archie had appeared 'on edge' and 'nervy', but he did not want to discuss his experiences. He wanted to forget things by distracting himself. Archie disliked any sort of unpleasantness and tried, in a very British kind of way, to avoid it by keeping up an appearance of jollity. When the marriage began to break down they could not discuss their difficulties frankly, although she could not see 'why we shouldn't live happily ever after'. Indeed, Agatha was so upset by the separation that she reacted with psychological denial and hysterical amnesia, forgetting who she was and being unable, for example, to remember her name when signing a cheque.

Agatha Miller had been brought up in Torquay by an upper class American father and his quirky middle class English wife. Agatha's eccentric brother disappeared abroad in the Army at quite an early age, while Punkie drew attention to herself by playing pranks and dressing up in various disguises pretending, for example, to be a vicar or a nun. The family had an apparently idyllic life in sunny Devon, picnicking on Dartmoor and occasionally travelling abroad. Yet there was some insecurity beneath the surface of Agatha's serene childhood: at the age of four she wrote that it would be misery if "someone I love to go away from me" and she had a recurrent childhood nightmare of a horrific manifestation of her mother, dressed as a man, staring at her with "steely-blue eyes". Then her father's money began to run out and, rather suddenly, in 1901, he died. Agatha was eleven years old at the time and, as the youngest in the family, had been his favourite. Punkie (twelve years older than Agatha) promptly reacted by marrying a rich man from Manchester, where she went to live, while Agatha and her mother found themselves alone and short of money in Torquay – "a middle-aged woman and an untried, naïve girl", as Agatha later described her situation.

Agatha had met her dashing young aviator, Archibald Christie, in 1912, and two years later, as he was about to leave England for the war, she had married him. After four years of harrowing aerial warfare Archie returned to civilian life and the couple settled outside London where their daughter Rosalind was born in 1919. But their marriage was unhappy and Agatha appears to have felt that her husband lacked empathy. Whereas Agatha actually enjoyed her fictional horrors, Archie had known *real* terror over the battlefields in France. The difference between fiction and reality may have contributed to their separation. It is rather strange that Agatha should blithely write about murder, rather as a game, in the post war England of the 1920s where hundreds of thousands of families were bereaved, and thousands of old servicemen were suffering the terrors of Post Traumatic Stress. Was her obvious enjoyment of the idea of death rather insensitive? Did it upset Archie, who had seen so much of the real thing? At that time few civilians realised the extent of the psychological damage caused by war. Admittedly, she avoided blood and gore in her books, preferring death by poison, but the obsession with murder remains central. By setting death at vicarage tea parties or in civilised drawing rooms, was Agatha trying to remove its sting? In 1926 Archie fell in love with someone who was, perhaps, more understanding of his traumatic wartime experiences, and began divorce proceedings. Distraught, Agatha fled from home and drove north, nearer to Punkie, to stay under a false name at a hotel in Yorkshire, apparently crashing her car slightly on the way. Strangely, she chose the name Teresa Neele – the same surname as her husband's lover. For a few days she forgot who she was. Like Punkie she could easily alter her identity. Whether she suffered amnesia due to a head injury or to the desire to forget, it was all entirely understandable. To make matters worse, Agatha's mother had died only a few months earlier. Anguished at being abandoned and desperate to avoid the media spotlight, Agatha achieved exactly the opposite and for some weeks became the centre of national attention. She felt like 'a hunted fox', she said. The tendency to travel in order to try to escape from problems, however, would remain with her.

According to her daughter, Agatha never got over her loss of Archie. By middle age, there had been two great crises in Agatha's life when important men had let her down. First, her father's financial ruin and death, and then her husband's infidelity and divorce. Her consequent insecurity became the primary source of her determination to make money as a successful author. In 1930, aged forty, she met Max Mallowan, a twenty-five year old archaeologist from Oxford, with whom she was to remain happily married for the rest of her life. Some women, no doubt, might fear disloyalty in a younger partner but in Agatha's and Max's case the reverse was true. The age difference between them enhanced her ability to control the relationship, thus reducing the risk of a third male 'desertion'. She now became archaeologist as well as writer: both careers dealing with mysteries and detection. She had always enjoyed such intellectual puzzles.

As a child, Agatha had been taught by her father and her older sister to read and to write and, as a teenager, she read voraciously, taking books from her father's well stocked library. She also learned to play word games: acrostics, rebuses, enigmas, cryptographs and riddles. She was not sent to school but largely educated herself, reading both fiction and non-fiction. Often alone when young, Agatha invented a large number of imaginary companions – indeed a whole school of invented school-friends. Being tall, gawky and not especially beautiful, she did not, as a teenager, attract much male attention. Yet the teenage Agatha had become ambitious and she began to think about a career – not an easy prospect for a poorly educated middle class girl in the Edwardian era. Her main model, as we have seen, was her sister Punkie who had had several short stories published in *Vanity Fair* before her marriage. Agatha's mother, also a would-be writer, and probably aware of Agatha's boredom, one day suggested she should write a story. Within days the eighteen year old had completed *The House of Beauty* – a Gothic tale about death, dreams and madness, inspired in part by her readings of Edgar Allan Poe. She proceeded to write other stories, sometimes using the name of her father's father, Nathaniel Miller, as a non du plume. All were rejected by publishers.

Agatha received encouragement, however, from a neighbour in Torquay, the successful novelist Eden Phillpotts, and in 1916 proceeded to write *The Mysterious Affair at Styles*. This followed the challenge from Punkie to write a detective story. During her childhood, detective novels had become very fashionable thanks chiefly to the appearance of Conan Doyle's Sherlock Holmes in the 1890s, and she had also enjoyed reading Wilkie Collins' two detective books *The Woman in White* and *The Moonstone*. *The Mysterious Affair at Styles* was eventually published in 1919, setting her off on her long and successful career as a writer of detective thrillers.

For Agatha, the main point of her books was the intellectual problems she posed for the reader. Her stories are riddles to be solved. She provided the clues and then challenged the reader to work out the correct solutions among several possible alternatives. This was very much an evolution of her childhood love of puzzles and conundrums. Like Punkie, she had also enjoyed confusing others with disguises, although in Agatha's case the disguises were usually in her books. Many of her characters disguise or swap their identities with others. It was the way both sisters had always interacted with people – playing games of hide and seek with the world – as mystifiers and teasers. Puzzles and their solution were the essential medium of the sisters' relationships. This, surely, was why she was drawn to the detective genre, and indeed to archaeology also.

Agatha was always shy. She had lacked her sister's and her mother's social adventurousness probably because she felt rather physically unattractive. Highly intelligent, but often alone, she had cultivated her imagination and her intellect. She was sensible but secretive. Being in the national spotlight when her first marriage had broken down had made her even more concerned about her privacy, but there was still a side to her, paradoxically, that yearned for attention and for excitements such as are to be found in the world of theatre – a world she still associated with the memory of her beloved father and her happy childhood. While her father was alive he had taken her to local theatricals and, as a teenager, her grandmother in Ealing had done likewise. This is probably why, in her latter years, Agatha converted many of her stories into plays. Once again her fascinating muse Punkie had led the way by suddenly writing a play, typically about faked identity, that appeared in the West End in 1922. (LT 46).

The loss of her father, and then the almost simultaneous loss of her adored mother and her first husband Archie, had devastated Agatha and increased her insecurity. Not only had she failed to understand Archie she had allowed herself to grow fat and unattractive. By her late thirties she had almost no loving friends except her dog Peter - her closeness to Punkie was mixed with rivalry and she was a distant and jealous mother to her own daughter. (LT 123)

What more is there to say? Like so many other authors Agatha had a parent (her mother) and a sibling (Punkie) who were would-be authors, so she was both emulating and competing with them, as well as joining in the family culture. Like other authors, too, there was a childhood background of financial insecurity and of real or threatened loss of social status. Similar circumstances are to be found in the lives of Jane Austen, Charles Dickens and Thomas Hardy. Like Daphne du Maurier she became deeply attached to places. Although Agatha Christie today is often described as a thoroughly English upper class woman, this is an image that Agatha herself created. In fact she came from the mixed background of an American father and an English mother whose maiden name was the foreign-sounding 'Boehmer'. Frederick Boehmer had married his step-mother's niece, from a family of orphans who had worked for their livings as nurses and hotel workers. Agatha's second husband's family also had foreign roots, coming from Austria. This is probably why her books celebrate the essence of Englishness. In the heavily class-conscious and xenophobic culture of the inter-war years, Agatha had had to perfect her own disguises. She was driven not only to make money but to better herself socially, ending her days as a titled lady, still outdatedly dressing for dinner at her home in Wallingford, or in the family's Georgian country house in Devon, separated from the bourgeois suburbs of the Torquay she had known as a child.

She had become the most widely published author of all time.

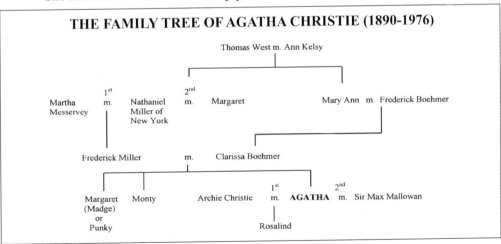

THE FAMILY TREE OF AGATHA CHRISTIE (1890-1976)

SOURCES

Agatha Christie: *Agatha Christie: An Autobiography*, New York, Dodd Mead & Co, 1977 and Harper Collins 1993.

Janet P Morgan: *Agatha Christie: A Biography*, London, Collins, 1984.

Andrew Norman: *Agatha Christie*, Pitkin Guide, 2009

Laura Thompson: *Agatha Christie: An English Mystery*. Headline Review, 2007

5

DAPHNE DU MAURIER (1907-1989)

Writer

Daphne du Maurier's tangled life of fantasy poses quite a challenge. Daphne was the second of the three daughters of the well-known Edwardian actor-manager Gerald du Maurier and his actress wife Muriel Beaumont. Daphne's grandfather was cartoonist and author George du Maurier who created the figure of Svengali in his novel *Trilby* (1894). Daphne was also a cousin of the Llewelyn Davies family whose boys served as the inspiration for the characters in JM Barrie's *Peter Pan* (1902) – a play in which Daphne and her sisters Angela (three years older) and Jeanne (four years younger) became immersed in various family and professional productions. These two literary creations, Trilby and Pan, permeated educated British society in the early years of the century and coloured all of Daphne's childhood. In many ways her father took the role of Svengali in attempting to control the lives of his three daughters, while Daphne, or a part of Daphne, would remain forever Peter Pan. On stage her father became memorable versions of both Captain Hook and Mr Darling.

Unlike so many middle children Daphne did not feel unfairly neglected by her family. She was fortunate in this respect in that she was her father's favourite. All the sisters, however, felt the lack of maternal love, but most of all Daphne. Their mother Muriel lived a life of total submission to the needs of her narcissistic husband. She is recorded as having few, if any, noticeable desires or feelings of her own, and her daughters grew up longing for more womanly love and affection. This is, presumably, part of the reason why all three girls became predominantly lesbian, although Daphne would always resist this identity, seeing herself as a boy in love with various women with whom she had relationships. We will have to explore Daphne's love life because it is so important as regards both Daphne's personality and her writings.

Daphne had had a strange childhood, brought up in the thespian world of the Edwardian era. Between the ages of four and seven, five close relations had died - her grandmother, two uncles and two aunts. This may have intensified her father's dependence upon her. Her biography of him, written after his death in 1934, is remarkable in several ways. The first is that it is written almost as a novel with long passages of quoted speech as if Daphne could recall the details of her father's daily life. Furthermore it begins in the 1870s, thirty or forty years before Daphne was born. In reality, the whole book is beautifully written fiction. But it seems to have some genuine psychological insights into the characters, not only of her father, but of her grandfather George, as well as of her aunts and uncles. It is all written in the third person and gives few clues as to her own very close relationship with her father. Yet according to Margaret Forster, the writing of this book emotionally drained Daphne. It was a tribute to the man she loved, yet she almost entirely left herself out of the story. She did not, however, withhold criticism of her father's character, portraying him as the spoiled child or 'ewee lamb' of his mother: nonchalant, overactive, tactless, amusing, he could never stand being alone or being inactive. He used constant denial and distraction in order to avoid serious issues about himself and others. She described him as 'changeful', 'inconsequent' and 'lonely'. Much of the time he was classically *camp* (as we would say today) and mimicked his actress colleagues by poncing around the stage in rehearsals 'his hips swaying, his eyes rolling, his hand patting an imaginary strand of hair' (DM 120).

There are some hints about herself:

There is, alas! a world of difference between the girl of eighteen and the man of fifty, especially when they are father and daughter. The one is resentful of the other. The girl mocks at the experience and detests the voice of authority; the man yearns for companionship and does not know how to attain it. (DM 206).

Yet the girls were not always unkind to Gerald. They adored him really, although Daphne became elusive, disappearing to Paris and to Cornwall (DM 208). Once she asked him whether it was true that boys kissed one another at public schools, and how very amusing it must be. 'He gazed at her in horror and had no answer' (DM 174). It was a teasing sort of sibling relationship as much as a parental one, with Gerald wishing that Daphne was a brother. (He missed his dead brother Guy almost as much as he missed his father.) He could be quite cruel to women sometimes, disguising his sadism with childish humour and converting it into an endless stream of practical jokes. It was all passed off as good fun.

Daphne imagines her father thinking about his daughters:

> *Why was Daphne always going to stay in Paris?* [Often, in fact, to visit her lesbian friend Ferdy]. *Whom did Jeanne have interminable conversations with on the telephone? They were not the companions they might have been... It was all very disappointing. He wished they were children again, playing cricket on the lawn... How little one knew about one's family. How little one knew about anyone. How little deep down, one really knew about oneself.* (DM 231).

The biography was also a tribute to her father in that its production demonstrated that Daphne was taking on the role of author just as her father had wished her to do. It was her first successful publication.

The usual psychological defence mechanisms such as repression, rationalisation, regression, reaction formation, projection, displacement, sublimation and denial that are used by most people to keep anxieties at bay, appear to have been insufficient for Daphne. She added two others – an obsession with safe places (nearly all in Cornwall) and the use of her formidable imagination. These gave her added security and protection. So, for over seventy years Daphne lived in a world largely of her own creation, clothing all important events in her life with fantasies of her own devising. Her imagination became a buffer between herself and the harsh realities of living, and her relationships with others were not with people as they really were but with her romantic ideas of whom she wanted them to be. Amazingly, Daphne knew that she was doing this.

One of her most significant creations was Eric Avon – the boy whom she imagined she was from the age of thirteen. All three sisters, and especially the two youngest, consciously wished they were boys, apparently believing that both their parents (and especially their father), had wanted sons. Jane Dunn, who has written a psychologically sophisticated biography of the du Maurier sisters, describes Daphne's alter ego, Eric Avon, in the following terms:

> *He was sporty and brave, captain of cricket at Rugby School, and his day of glory came each year at the imaginary cricket match between Rugby and Marlborough School... Jeanne and her friend Nan were drawn into this fantasy. Renamed David and Dick, the Dampier brothers, they bowled and batted for Marlborough, the opposing team, and invariably lost...* (JD 42)

Eric was three years older than Daphne and seems to have been very much the typical Boys Own hero of the Edwardian era. He was self-sufficient, resolute and daring. Eric was not what her father was, but what he partially *wished* he was. Indeed Eric was the sort of chap that Gerald's heavily suppressed homosexual side might have admired and loved. Furthermore Eric was rather like Gerald's two business partners, Tom Vaughan and Frank Curzon. (J.D. 43) Her father even described Eric in a poem written for Daphne in which he admits how he had wanted her to be his son. He wishes she could:

Do deeds of daring have much fame,
And she knows she could do the same
If only she'd been born a boy.
And sometimes in the silence of the night
I wake and think perhaps my darling's right
And that she should have been
And, if I'd had my way, she would have been, a boy. (J.D. 44)

Years later, when Daphne met Tommy, her husband to be, she instantly fell in love with him because here was Eric in the flesh – brave handsome Tommy who had endured horrors in the Great War and would go on to endure further horrors as a parachute commander at Arnhem. She felt, she said, as though she had 'known him for years' (J.D. 163). Daphne would often refuse to recognise the sensitive, shell-shocked and depressed real Tommy who needed her womanly love, because she was still clinging to the fantasy of Eric Avon.

Eric Avon was, of course rather like her other hero, Peter Pan. He too, was a loner who never grew up. Eric was, however, far more conventional and class-conscious than Pan. Even years later, when Daphne was in her forties, she fell in love with her American publisher's wife, Ellen Doubleday – or the fantasised version which she projected onto the long-suffering Ellen – and Daphne suddenly felt she was Eric again – 'a boy of eighteen … with nervous hands and a beating heart, incurably romantic, and wanting to throw a cloak before his lady's feet'. (J.D. 275) Like Pan, she built her life by the sea, surrounded by boats and the descendants of pirates, thus escaping the cloying, confusing and dangerous grasp of her father – was he Mr Darling or Captain Hook?

Sense of identity and gender, sexual orientation, personal success and good looks are important issues for all of us as teenagers. For Daphne they confused her all her life. Who was she? What gender was she? Was she lesbian? Was she beautiful and attractive to others? Was she a success? Two important reasons why Daphne never succeeded in finding satisfactory answers to these questions was her very strange father and her even stranger relationship with him.

Sir Gerald du Maurier, the successful actor, had been the youngest and most pampered child in a family of two boys and three sisters. His older brother Guy wrote a successful patriotic play in 1909 and died heroically, aged fifty, in the Great War. Daphne had been eight when her uncle died. Maybe he, too, had once been a bit like Eric Avon.

Gerald was different. He relied upon his business partners to build the material success of his career, while he went from one theatrical triumph to another, beginning with his roles in *Peter Pan* in 1904 – and what roles these were: as Hook, the epitome of evil, and as Mr Darling, the embodiment of respectable paternity. Gerald started the tradition of playing both characters in the same performance. Gerald was charming, self-centred and a social climber. He completely dominated his snobbish wife Muriel and together they presented to the world the image of the supremely successful Edwardian family. Gerald notoriously flirted with the actresses with whom he worked, and perhaps had affairs with them, but was strongly opposed to homosexuality, shielding his three daughters from any knowledge of sex, and becoming extremely jealous of their later adult relationships. Daphne was his favourite child and he flirted with her to such an extent that it sometimes upset those who saw it. 'He couldn't keep his hands off her' the tennis star Bunny Austin once complained, (J.D. 232) and there were rumours that their intimacy went further.

When young, all three sisters showed a conventional interest in men but their relationships were mostly flirtations based on romantic fantasies. None of them seemed to know what physical sex was, nor wanted to try it. Daphne's first passionate emotional relationship was with the headmistress of her French finishing school when she was aged seventeen. Fernande Yvon (Ferdy) was a lesbian who preyed upon her girls, and her tactile, but perhaps not fully sexual, friendship with Daphne continued for years.

In as much as Daphne had never felt loved by her mother, her female relationships tended to be with older women – Ferdy, Maud Waddell (governess), Molly Kerr (actress), Ellen Doubleday (American beauty) and Gertrude Lawrence (actress). Later there were friendships with county ladies in Cornwall. According to Jane Dunn the affair with the delightful and easy-going bisexual Gertrude was probably the only one which became fully physical. But then Gertrude was ahead of her time, unusually relaxed about sex and taking it all in her stride. In her relationships with men Daphne led them on, and the men ardently pursued her, but mostly without consummation. Relationships were, however, occasionally completed – such as the adultery with her friend Christopher Puxley, but even this, seemingly, lacked any real sexual passion on her part. With both sexes, Daphne created a love story, and then applied all her creative fantasies to her chosen actors. She cast Ellen in the main role in one affair, while Christopher starred in another.

Daphne continued to live in her artificial world, protected from reality by her own imagination. Years later, after using her distorted image of Christopher as the main inspiration for the cultured and piratical main character in her novel *Frenchman's Creek* she admitted that:

> *Anything less like the Frenchman, really, than that poor man, there couldn't be, but I Gondalled* [imagined] *him into it, and saw him that way.* (Malet. Letters from Menabilly. P134)

Such insight is, perhaps, what makes Daphne a remarkable author.

Whatever else remains difficult to understand about Daphne's love life, we can, I think, say with some certainty that none of her affairs, either with men or women, were lust-driven. Indeed, one wonders whether she was ever aware of the purely physical attractions of others, or even whether she experienced the genital pleasures of sex at all, either in marriage or in any of these other relationships. Years later she admitted that she had always most enjoyed the foreplay in a sexual relationship "and was not much bothered by the rest," (JD151). Such very private matters might not be of much importance in most people but, for Daphne, they affected her world of imagination which, in turn, was the source of her best writing. All the du Maurier girls had grown up in a world where sex was a taboo subject and they did not learn the facts about sexual intercourse until they were well into their adolescences. This is unimaginable today but in Edwardian times such ignorance was quite possible. Daphne's older sister, Angela, far more outwardly emotional and sociable than Daphne, also took years to discover sex. It was not until 1935, aged 31, that Angela had her first frankly sexual relationship with the remarkable South African actress Marda Vanne, who told her:

> *It seems you expect me to feel more than lust for you. Is not lust a decent honest thing?* (J.D. 196)

Like some other good-looking 'lipstick lesbians', Marda could enjoy the physical pleasures of sex without the complications of romantic love. It was a breakthrough for Angela and helped her to begin to shake off all the shame and twisted fictions surrounding sex and love that had been forced upon her by her parents. Maybe her father's death the previous year had made all this possible. How did Angela's enlightenment help Daphne? Apparently not at all. Daphne remained frightened by lesbianism, denied that she was a lesbian, avoided meeting Angela's lesbian friends and even continued to refuse to use the 'L-word' itself. Yet throughout her life she had intense relationships with women. Like her sister she was drawn to women, enveloping them in her fantasies and usually, once the intense phase of the relationship was over, converting them into long term friends.

Her relationships with men were, on her part at least, far more superficial. She had a heroic husband who helped her to make her life appear to be conventional, but she failed to understand his deepest needs, and often found his presence irksome. The other male admirers she merely seemed to play with.

Was Daphne trying to convince herself that her fascination with women was not basically lesbian but merely Eric Avon's normal heterosexuality? By turning herself into a young man in her imagination she could have romantic and gallant relationships with lesbian and heterosexual women while avoiding having to call herself a lesbian.

What one can say with some certainty is that Daphne did a lot of things that she knew her father wanted:

- In her imagination she became a boy called Eric Avon (or, later, Niall).

- She became a successful writer like her father's father – so continuing the du Maurier tradition, and filling the psychological gap in Gerald's life created by his father's death.

- Outwardly she appeared sexually restrained and conventional.

Yet despite all this conformity to Gerald's wishes Daphne could not help herself from becoming closely involved with various, mostly older, women – or at least with her fantasies of them. One could speculate that these relationships with women, only a few of which were probably consummated physically, would have had Gerald spinning in his grave. He had detested the idea of lesbianism. Was this why Daphne imagined it was Eric Avon who was having these affairs? This would, of course, make it all normal and heterosexual and so not so shocking for Gerald.

Perhaps the most economical way to explain Daphne's complicated love life – so full of fantasy and yet so lacking in sexual passion as it was – is to say that her need for women was, like her sisters', based upon the search for maternal love. In every case Daphne's older women were outstanding people (or so she imagined them) who gave her what Muriel could not give. She felt that Muriel had never provided understanding, warmth, creativity, or even social standing – just dull and clockwork obedience to Gerald, and hostility. In the Oedipal triangle between her parents and herself, Daphne usually suppressed her irritation with her mother, yet her mother sometimes showed outright jealousy and steely anger towards her. In later life Muriel descended upon her daughters in Cornwall to be cared for, but it was mostly Jeanne, and occasionally Angela, who did the caring. Using her writing as an excuse, Daphne stayed away, occasionally chipping some money into her sisters' coffers.

At times Daphne appeared very selfish, as indeed she was. But her withdrawal from society, her employment of servants to care for her own two daughters, her early indifference towards her war-damaged husband and her solitary self-confinement to her writing desk, were all parts of her elaborate defences. She was selfish because she had to be. She had to protect herself from life. She knew that for her, real human relationships could prove to be a minefield and so were better avoided. Her novels reflect this frigidity – there is a swagger, a menace and an emptiness about them. Her writing depends mostly upon a feeling for *places* and on Daphne's ability to create an *atmosphere* of dimly discerned danger. Alfred Hitchcock, of course, responded to these qualities and, very fortunately for Daphne, made films of her stories. Without Hitchcock she might be a forgotten writer today.

What else should a psychologist take note of? Daphne was one of a trio of sisters and one finds, as is common in such cases, fierce rivalry and competition between the three of them. They compete for parental attention while at the same time subtly clinging together in a band of family loyalty. Daphne had won the competition for father's favourite, while Angela desperately searched for love outside the family, and Jeanne devoted herself to caring for Muriel. All competed in career terms, too, with Angela's books and Jeanne's paintings being largely ignored by the critics. Daphne would both encourage and subtly denigrate her sisters' work.

There was something very irritating about Sir Gerald du Maurier, as Cecil Beaton noted in his diary in January 1923 – "he is so conceited and so ridiculously affected. He gets completely on my nerves". Success had come too easily for Gerald – his father's name and contacts had given him a good start and Tom Vaughan and Frank Curzon had done all the hard graft for which he got the credit. He had certainly been spoiled by his mother. He did not want his own daughters to grow up, was pathologically jealous of their admirers, shielded them utterly from any knowledge of sex, was thoughtless of their feelings, alternated flamboyant chivalry and charm with studied indifference, and swung in mood from waspish depression to bumptious elation. Daphne must have felt reassured that her father was so interested in her, but how did she react to his constant tactile stimulation? Did this trigger feelings of sexual arousal in her as well as generalised affection? Full-bloodied sexual and affectionate feelings were to be rarely experienced by her in later life – were they under lock and key, banished forever because of their guilty association with incest –

a subject that fascinated her to the end? Perhaps she had felt primal disgust rather than excitement at her father's approaches. How often does disgust at a parent's sexuality turn off a child's own incipient sensuality? Freudians might say that such disgust is a product of guilty interest, but can it also be more basic than this? Disgust can exist as a natural reaction to vomit, dirt and bad smells, for example, and can be powerful. Daphne would, in later life, leave several hints that she found all genital sex to be disgusting, or at least that she was disgusted by full heterosexual intercourse. She had quite liked foreplay with Puxley but never the full thing. (Disgust at its most basic is a defence against catching diseases and so it is an instinct that has clear survival value.) Daphne had not been told about sexual intercourse until she was eighteen when, informed by a school-friend, she exploded: "What an extraordinary thing for people to want to do!" (J.D. p28) She wrote about the sexual act – "Oh, isn't it all unwholesome?" (Letter to Tod 4/2/24).

Daphne may have been secretly aroused by her father's approaches but she may also have been simultaneously disgusted. It was almost certainly a matter of intense ambivalence. There was also the question of his Svengali-like power over her. That too was something she both enjoyed and detested. In her third novel, *The Progress of Julius*, written when she was twenty four, is her remarkable description of a daughter's reaction to her powerful father:

> *[She was] aware of Papa who watched her, Papa who smiled at her, Papa who played her on a thousand strings, she danced to his tune like a doll on wires – Papa who harped at her and would not let her be. He was cruel, he was relentless, he was like some oppressive, suffocating power that stifled her and could not be warded off... she was like a child stuffed with sweets cloying and rich; they were rammed down her throat and into her belly, filling her, exhausting her, making her a drum of excitement and anguish and emotion that was gripping in its savage intensity. It was too much for her, too strong.*

Jane Dunn is fairly unequivocal – Daphne found Gerald simply 'irresistible'. (JD 35). But why was Gerald so universally flirtatious with women while being so secretive about sex in general and so condemnatory about any form of homosexuality? Almost certainly it was because he was himself a repressed homosexual. He was a Don Juan. Of course, not all womanisers are repressed homosexuals – some are genuine heterosexuals whose libido is intensified, usually by hypomania. But in the case of Sir Gerald du Maurier the combination of his strident homophobia with his 'camp' femininity, suggests that he pursued women incessantly because he wanted to conceal from himself his own homosexuality. (Daphne refers to his love of gossip, intrigue, drama, confidences and of female company itself, as further signs of his femininity (DM 190).) So this was another unspoken complication that the poor du Maurier girls had to deal with. Was part of Daphne's unconscious reaction to turn herself into Eric Avon – the sort of boy that her homosexual father would find attractive? The trial and conviction of Oscar Wilde in 1897 had been a scandal of immense proportions and had inflamed a violent prejudice against homosexuality throughout the country. As a result, the young Gerald du Maurier, twenty four at the time, must have feared his own gay tendencies intensely. No wonder that he outwardly appeared to detest both male and female homosexuality.

We still do not know for certain why the three sisters were so sexually unusual. Was it their hormones, lack of maternal love or the peculiar influence of their prudish, flirtatious and Don Juan father? Any hints that Daphne's sexual confusions were in fact fuelled by her unusual hormonal set-up might be supported by the evidence of her savage post-natal depressions, the worst of which was after the birth of her longed for son (MF 157). Or is this too sensational? Gerald had loved his father and often told Daphne that "You remind me so of Papa" (J.D. xvii), as he urged her to become a writer. So was she simply trying to fill the gap in her father's life that had been created when her grandfather died? All three girls turned out to be bisexual romantics, and all three may have been a little frigid. Jeanne and Angela never became celebrities, however, while Daphne went on to win all life's prizes, except for peace of mind.

Other Matters

So Daphne grew up as a loner living in a world of her own imagination. She was wary of other people and wished to get away from the histrionic and stressful company of her father's actor friends. The personalities of actors can fluctuate; there can be a lack of consistency and depth that may confuse a child. This is partly why she escaped to Cornwall. Daphne was a thinker and a searcher after truth, yet handicapped by her own fear of truth. Instead of casting a cold analysis of reality she played a solitary game of hide and seek, alternating insight with fantasy. Desperately, she tried to understand her own transsexuality. Although she had not known the facts of life until eighteen, her heterosexual instincts had first been aroused four years earlier, Daphne subsequently recorded, when her thirty six year old cousin Geoffrey had lain beside her on the beach and squeezed her hand under a rug:

> *No kisses. No hint of the sexual impulse he undoubtedly felt and indeed admitted... but instead, on my part at least, a reaching out for a relationship that was curiously akin to what I felt for D(addy).*

She wrote (J.D. 49) later:

Nothing, in a life of seventy years, has ever surpassed that first awakening of an instinct within myself. The touch of that hand on mine. And the instinctive knowledge that nobody must know.

When she was 21 she allowed Geoffrey to kiss her passionately one night when she was in her pyjamas. This was probably the only time it happened. Apparently she did not yield, as many would have done, but reacted with apparent coldness and detached surprise. "Men are so odd" she wrote in her diary (J.D.50), adding, "the strange thing is [kissing Geoffrey] is so like kissing D[addy]". Surely this suggests her frigidity was a reaction that she had learned to deploy when aroused by her father.

What else is there to say? Taboo and incest are enduring themes in Daphne's stories. The idea of incest in particular became a fascination for her. This suggests to me that she was far less disgusted than excited by her father's advances. She had been aroused and remained so throughout her life. So by being a boy in love with women, and by being cold towards her husband and other men, she was also being loyal to Gerald. Daphne was often withdrawn, intellectual, introspective, cynical, humorous, wary and observant of others. Once she admitted "I like women much better than men" and yet insisted: "If only I was a man!" (JD 71). In fact, Daphne led quite a dull unadventurous life outwardly, yet once wrote – "life's no fun unless there's a spark of danger in it" (JD 78).

Her relationship with Mlle. Fernande Yvon (Ferdy) had been, so it seems, a "hugging" relationship. She had told Tod: "I get on the back seat with her, and she puts her arm round me and makes me put my head on her shoulder. Then sort of presses me!" Again, the maternal quality seems to be important for her. Even with Fernande, so Daphne told Ellen Doubleday years later, she had reacted *not* as a girl but as a boy. She was both boy and girl and:

...at eighteen this half-breed fell in love, as a boy would do, with someone quite twelve years older than himself who was French and had all the understanding in the world, and he loved her in every conceivable way up to the age of twenty three or so ... then the boy realised he had to grow up and not be a boy ... and the boy was locked in a box" ... [although when alone at Menabilly] she *"opened up the box sometimes and let the phantom who was neither girl nor boy but disembodied spirit dance in the evening when there was no one there to see. (JD 90).*

Notice also that Daphne recalls Ferdy's "understanding". That, too, was something she felt she had never received from her mother. There is a great deal in this passage. She describes Eric Avon almost as a ventriloquist's doll – something created by someone else – and as "disembodied", as if the body but not the essence, were unacceptable to her father and herself. Romantic love and physical love were always to be separated in her life, and the latter put in a box and suppressed. As Jane Dunn reports:

> *Daphne's first sexual experiences were with a woman and, although she continued to find both men and women attractive, she was never entirely to enjoy the complete heterosexual experience...* (JD 92)

In a letter to Tod in November 1931 Daphne said that enforced sexual ignorance was the reason for the mess that people made of their emotional lives. (JD 124) She was, of course, thinking of her sisters and herself. Because of her father's obsession with her and because various people, male and female, had found her attractive during her teens, Daphne drew the wrong conclusion. She concluded that she was especially alluring, not realising that most girls are attractive at that age, simply because of their age. (It is the natural age for breeding and male instincts run true to this.) Daphne as a teenager, as she said, knew "nothing at all – but Nothing" (JD 127) Her ignorance of sex and misunderstanding of human nature was so complete that once, in order to shake off the amorous advances of an elderly millionaire, she had stripped off naked in front of him and dived into a lake. She was then surprised that this had the opposite effect to the one she thought she wanted. (JD 133)

As Gerald approached sixty he lost his two business partners, Frank and Tom, and became disenchanted and depressed. These contemporaries had been father figures for Gerald, filling the gap he had felt when his father had died when he was 23. Then his affectionate friend the author Edgar Wallace had died. So things were bad for Gerald. He turned to Daphne for support, rather than to Muriel. But Daphne shrank away from him. Instead, she embedded herself in the Neverland of Cornwall, initially refused to go to London to join her parents and began to write her first novel, *The Loving Spirit*. Writing now mattered much more to her than sex or romance. As Dick (Daphne) in *I'll Never Be Young Again* says "this power of writing [is] more dangerous than adventure, more satisfying than love" (JD 170). She was also infatuated by places and Dunn claims that her love for Menabilly "was more powerful than her love for any man" (JD 260). Later, she did return to London but stayed away from Gerald while she was being courted by both cousin Geoffrey and Carol Reed. When Gerald heard that Daphne was to marry he "burst into tears and cried 'It isn't fair!'" (JD 168). When he died in April 1934 Daphne refused to attend his funeral and "instead took a basket of caged pigeons to Hampstead Heath and set them free." (JD 181) Did this indicate that she felt liberated by his demise? In fact the sudden death of the great love of her life must have been devastating for her, but she hid this. Daphne kept some of his clothes and wore them for years. She also wrote his biography, saying it was done to keep him alive.

Yet Daphne's novels were often more about identity and power than love, and she thought of *Rebecca* as being concerned with fear, jealousy and hatred also. She claimed that she valued power and independence above love. She liked the world of ideas, and writing a novel was like giving birth. "What I write is me" Daphne said (JD 274). Yet wasn't her writing also doing what her father had wanted – reminding him of his much loved father and keeping up the family tradition? One of the great paradoxes of Daphne's life is that her novels did not fully reflect the spiders-web of her own romantic fantasies

Dunn says: "Her heroes and heroines were unsympathetic and loveless, [her men] either weak and ineffectual or brutish and bullying. But the dark and menacing relationship between the sexes… was fascinating and distinctly hers" (JD 247) It was partly Pan and Wendy's relationship with the strange figure that combined Mr Darling with Captain Hook, so it was also her relationship with her father. For Daphne, Ellen Doubleday briefly became "the mother I always wanted". Daphne would hang all sorts of imaginary attributes upon such ro-manticised figures or "pegs" as she called them. One of the women inside Daphne was 'hard and down to earth' as she said, and the other was timid (280). It was Daphne's Eric Avon who was the romantic figure who would ride out to fight dragons so as to protect fair damsels such as Ellen.

Daphne depicted her fantasy of Ellen's character as Stella in her play *September Tide* and then fell in love with the actress Gertrude Lawrence who played the part, re-enacting as she did, her late father's real life role as one of Gertrude's lovers. Daphne was always aware that she was an actress in the play of her own life and that she was acting all these roles. She wrote to Ellen "you *are* a complete woman, and I have never been. I've only put up an act at being one."

The chronology of Daphne's unusual love life can be summarised as follows:

Age

13 years – She first imagines herself to be Eric Avon. By being Eric she hopes to secure *both* her parents' love, but particularly her father's.

14 – Older male cousin Geoffrey arouses her heterosexuality by holding her hand under a rug.

17 – Her affair with Fernande Yvon begins.

18 – She is first informed about the facts of heterosexual intercourse and is amazed.

21 – She allows herself to be kissed passionately by Geoffrey, but claims not to be moved.

24 – She falls in love with Tommy 'Boy' Browning and marries him.

27 – Her much loved father dies.

40 – In her role as her alter ego Eric Avon she falls in love with her image of Ellen Doubleday as a mother figure.

41 – She falls in love with Gertrude Lawrence, and identifies with her father as she does so.

Eventually Daphne tried to get rid of her obsession with Ellen by basing on her the main character Rachel in her novel *My Cousin Rachel*, and then killing off Rachel! Insightfully, Ellen had accused Daphne of turning her into a mother substitute and a reinvention of Ferdy, her first love. Then her other girlfriend, Gertrude Lawrence, suddenly died in September 1952, and Daphne lost not only another lover, friend and 'peg', but also all the associations with her father. We can see that Daphne subsequently avoided other deep relationships almost entirely and enjoyed, instead, a prolonged love affair with the house at Menabilly and a series of shallower fantasy-based relationships with women. After the double loss of Ellen and Gertrude, Daphne felt devastated and started writing several short stories, including *The Birds*, that reached deeper still into violence, fear and the macabre. She had been bereaved of the two greatest loves of her life – her father in 1934 and Gertrude in 1954. Both their deaths had been sudden and unexpected.

In her correspondence with Ellen, Daphne dwelt upon the two key experiences of her childhood – the lack of love from her mother and her father's controlling favouritism. Indeed she wrote even more about her mother than her father. Tod (her nanny) had been of the opinion that Daphne was afraid of her mother and this may well have been the case.

In such an Oedipal situation Daphne as a child had instinctively feared her mother's jealousy, which had been aggravated by her father's open flirtations with Daphne. (JD 335) This fear only mellowed in the mid 1950s when Daphne found herself nursing her ailing and senescent mother and realised that Muriel deeply appreciated this care. At the end of November 1957 Muriel unexpectedly kissed Daphne twice on the cheek. Daphne felt "all the queer strains between us … were somehow wiped out with that brink-of-death kiss" (JD 336)

But it was Tommy's sudden collapse, also in 1957, when alcohol and PTSD finally overwhelmed him, that had a really destructive effect on Daphne. In middle age Tommy had become depressed and dependent rather as Gerald had done a quarter of a century earlier. Discovering that Tommy, bereft of wifely love, had been finding some solace in the company of other women in London, Daphne was overwhelmed with guilt and realisation. In her search to understand, Daphne tried to explain it all in terms of her own novels. Tommy's breakdown "had so shaken me from my dream-world that I began to think I was going potty, it seemed to me everyone was an enemy". (Letter to Ellen. 18 Dec. 1957).

Her elaborate strategy to avoid her own disintegration, that had worked well for so many years, - her withdrawal from society, the defensive barrier of her imagination, her dedication to writing, and her obsessive love for Menabilly – all suddenly felt hollow. The world of make-believe which, she said, she had cultivated since the age of five, suddenly began to fail her.

When Tommy had retired in 1962 from his job working for Prince Philip, he had come back to live in Cornwall, still depressed and alcoholic. It was only after he died at Menabilly a few years later that Daphne, to her surprise, discovered how much she had loved him. They had become attached, and she missed him. Her final decade was marked not by mellow understandings but by emptiness and quiet despair. She died in 1989. It would be gratifying to believe that her mother's dying kisses, and her nursing of Tommy in his final days, perhaps also her final achievement in being made a Dame of the British Empire in 1969, together marked a resolution of all Daphne's yearnings for maternal acceptance, heterosexuality and worldly success. But other factors, principally depression, supervened.

All three sisters had tried to avoid their father's influence by escaping to Devon and Cornwall. Yet all three had, to a greater or lesser extent, felt that they had to carry on the torch of du Maurier creativity and ambition by becoming artists and writers, and all three had, in order to meet their father's wishes, toyed with being boys. But it was Daphne's yearning for her mother's love that had made her, despite her reluctance to become a lesbian, seek the motherly love of other women. (We do not fully understand what makes a lesbian, but yearning and competing for maternal love is certainly a common feature.) So there were three special motives driving Daphne all her life: first, the yearning for maternal love, secondly her desire to please her father by being a boy, and finally, her ambition to be a successful writer like her grandfather, also to please her father. In retrospect it is clear that her feelings for her father were mostly extremely positive.

With complex cases such as Daphne's, it often helps to set down a chronology of the psychologically significant events:

Salient Chronology

1907 – Daphne is born in London. She is named after actress Ethel (Daphne) Barrymore, who had once rejected Daphne's father's advances.

1910 – Aunt Sylvia Llewelyn Davies dies.

1911 – Younger sister Jeanne is born.

1913 – Aunt Beatrix dies.

1914 – Grandmother Emma dies.

1915 – Uncle Guy dies in the war. Daphne calls to her father not to leave her.

1916 – The family move to Cannon Hall, Hampstead. Daphne's father Gerald enjoys huge successes as England's leading actor-manager.

1917 – Gerald stars in *Dear Brutus*.

1918 – Maud Waddell (Tod) is employed as governess.

1920 – Daphne creates Eric Avon as her chief alter ego.

1921 – Cousin Geoffrey Millar holds her hand under a rug. Daphne writes *The Seekers*, portraying herself as a boy seeking love from "Tommy" (a character who resembles Gerald).

1922 – Gerald is knighted.

1925 – Goes to a school in Paris which is run by Fernande Yvon (Ferdy). Falls in love with Ferdy who reciprocates. Learns the facts about heterosexual intercourse for the first time.

1926 – An unknown man courts her. First visit to Fowey. Ferryside purchased. Anger with Gerald's jealousy and possessiveness over her relationships with men. Muriel's overt anger at Gerald's affairs with actresses.

1927 – Gerald becomes depressed and dependent on Daphne.

1928 – She writes short stories critical of men's unfaithfulness. Continues flirtation and kissing with Geoffrey.

1929 – Escapes to Fowey. Fascinated by Menabilly. Tom Vaughan dies. Gerald's depression worsens. She meets Carol Reed and starts romantic friendship with him. Gerald expresses anger towards Carol. She realises her mother's hostility is because Gerald loves her (Daphne) so much. Attempts to lock up "the boy" inside her and tries to suppress her "Venetian tendencies" (i.e. lesbianism). Ferdy scoffs at Daphne's short stories. Sex with Carol continues and he suggests marriage. Relationship with her mother worsens.

1930 – Daphne feels unloved by both parents. For a short time Jeanne is Gerald's favourite. *The Loving Spirit* is accepted by publishers. Writes *I'll Never Be Young Again* while in London, in which she examines what sexual passion is all about. Disgust with sex. Ambivalence. Horror at female sexual appetites. Questions the relationship between sex and love.

1931 – Writes *The Progress of Julius*. Julius has "a voracious passion" for his daughter. Meets Major Tommy 'Boy' Browning at Fowey. Daphne is attracted by his dominance and good looks. She feels she is in love. They marry. Gerald, allegedly bursts into tears and cries "It's not fair!". Daphne now tries to improve her relationship with her mother.

1932 – Unexpectedly, Tommy begins to show dependence on her, and the symptoms of PTSD (nightmares of First World War). She feels annoyed by Tommy's need for love, but enjoys sex with him.

1933 – A boy is expected but Tessa is born. Nanny (Margaret) installed. Daphne does not cuddle Tessa, and becomes depressed.

1934 – Gerald becomes ill. Operation reveals colon cancer. Gerald dies. Daphne shows few signs of grief. She believes that in some way Gerald is not dead, he is somehow around her. She does not attend the funeral but releases some pigeons from a cage on Hampstead Heath, imagining Gerald is equally free. Signs contract with Victor Gollancz to write Gerald's biography. Finishes *Gerald: A Portrait* in four months. Acclaimed by the critics. The book glosses over Gerald's passionate love for his daughter but paints a portrait of a charming and nonchalant actor who reaches the top of his profession. The pinnacle of his career, she believes, was his portrayal of Will Dearth in JM Barrie's *Dear Brutus* in 1917 – the role of a father infatuated with his fantasy daughter.

1935 – *Jamaica Inn* published. Success.

1936 – Goes to Egypt with Tommy. Hates it.

1937 – Returns to England. Birth of Flavia. Depressed. Returns to Egypt. Starts writing *Rebecca*.

1938 – *Rebecca* published. Huge success.

1939 – Joins Moral Rearmament.

1940 – Craves a son. Kits is born. Although delighted she is depressed again.

1941 – Starts affair with Christopher Puxley. Publishes *Frenchman's Creek*. Adores Kits and sees resemblance to Gerald.

1942 – Family moves to Fowey.

1943 – Publishes three lesser known novels. Takes lease on Menabilly and moves in. Almost alone in the house with Nanny and children.

1944 – Tommy commands Arnhem landing as Lieutenant-General. He is then posted to Ceylon. Tod moves into Menabilly.

1945 – Daphne ends affair with Puxley.

1946 – Publishes *The King's General*. Tommy is knighted. Nanny (Margaret) leaves. Tommy returns home. Marital tensions. Tommy shows more signs of PTSD. He resents Tod but tolerates Ferdy. Daphne often dreams of Gerald.

1947 – Tommy gets a job with the Royal Family. He takes a flat in London. The Brownings appear to be the perfect couple: much laughter and apparent happiness. Daphne still sees Ferdy and Carol Reed. She meets Ellen Doubleday and falls in love.

1948 – Daphne is sued and acquitted of plagiarism (*Rebecca*) in America. Stays with Ellen. Writes play *September Tide*. Gertrude Lawrence stars as Stella – a role which reminds Daphne of Ellen. Tommy is depressed and alcoholic. Daphne falls in love with Gertie Lawrence.

1949 – Publishes *The Parasites* which deals humorously with her three personas of Maria, Niall and Celia. This book is slated by the critics. Indicates her fear that she is a social parasite herself.

1950 – Starts writing *My Cousin Rachel* in the midst of her affair with Gertie. Corresponds frequently with Ellen.

1951 – Publishes *My Cousin Rachel* which deals with male jealousy. Great success. Visits Ellen and Gertie in America. Relationship with bi-sexual Frank Price. Admits to Ellen that she prefers "Venice" (lesbianism) to "Cairo" (heterosexual intercourse).

1952 – Publishes *The Apple Tree* which deals with her feelings about her marriage to Tommy – "their minds not meeting", and his jealousy of her love for her children. Her stories now give more power to women and less to men. Gertie dies suddenly aged 54. Daphne is devastated. Admits to Ellen that she was in a physical relationship with Gertie. She equates the importance of the loss with the loss of her father Gerald.

1954 – Reads Jung. Tries to make friends with her boyish persona No. 2. When she was writing she felt all No. 2.

1955 – She finds Tommy intensely annoying. Still feels no inspiration for a new book.

1956 – Writes *The Scapegoat* which deals with Tommy's and her own conflicts between inner (real) and outer (artificial) selves – "We are both doubles. So is everyone".

1957 – Publishes *The Scapegoat*. Good reviews. Tommy's drink problem worsens. He has women in London. He collapses. Daphne feels guilt. Sees herself as the first Mrs de Winter. Confesses about Puxley to Tommy and explains her Venetian affairs as part of a "nervous breakdown". Daphne's mother kisses her and dies shortly afterwards.

1958 – Imagines plots against her. She writes about the distinction between liking someone and wanting sex with them (...a typical no. 2 distinction). Tommy's depression worsens.

1960 – Publishes *The Infernal World of Branwell*. Irritated by Tommy's psychiatric troubles: "pathetic ... there is really nothing wrong with Boy ..."

1961 – Convinced she is short of money and can write no more. Surrounded by grandchildren who should be, but were not always, quiet, polite and imaginative.

1962 – The Queen and Prince Philip visit Menabilly. Daphne feels she is unsuccessful as a writer. Tommy's physical condition is treated but his psychological problems (depression) are not effectively treated. Daphne loves television, especially fast car chases and thrillers.

1965 – Tommy's left foot is amputated. Tommy dies. Daphne does not attend his cremation. She scatters his ashes in Menabilly garden. Feels shock and guilt. Condolence letters from Eisenhower and Montgomery.

1966 – Takes two short cruises to Greece. Makes friends with the Wolfendens. Visited by Ellen. Grows closer to her sister Jeanne and Jeanne's partner Noël.

1967 – Victor Gollancz dies. Daphne dislikes her daughter's divorce. Starts writing a new novel about Dick, a male narrator, who lived at Kilmarth and takes a time-travelling drug. Dick dislikes women and "the dreary road to copulation". Daphne feels she *is* Dick.

1969 – *The House on the Strand* is published to great acclaim. Obliged to leave Menabilly and move to Kilmarth. Made a Dame of the British Empire. Mourns the loss of Menabilly.

1971 – Publishes *A Borderline Case* about a woman who makes love to her father without realising his identity. Daphne says, in a radio interview, that not being able to give free reign to incestuous feelings is some kind of tragedy. Incestuous desires are normal but never can be fulfilled.

1972 – Her routines become obsessional and self-restricting.

1978 – Ellen dies. Daphne becomes more depressed. She takes Largactil in addition to sleeping pills and anti-depressants.

1981 – Depressed by her lack of creativity. Becomes irritable and controlling. Mourns her creative past. (Death of No.2).

1989 – Dies.

Comments on Chronology

This chronology emphasises the huge importance of Daphne's love for her father Gerald, and his for her.

We can see that there were many family deaths during Daphne's childhood which must have made her feel insecure. To make matters worse her mother

Muriel (presumably already incensed by Gerald's obsession for Daphne) provided no comfort, only hostility. Increasingly, the young Daphne turned to Gerald, desperately imploring him not to leave her. Gerald never made a secret of his wish that Daphne should be a boy. So, partly to attract him, she invents her alter ego of Eric Avon (later also called Niall apparently), the character she uses to flirt with both men and women. Eventually she escapes to Cornwall, and lives almost alone with the children and Nanny – what exactly was her relationship with poor Nanny? (FL 82). Nanny not only looks after the children but is fellow renovator of Menabilly and housekeeper, too (FL 57).

Daphne uses the confusion of her identity crisis as material for her novels, as she tries endlessly to understand herself. She feels love for Gerald but also anger at his disloyalty to her through his affairs with actresses. Around 1925 her love affair with her father begins to breakdown, as she meets Ferdy. She marries Tommy, partly I believe, as an attempt to suppress or conceal her own lesbianism. Gerald's death deeply upsets her. Behind her passionate obsession for her father lies her even more fundamental longing for her mother.

She loved Menabilly. Her daughter Flavia recalls her kissing its ivy-clad walls when she first saw the deserted house in 1943 (FL 56). Apparently Daphne said the house had been empty for some twenty years – that would be around the early 1920s when Daphne's love affair with her father had disintegrated on account of his apparent disloyalty with other women, his jealousy and his decline into depression. Did "Mena" become, for Daphne, an embodiment of her dead father? I believe it did. She had always said he was still around her and that houses could exude the essence of certain people.

After the war, Tommy returns home suffering from PTSD and their marriage fails, although they shun divorce. She falls in love with Ellen Doubleday and Gertrude Lawrence and is devastated by Gertie's unexpected death, and then by Tommy's.

Daphne carried the past around with her so this chronology has to be viewed as cumulative.

General Comments

Daphne's life was full of fantasies, half-hidden associations and special family code words. The latter were chiefly to do with sex and class – both subjects one could not discuss openly in the 1930s or 1950s. (These were periods of intense snobbery and puritanism). So, "Cairo" was sexual intercourse, "Venetian" meant lesbian, "waxing" was making love, "spinning" was petting and "honky" meant vulgar working-class. Nicknames too, abounded: "Moper" for her husband, for example, "Bing" for herself and "Boo" for her son. Then there are the names of her fictional characters, so many with possible connotations that they could themselves be a subject for a book. Finally, the real and fictional place names that were so important for her, most prominently, the strangely masculine name of her beloved Menabilly which she translated in *Rebecca* into 'Manderley'; a mutation from 'Men' to 'Man'. Like many great writers, she found language itself to be an endless Aladdin's Cave of symbolic and other delights. Strange, too, that when she met him, her husband's nickname was 'Boy'. She was already referring to Eric as her 'boy in the box' or 'the boy'. So had this drawn her to Tommy? Had she seen their liaison as partly a marriage to her principal alter ego? If so, this might help to explain her doppelgänger obsessions at that time.

Although Daphne was aware of world events, her books focus upon personal relationships. Her own inner obsessions, too, were with personal and family relationships rather than with philosophical or political ideas. Because these relationships were, in her case, intensely troubled she would always be thinking of them and of her family (about which she wrote several books). She was constantly trying to understand herself. Ironically, her books lack, in consequence, any typically masculine interest in politics or philosophy. She was so wrapped up in her personal dream world, Daphne had hardly noticed the war, and never seemed to recognise (at the time) the hugely courageous role in it played by her husband. It was as if she was a passenger or parasite on world events, pampered and cocooned in fantasies.

Just below the surface Daphne resented men. Was this because she felt her father had titillated her, been disloyal to her, dominated her and had then died and left her? Her novels and short stories often depict women as timid and doe-like, while the men are powerful, aloof and sometimes murderous. In life she managed to conceal most of her anger, but it was there: anger with men and anger with female rivals too. Yet why the anger with men in general? Modern interpreters might look at once for male "abusers". Yet only her father (whom she adored) could possibly fit this category. It was more Daphne who abused men (her husband, and several lovers) than the other way around. Her real abusers, if there were any, (I hate the word "abuser", often used unthinkingly to condemn rather than to explain) were women: first, and very obviously her mother and then her French school teacher, Ferdy, who mocked her literary ambitions and seduced her.

It is certainly possible to see Daphne as a heroic figure. She was a very deeply disturbed woman, yet she succeeded in turning her neurotic problems into wonderful novels and short stories. She had grown up in a confusing and histrionic environment, adored and erotically loved by her charismatic father, and hated by her jealous mother. Like her father she had tried to conceal her homosexual feelings behind a number of heterosexual affairs and by marriage to a highly conventional man. Everything of importance that she did was, ultimately, to please her father: as a boy, as a writer and as the conventional lady of the manor.

Unlike so many deeply confused and neurotic people Daphne led a highly successful life as both author and parent. With steely determination she proved herself to be a jolly mother and a kind and humorous human being. Her alter ego Maria, with iron will, controlled her outer life, obsessionally suppressing the boy in the box and Daphne's true sexual and angry feelings.

Flavia's wonderful memoirs give us a picture of a happy family home with faithful servants, a large house with bats and rats in the attics, solitariness, picnics and sailing, dogs and horses, and of children going away reluctantly to boarding schools. Flavia refers to her mother constantly as Bing (never Mummy or Mama), and Daphne comes across as a secluded writer who, when she rarely sees her children, acts like one of them, like a brother who plays cricket with them, laughing, mimicking, and giggling with them at the pomposities of adults. Daphne delegated their care – and indeed all traditional household duties – to Tod and the other servants. Presumably because of her strong male identity Daphne was quite incompetent when dealing with such matters as her children's clothes, their food or general welfare. Generally, Daphne was left alone to write – "her need for space, for freedom, was greater than her need for us" (FL 15) writes Flavia. Daphne adored her son Kits but seemed "a little bored with us girls. She liked to be alone whenever possible" (FL 168). Bing never became cross or impatient and "had a feeling for fun" (FL 38). She did, however, discourage the offspring from playing with the local village children. "She called them 'honks', and I suppose was as bad as Gran over what she referred to as a 'different class'. Tod was her ally in this …" (FL 106). Daphne also "despised girlish ways" and persuaded Flavia to develop into a tomboy, dressing in boy's shirts and corduroys, climbing trees and exploring the woods – "my hair cut straight and bobbed". Later, finding she had no skirt or dress, Flavia and Daphne were put into a panic whenever Flavia was invited out, which was only very rarely. Their few visitors were mostly family members such as Aunt Angela or the bad tempered Gran (Muriel).

Flavia portrays her father as mellowing as the war years receded. From being driving and quick tempered he gradually revealed his fondness for books and ballet, and travelled everywhere with his beloved childhood teddy bears. He also revealed that he had a predilection for tomboys like Bing and Joan of Arc – perhaps the main way in which he resembled Gerald, and one of the few reasons why he and Daphne had shared some love.

Clothes remained a problem for Daphne and her daughters. When she went to visit Ellen or Gertie in America (with both of whom she was in love) these two beautiful women would give her gorgeous cast-offs for herself and her children to wear. They were both amazed at her lack of a social life in Cornwall where nearly all social invitations were refused.

It is a little difficult to see which alter ego was the one Daphne chose to show to her children. Surely it was not Maria, if she was really the actress lady of the manor. So exactly who was the fun-loving "brother" who hated hurting people (FL 97), dreaded other people's anger (FL 99), but was totally hopeless as the manager of a household (FL 188)? Was it really Eric – the boy in the box? Daphne once told Flavia that her number one persona was conscious and her number two was unconscious. If her numbering was consistent this suggests that, sometimes at least, Eric/Niall *was* unconscious (FL 169).

Flavia's description of Daphne's declining years is moving – "I watched with ever increasing dismay and agony the slow deterioration of the once bright, cheerful and loving 'Bing' into an unhappy, lonely and frightened little soul, taking less and less interest in her family and surroundings". (FL 205).

Growing up as a child of actors is rarely easy. Being forced (as the du Maurier girls were) to act parts in a play as confusing as Peter Pan, while they were still children, can only have made matters worse. Acting is a psychologically disruptive occupation or, as Gerald du Maurier himself once put it – 'a highly strung, nervous business and no good to one's internal arrangements.' (DM 96) For these reasons alone, it is hardly surprising that the du Maurier girls experienced life-long difficulties with sexual orientation and gender identity. From her early years Daphne had become used to Peter Pan being portrayed by actresses. This was almost an invitation to her as a child that she could also play a male part in life. I suspect that childhood acting experiences may have long-lasting psychological effects. Nevertheless, it was Daphne's emotional involvement with her father and the rejection by her mother that lay at the heart of her confused but creative existence.

Ruminations

Daphne has been fortunate in having two of the most psychologically sophisticated of biographies written about her, as well as some moving memoirs by her daughter Flavia. My role is not to repeat the biographies but to try to resolve their differences and to go deeper. Margaret Forster's pioneering work, published in 2004 - as both A.L. Rowse and Anita Brookner pointed out at the time – also commented upon the connection between Daphne's inner life and her novels, or how she "put her demons to work for her" as Brookner says. This area deserves a book of its own. We have more than enough to deal with when considering Daphne herself. Part of the psychologist's job is to clarify and, in Daphne's case, much of the obfuscation lies with her affairs of the heart. She forces us to distinguish between some half a dozen different but usually inter-meshed feelings that are of universal human importance – gender identity, dom-inance, self-identity, lust, admiration, affection, attachment and friendship. In our culture today, men sometimes find it easier to separate these strands than women do. With Daphne, they all tended to be entangled to an almost infinite degree and made even more complex by her wanton use of conscious and de-liberate fantasy as a further layer of complication.

Like her father, Daphne often felt restless and dissatisfied. In his case I be-lieve this was because he was denying his true homosexual nature. In Daphne's case it could have been similar or different. Similar if her dissatisfaction was merely an unconscious imitation of his dissatisfaction (she identified closely with him) or because she too was suppressing homosexuality. On the other hand it could have been different in that it indicated some slightly different form of self-suppression – of sex (lust) *in general*, perhaps; or was it a longing for motherly love or for her father, Gerald? Maybe it was all these things. Daphne herself never worked it out. She continued in this adolescent confusion to a greater or lesser degree throughout her life. As Brookner indicates, artists can use such confusions as an endless source of inspiration. Daphne did so. "I long for something so terribly" the fourteen year old wrote to Tod, her nanny, "and I don't know what it is." (MF 16) It was like her father's "yearning to which he could give no name" (MF 5) She started to write a book about "a boy who is searching for happiness, at least not exactly happiness, but that something that is somewhere, you know. You feel it and you miss it and it beckons and you can't reach it…" (MF 21)

As regards *gender identity*, Daphne actually seems to have frequently con-vinced herself that she was a boy inside. Her body was a mistake, she thought. Her thoughts and her feelings were a boy's. Such experiences today are seen as part of a Gender Identity Disorder called Transsexualism. Its causes, whether genetic or environmental, are hotly disputed, and its links with homosexuality are obscure. Many transsexuals are not considered to be homosexual. *Domi-nance*, too, was an obsession. Daphne seems to have enjoyed dominating her sisters but to have liked the authority of her nanny. She was ambivalent about her father's power over her. Power is often a matter of obsessional interest to lesbians but with Daphne it merely continued to be one of the many issues in her life, and one she sometimes dealt with in her novels, where men are often seen as having power over women. With her *self-identity* (of which gender iden-tity is only a part) Daphne played continuing fantasy games, often identifying as a young heroic male, a respectable county lady and as a loving mother. One of the most touching aspects of Daphne's life is her successful role as a caring parent who, despite her inner turmoils, managed to give her children a stable and comforting home. She often neglected them but, when she did see them, she was invariably kind and cheerful. They became used to the chameleon like shifts in her personality.

She never, so it seems, let lust off the leash. She saw it as "foul" and "vile", and all her relationships lacked this dimension. *Affection*, however, was certainly there, but it flickered occasionally and was to an extent triggered by her fantasies of other people. She hated sentimentality or what she sneered at as "sloppiness". This was, perhaps, to reduce her childhood pain at being deprived of maternal love. She hadn't received love so she ridiculed it. *Attachment*, although she was sometimes unaware of it, was certainly present in her relationships with her husband and family and, more idiosyncratically, in her attachment to places. (It is a common feature of attachment to persons that the holder of such attachment is often unaware of it until it is threatened or broken.) One of the greatest attachments was to the house of Menabilly itself which I suspect became a symbol of her father. She had friends, too, and managed to turn many of her fantasy-bedecked lovers eventually into long term friends. She was not, however, someone who made friends quickly or with those who were over anxious to please her.

Daphne's main concern as a young adult continued to be her unidentified yearning for "something that is somewhere". According to a letter written to Tod when she was seventeen (MF 23) this feeling clearly had something to do with love, lust, marriage and, in particular, her father's "affairs" with actresses. But it is probable that, amazingly, at this age, Daphne had not even learned what sexual intercourse actually entails. Yet it helps to begin to identify this "something that is somewhere" with her concern about her father's heterosexual activities. Was she half-instinctively *concerned about his loyalty, not to his wife (as Daphne stated) but to herself, Daphne?* Unlike her sisters, she had gone everywhere with him as a teenager, to receptions, dances and parties – but he had a "stable" of actress friends with whom he also consorted. Was it this, his "disloyalty", which was making her so sullen and solitary?

How far was Daphne a lesbian? She hated the idea of being lesbian (or 'Venetian' as she called it) and went to some lengths to deny it. This was because her father, whose love she cherished, was overtly homophobic. Her crushes upon women she tried to depict as the heterosexual relationships of her male alter ego (Eric Avon or Niall). She did not mind being male but she did *not* want to be 'Venetian'. Her first 'Venetian' experiences were with Ferdy in Paris. She loved Ferdy "in every conceivable way" she said, (MF 31), but insisted that the Venetian "strange thrills" which she experienced with Ferdy, were Eric's and not hers. Furthermore, she claimed that she had also experienced such thrills with her father and with other men. Daphne was forever caught in a bind; she yearned for her father's love, knew that he wanted her to be a boy, yet also knew that he overtly detested lesbianism.

In a fascinating letter dated July 4th 1957, (MF 420) when she was aged fifty, Daphne wrote about her fantasies to her friend Maureen Luschwitz (who had been her husband Tommy's PA and had now married). She clearly intended this letter to be in the public domain. It provides a careful key as to how her fantasies are expressed in her novels. (She reveals that Rebecca was largely Tommy's ex-fiancée Jan Ricardo, while she herself (Daphne) was the narrator, and Tod was the inspiration for Mrs Danvers.) Although this letter seems to go into considerable introspective depth it hardly emphasises her relationships with her parents. She describes her visit to the oracle at Delphi and seeing the carved Greek words for "Know Thyself", which she then tried to put into practice. She realised that "no one I had ever loved was real (except the family)".

This letter raises so many issues but I feel that some of these are, if not deliberate red herrings, at least distractions. The truly useful elements in this letter seem to be:

- A repeated fear of rape or violence from men such as her husband (she refers to Tommy's revolver and Tommy gun, and to the rape experiences of the mythological Daphne.)
- Her realization that features of her close relationships with both men and women (except her family) were fantasies and unreal.
- An admission that, at the level of fantasy, she had inner selves. "Maria, Niall, Celia were the three people I know myself to have been" and that "Niall, the boy, was the one who turned to Ferdy and later to Ellen and Gertrude". (Exactly what she saw as the differences between these alter egos, still remains unclear.)
- A realization that her love for her father (and for Nelson Doubleday, Ellen's husband) were also "boyish". (Nearly all her loves, both male and female were, therefore, fantasised as being experienced by the boy inside her.)
- Her fantasised relationships were, she says, partly due to her "fear of facing reality", for example concerning her (Oedipal) jealousy of her husband's previous lover Jan Ricardo (and, presumably, concerning her parents too).
- Her neglect of her depressed husband (nicknamed 'Moper' by the family) was, she says, because she was trying "to work out the problem of Niall".
- A threat to kill her father (and herself) from the combined fantasy figure of Ellen and Gertrude. (These were, after all, partly mother-figures and so could be jealous of her love for her father.)
- Her revelation that everyone "has his, or her, darkside 'that will be destructive unless' we recognise it in time". (She knew she had hidden angers, ultimately with her rejecting mother and tantalizing father.)

- She sees her husband (and perhaps her father) not only as potentially violent but as "the man who takes, and takes, and takes".
- A feeling that looking after her mother is irksome – she (Gran) has become "so dependent on me that it's torture." (Daphne, in both 9 and 10, is expressing her feeling that no one really *gives* to her, but only takes).

We learn from this letter about Daphne's lifelong search for (maternal) affection, her consciously divided personality, her exploitation of her own fantasies and personas for the purposes of writing, her frequent male gender identification, and of her fear of her own and others' violence. We also gain a glimpse of a highly layered inner world, like an expensive cake, full of fruit and glitter and cream. The basic ingredients, however, remain simple – jealousy, anger, fear and the rapacious craving for love. The cake has at least three layers: in the middle are her desperately genuine fantasies about being a boy, and her love affairs. On top are her deliberate and playful fantasies, while the base is composed of her largely unconscious feelings for her parents.

There are then three apparent possibilities as regards Daphne's sexual orientation:

- She was predominantly lesbian and her heterosexual relationships were a cover to convince herself and others of the opposite. Her whole life was therefore a lie.
- She was basically heterosexual and the homosexual adventures were due partly to her overall sexual frustration, combined with her undoubted longing for maternal love.
- She was bisexual, and both orientations were full bloodied, although never entirely fulfilled.

There is, however, a fourth possibility that I slightly prefer, and that is that she was, as she always said she was, a *genuine transsexual*, and that her (in reality rather half-hearted) sexual adventures flowed from this. As far as I can see, all her intimate experiences were either fully or partly experienced in her boy identity. (Even those intimate experiences within the family such as with her cousin and when her father touched her, were experienced largely by Eric/Niall.)

Does it make any real difference which theory is adopted? Well, in the first place, I feel we have to acknowledge the link between her world of fantasy and her writing. That is quite important. More importantly, however, for an understanding of Daphne the person, we need to find what was making her feel her constant longing for "something that is somewhere"? It seems this chronic yearning disappeared temporarily

- When she was with her true love Gertrude (when Daphne was in the role of Eric/Niall)
- When she took Eric/Niall out of his "box" on some other occasions.

• When her dying mother kissed her.

Would it have also disappeared if she had been able to have a full bloodied and entirely guilt-free sexual and loving relationship with her father? Probably. But that was impossible for cultural reasons. Her conscience (superego) would never have allowed this to happen. There was always a crushingly conventional side to Daphne (No.1) that had to maintain her respectability. The era itself was very respectable and she (No. 1) strongly conformed to this.

Part of Daphne's problem was the non-sexual part of her identity. As an ("incomplete") woman she saw herself as Celia, like the second Mrs de Winter (in *Rebecca*) – a timid little wimp. It was only as a boy that she showed any normal strength of character. She was so many people – three at least by her middle age. Were Niall and Eric distinct characters? I doubt it. So we have: Maria, Celia and Eric/Niall. Her outward living self (the confident county lady) was probably the Maria part of No.1, and her writing persona was No.2 (Eric/Niall). Eric/Niall increasingly remained in his box after 1960, and around 1977 her writing self disappeared entirely, leaving only the county lady – an empty shell or outline of what had been before. When she felt confident it was Maria. When she was timid it was Celia.

The search for "the something that is somewhere" had failed. What had it been really? Surely her half-conscious craving for maternal love and some sort of consummation of her titillating relationship with her father: an Oedipally impossible combination. In Daphne's early twenties her father had become clinically depressed. He was in financial difficulties, several plays had failed and his business manager had died. He turned increasingly to Daphne. At the conscious level Daphne hated his growing dependence on her. Yet at the same time it must have stirred her longing for him. She wrote some short stories at this time in which she expressed revulsion at how men use women and how girls suffer because of men's lust and disloyalty with other women. Surely this was inspired by Gerald. Daphne tried to escape by dallying with cousin Geoffrey again and then having her first consummated romance with the young film director Carol Reed. He was as she liked her men to be – tall, strong and good-looking. Gerald reacted with furious jealousy and, strangely, thought Daphne, her mother Muriel appeared to back Gerald. She found herself drifting even further from her mother. But this was the beginning of the end of her youthful love-affair with her father, too.

It is interesting how Daphne's first stories relentlessly depict women as victims of masculine heartlessness. Yet, on the face of it, she herself had never been such a victim. She had enjoyed the advances made by Geoffrey and Carol. It was they (and certainly her father) who had become dependent upon her and not the other way around. She had enjoyed the relationships with Geoffrey and

Carol but had not been swept off her feet by them. So where was all this bitterness about men coming from? Its intensity was almost delusional. Could it have reflected the internal relationship between her alter egos – between Celia, Maria and Niall/Eric? Was Niall/Eric abusing the girls? This seems unlikely. Niall/Eric was the fantasised model of chivalry. Far more likely that this bitterness was something to do with her father, who certainly loved her but still flirted with other women. How far these affairs of Gerald went is uncertain. Perhaps, just as Gerald imagined that his daughters were totally promiscuous (when they were not), so Daphne also exaggerated the intensity of her father's relationships with his stable of actresses. He may have had sex with none of them, although he wanted the world to think otherwise as a cover for his homosexual inclinations. By the end of the 1940s Daphne could admit to certain people that she was attracted to both sexes: 'I seem to have fun either way' she told Ellen, 'I glory in my Venice (lesbianism) when I am in a Venice mood, and forget about it when I am not.' But it was not really as casual as that.

When Tommy had returned after another gruelling war Daphne's marriage had appeared to be on the rocks. Partly for reasons of respectability Daphne was determined to avoid a divorce. (Divorce was still rare in the 1940s and still carried a heavy stigma.) She said she felt Tommy now found her unattractive, but it was more the other way around. She realised how little they had in common, and confessed her marital difficulties to Tod and Ferdy. She no longer could fancy him. The sight of Tommy's attractive staff officer, Maureen Luschwitz, caused Daphne to jump to the helpful conclusion that Maureen was Tommy's mistress. Anyway, she seems to have used this as the excuse for allowing the marriage to lose its romantic and sexual ingredients. She had dressed up in elegant female clothes to meet the home-coming Lieutenant General Browning at Northolt airport (July 1945) but he had failed to embrace her. There was to be no 'Cairo' (sexual intercourse) between them for weeks after his return. Daphne felt rejected. Her attempt to be a pretty young woman for him had gone unrewarded. She was once more struggling with the boy in the box who wanted to come out. Shortly after Tommy's return, she (or the boy in the box) fell in love first with Ellen and then with Gertrude.

There are several ways to interpret the deterioration in marital relations between Daphne and Tommy. The most obvious are that:
- Daphne and Tommy had fallen out of love. She hated finding out how needy and dependent the PTSD Tommy had now become. The war had this effect upon thousands of couples. Some wives showed little understanding of the battle horrors experienced by their menfolk.
- Daphne's affair with Christopher Puxley had shown her how different some artistic men were from her apparently hard-headed and yet needy

military husband. The dissatisfaction and guilt now came between them.

• The fear of a rival (Luschwitz) in supposedly gaining the love of a father-figure (Tommy) had triggered all her old childhood problems with sibling rivalry (It was her jealousy of Jan Ricardo and of her mother and sisters all over again.).

• She was now having to realise that she was overwhelmingly a Venetian (lesbian) and that all her attempts at heterosexuality were principally efforts to prove to herself and the world that she was 'normal'. She admitted that she had been 'living a lie'. (This was the same denial strategy adopted by her father Gerald towards his own basic homosexuality.)

• Daphne blamed, once again, 'the boy in the box' i.e. her *transsexuality*. She may well have been right to do so.

• Her strong feelings for Gerald, her father, were always in the background. Did she unconsciously feel the guilt of her 'disloyalty' to Gerald by marrying Tommy? Did part of her want to separate from Tommy for this reason? Was being the boy in the box part of getting back to being close to Gerald again?

In order to test these six hypotheses, and the exact relationships between them, a psychologist would have to explore them with Daphne, which we can't do. I would put my money on the last three scenarios, although the first three played their part at a more conscious level.

There were, it seems, two tricks that Daphne frequently played on herself to convince the world that she was not a 'despised' lesbian:

(i) Her heterosexual relationships with men. She once admitted – 'nothing is more amusing than to have fun with glamorous or menacing (attractive) men, but that's a diversion, it's not home.' (MF 251)

(ii) Her boy in the box. It was, she convinced herself, not her female side that fell in love with Ferdy, Ellen and Gertie, but herself as Eric (later to grow into Niall apparently). Thus these relationships (at fantasy level at least) were also heterosexual. 'Nobody could be more bored with all the 'L' people than I am…I like to think my Jack-in-the-box was and is unique' (MF 229) she said. Daphne's inner boyishness continued to old age (MF 339) in her love of television thrillers and films with fast car chases.

Even her incestuous feelings for her father may have been in part a ploy to deny her lesbianism. Respectability for a newly arrived titled county lady in the 1950s was vitally important.

The search for a loving mother manifested in at least three of her close friendships with women: with Tod, with Ferdy and with Ellen. She told the latter: 'you are the mother I always wanted!' Daphne lamented that 'I can't remember once being held by her (her mother), feeling her arms around me, sitting on her lap. All I can remember, from the very beginning of time, is someone who looked at me with a sort of disapproving irritation, a queer unexplained hostility', (MF 227) (This presumably was Muriel's jealousy of her husband's flirtatious closeness to Daphne). In contrast, her sisters, according to Forster, sometimes enjoyed affectionate moments with their mother.

Daphne spent her life trying to understand herself. During the 1950s she began reading Adler and Freud and Jung. She wrote to her teenage daughter Flavia in 1954 that she had always felt herself to be two distinct personalities: 'When I get madly boyish, number 2 is in charge … (and) he certainly has a lot to do with my writing' (MF 276). He can also cause trouble by making fantasies about others and by causing her to alter her behaviour to please whomever she meets. (This chameleon tendency was familiar to her family and friends). She feels she has always been an actress in life – 'as if one was watching oneself in a play. It is fearful but I know I am always doing it.' (MF 277). From these and other remarks we can see that the number 2 personality is the boy in the box (Eric and Niall), the lover, the actor and the writer. No.1 appears to be comprised of two female personas – Maria the confident actress and Celia the artist who is a shy unassertive slip of a girl.

Daphne's husband Tommy haunted her life. For twenty years or more he was depressed and alcoholic. The two world wars had destroyed him. He had suffered in both and never recovered. He might have done better if he had had a wife who really loved and cared for him. But she didn't. At many times Daphne could hardly stand him. She found him bad-tempered and frightening, and had little ability to cosset him or to share his inner or outer lives. After the Second World War, Lieut. General 'Boy' Browning was knighted and his outer life as Prince Philip's military secretary was one that thousands of wives would have relished. But Daphne, invited to Windsor and Balmoral, hated every moment of it. She had few long lasting emotional attachments to any male (other than to her father) and in reality disliked most of her old male lovers and suitors. She thought sex might build a bridge but in fact the chasm between herself and them widened over the years. Almost her only lasting and positive relationships with men (other than Gerald) were, firstly with her son (whom she adored), and then with older father figures such as her publishers Nelson Doubleday and Victor Gollancz, both of whom could help her with her career. She meekly acquiesced with most of their highly helpful proposals, usually using her persona 'number 1'. (Celia) These were non-sexual relationships. She tried hard to have heterosexual relationships but they never worked for long. With her male admirers (like cousin Geoffrey, Carol Reed, Christopher Puxley and Frank Price) she rarely seems to have allowed full intercourse (although enjoying petting sometimes) and the relationship occasionally deteriorated into contempt and even to downright cruelty on her part (as with Puxley and Price). With Tommy it went well at the start but, when he returned after the war, things were never the same. She used his nickname 'Moper', showed him little sympathy or concern, and just felt deeply estranged and irritated by him. At times the marriage only held together because both of them wanted to avoid the disgrace of a divorce which would, incidentally, have cost Boy his job at Court. (Such was the prejudice against divorce at the time). I am increasingly of the opinion that the whole of her heterosexual career was, like her father's, a cover for her deeply homosexual inclinations. Most of her lastingly happy *emotional* relationships were with women – Ferdy, Tod, Ellen and Gertie. Clearly non-sexual relationships with Maureen, for example, local friends and Daphne's own daughters, were also positive.

What then, was the cause of Daphne's homosexual orientation? We still know for certain so little about the causes of homosexuality in general. Theories abound but no scientific certainties have been established. Genetic and hormonal factors have been suggested and contradicted. So have many environmental causes. The female sexual drive (unlike the male sexual drive) is usually not centred on the desire for physical sexual intercourse, so much as on an emotional need for security and attachment. This applies to lesbianism also: *it is a search for a relationship*. The lesbian, like an infant, is deeply insecure. She yearns for security. Where does this insecurity come from and why does it become a search for *same-sex* security rather than heterosexual security? There are as many theories as fish in the sea, but, based upon lesbians I have known, in my opinion the usual features are:

An unloving and critical mother

Also, possibly, an absent or frightening father, although he may simply be detached or unreliable. (About one third of lesbians allege a threat of incest with a male.)

Female sexual orientation is also linked with gender identity. About half of adult lesbians say they have been tomboys in their childhood. Some writers suggest it is experiences of insecurity based upon maternal rejection (1. above) *in the first four years*, that is critical. Obviously, in Daphne's case, this was true as regards her relationship with her mother. From infancy her mother, Muriel, seems to have taken against her. Whether or not this happened before or after her father began to display his passion for Daphne is uncertain, but it is clear that the Oedipal situation developed quickly, fuelling Muriel's hostility towards Daphne.

There remains one further mystery. Why, if Muriel was a little more loving towards her oldest and youngest daughters, than she was towards Daphne, did all three, and not just Daphne alone, become bisexuals with predominantly lesbian preferences? If these reports are correct, not only did her sisters have a loving mother but they also had an affectionate and unseductive father. According to this theory, conditions (1. and 2. above) were not met in Daphne's sisters' cases, and so neither Angela nor Jeanne should have been lesbians. But, in fact, they were, and far more openly than Daphne.

In general it appears that women's sexual orientation and preferences are more malleable than mens'. They are more passive and reactive. Men tend to be either homoerotic or heteroerotic, whereas, to put it simply, women (depending on circumstances, external stimuli or culture, for example) are more flexible and are more easily bisexual - as all the du Maurier sisters were, behaviourally speaking. Sexual relationships can grow naturally out of friendships in the case of women.

Just a word about localities. Daphne is a very good example of someone for whom locations come to play a very important part in their emotional and fantasy lives. In the first place Daphne escaped to Cornwall in order to avoid her parents. Unconsciously, however, she could well have been drawn to Cornwall because it seemed like JM Barrie's Neverland: the sea, old fashioned sea-farers and boats, not to mention Cornish folklore stories of fairy folk and of the sinister wreckers. Some of the piskies of Cornwall were reputed to care for love-starved children rather as Tinkerbell does in the play *Peter Pan*. As for pirates, Cornwall had pirates and wreckers at least until the generation before Daphne was born. They were still within living memory. Daphne had been brought up as a child saturated in the story of Peter Pan written by JM Barrie who was a family friend. Her cousins were the boys who inspired Barrie to write the play in productions of which she had acted as a child. Daphne (or the boy part of her) loved adventure and excitement, although rarely had any, other than her fantasy-entwined relationships. She turned to places instead of people, as they proved less disillusioning. Yet Cornwall, as Neverland, always reminded her of her childhood. Menabilly was, of course, central to this feeling and, so I believe, the house represented her father for her. This is why she clung to the place so tenaciously. Consciously she had the view that buildings could store the essence of people. Living there alone with nanny and the children she could have her father all to herself.

Dressing, for Daphne, mattered considerably. Throughout her life she wanted to wear trousers at a time when it was unusual, and often considered shocking, for a woman to do so. As a child she had insisted on wearing boys' shirts, ties, shorts, socks and shoes. In Cornwall she could wear old sweaters, rubber boots, seaman's caps and, inevitably, trousers. Being invited to attend smart functions or to visit Royalty (her husband's work) she was always thrown into a panic. She hated wearing skirts and dresses, and always felt ill at ease doing so. This,

I take, as evidence of her enduring *transsexualism* or male gender identity
Daphne was always conscious that her life was, in some respects, a lie. On the one hand, she wanted to be a confident boy (persona "No. 2") but her upbringing (and her mother's middleclass respectability) made her ashamed of any behaviour that deviated from the strict conventional normality for the period. Neither parent, although actors, were social rebels. Her brilliantly talented father had been knighted and she knew of his violent dislike of homosexuality. So Daphne felt driven to conceal both her desire to be a boy and her romantic interests in other women. To meet these demands (principally to fit the family's newly acquired upper class standing) she had to adopt persona "No 1" – some of which was the respectable, timid, shy, reclusive county lady living in a fairly large country house. It was the first time that any member of the du Maurier family, in at least a hundred years, had reached such a pinnacle of social status. As far as locals were concerned Daphne was Lady Browning of Menabilly Manor. No modern reader should underestimate the importance of social class in the first three quarters of the twentieth century. Daphne, through her considerable income as a successful writer, could afford all the trappings of gentility. Her husband was also a member of the new gentry and his heroic war career, his job with Royalty and his knighthood, all helped the family to join the elite of British county society.

I know that Daphne always tried to convince herself and others that class did not matter to her. But it did. She constantly disapproved of 'honkiness' (the vulgarities of the rougher elements of the working class). Being reclusive, slightly eccentric, outwardly attacking overt snobbery and using family code words to conceal her puritanical and class concerns, were all acceptable features of British upper class culture of the time. Yet Daphne was still slightly a rebel – or persona 2 was. Neither she nor Tommy voted Conservative. The Maria part of persona 1, however, usually dominated No. 2. So although persona 1 tried to keep persona 2 in its box there was always going to be tension between these two elements of her personality. Her basic inclinations (No.2) were in conflict with her conscience (No.1). In Freudian terms her id (No.2) was being suppressed by her superego (No.1). The 1930s and 1950s were periods of stifling conformity and class consciousness.

The causes of male homosexuality are just as uncertain as those of lesbianism. Among the most likely of the environmental causes are a traditional Oedipal triangle where a pampering mother, who adores her son, provokes intimidating jealousy towards the boy from his father. All boys tend to be attached to their mothers in infancy (as girls are also) and hence imitate and identify with them (as their sisters do also). Whereas most boys naturally grow away from their mothers and re-identify themselves with their fathers (or some other friendly male), homosexual youths fail to do this and continue to be attached to and identified with their mothers. (Some boys only *partially* succeed in this dis-identification and become effeminate or irrationally irritated with their mothers, while never fully identifying themselves with their fathers.)

In Daphne's case what may have happened is as follows:

- Her father showed favouritism towards her in infancy.
- This provoked jealousy from her mother who withheld love from Daphne. This further encouraged comforting from the father.
- Daphne responded by looking for love from her father and from older female mother figures. Perhaps her affection for her father might have become sexual if circumstances had been different.

Vicious cycles ensued.

So Daphne was the victim not only of the usual dynamics for the lesbian (a rejecting mother) but also the full Oedipal triangle (which included adoration for and from her father). The latter produced identification with the father which led to her *transsexualism* (her fluctuating conviction that she was a boy, Eric Avon, persona No. 2 etc.) The 'natural' thing for her to do as a boy, of course, was to dis-identify from the mother and transfer her self-identity to her father. This process reached its climax when Daphne, acting as Eric, took one of her father's old mistresses, Gertrude Lawrence, as her own lover.

Although we have worked out what Daphne's personas No. 1 and No. 2 were about – the female and male versions of herself respectively, I have found few clues about the distinctions between her sub-identities as Celia and Maria, or Eric and Niall. She was Eric by the age of twelve and may simply have grown into being Niall later on. These were convictions and not just fancies. On and off she really was convinced that she was a boy. The feeling fluctuated over time. She often tried to suppress the boy in the box but at times he was real. She was much happier as the boy but tried to suppress him. With iron control Lady Browning (persona No. 1) kept the lid on the box. Maria was the actress who always presented an unruffled and courteous appearance to the world. Was Celia the timid and awkward slip of a girl? Were there other personas? Maybe. Over the course of forty years there were times when she had seemed very reclusive as No. 1 and times when, also as No. 1, she thoroughly enjoyed partying. Perhaps she was moving from Celia to Maria. It seems likely that both Celia and Maria were parts of No.1, the former shy, the latter strong and confident.

We all have different sides to our personality, and cases of *splitting* or *multiple personalities* can occur. But with Daphne, although her identification with such personas was intense, each persona consciously knew of the others. There were no barriers of amnesia between them.

Had she liked Tommy partly because his nickname was 'Boy'? Possibly. Did she love Menabilly so much because of its masculine name? That could only have been part of the reason. The importance of places, especially houses, among insecure people, who find other people difficult, is not to be underestimated. As an issue it has been rather overlooked. Yet the material house, as nest, as haven, can be a psychologically powerful source of security, especially following bereavement or other separation. Daphne was most relaxed when alone at home with her dogs: as usual, animals come to the rescue for saints and solitaries. As soon as she was with people she had to act the part of No. 1 (or sometimes No. 2), but away from Menabilly there was always separation anxiety.

Towards the end of her days she often seemed obsessed by the question of incest. Female sexuality merges more easily with friendship and affection than does the male sexual drive. The love unsatisfied for her father continued, somewhere at the back of her mind, to seem to be the other solution to her childhood lack of maternal love. Girls like her, lacking a loving mother, could either seek mother-surrogates or switch to daddy's love. She did both.

Conclusions

Daphne, in the twenty first century, has become a cult figure internationally. In as much as she wrote about *human relationships* her work attracts women even more than men. A recent Companion about Daphne, edited by Helen Taylor, has six male contributors and thirty female ones. Increasingly, the brilliance and importance of Daphne's work is being recognised. In the Companion, Daphne's insightful children are interviewed and Flavia speaks of how her mother "liked anything as a rule she called 'slightly boyish'" and would try to persuade her to wear boyish clothes and hair styles (HT6). She says she "never saw Daphne lose her temper or get cross or irritated at all" before her final illness (FL 16). It seems that Maria was in control (HT9). Daphne comes across as an excellent mother in so many ways, although she failed to support her children's ambitions or to encourage their talents (HT16). (Perhaps this was a repeat of Daphne's sibling rivalry.) Daphne's social awkwardness as regards proper clothing, or when to come down for breakfast when staying away at friends, is remembered by her daughter. (This seems to be the doe-like Celia persona rather than the poised Maria persona.) (HT 212).

Helen Taylor rightly points out that the publication of Daphne's diaries in 2029 will probably make all our descriptions appear inadequate. She identifies some of Daphne's important literary themes as: "incestuous desire, doppelgänger figures, dynastic and dysfunctional families, polymorphous or multiple sexualities, and fractured notions of appropriate class and gender roles…" (HT xx).

Celia Brayfield's analysis of Daphne's novel *The House on the Strand* of 1967 reveals another familiar theme of a homosexual (Dick) trapped in a heterosexual marriage (HT 212). Sheila Hodges was, for nearly forty years, Daphne's editor, and she helps to define some of Daphne's personas (HT 25) as revealed in her novel *The Parasites* (1949). Maria is here the eldest of three siblings and an actress who reveals she is "always being someone else" while "the real me, is making faces in the corner." "This was true of Daphne herself" says Hodges, "the face she presented to the world was courteous and unruffled... but behind this calm exterior was a dark, often perturbed mind". So Maria was the actress acting the serene, sensible, well organised and generous lady of the manor who was, for most people, Daphne du Maurier. Niall is portrayed as a popular composer while Celia is an artist. All three personas are accused of living in a world of fantasy and of being parasites. They love their father (who resembles Gerald). Hodges brilliantly describes Daphne's fear of separation from her father, as expressed through some of her characters and by Daphne herself as a child. When he had intended to go up to the roof of his London house during an air raid in the First World War, eight year old Daphne had stretched out her arms and cried "Don't go... don't go... don't ever leave me!" (HT 29). Almost identical words are given to a girl addressing a man with whom she has been making love (in fact her father although she does not realise this) in *The Borderline Case*, to a small girl in *The Parasites* and to another in *The Loving Spirit*. In the excerpt from *The Parasites* the little girl appears to address Niall as well as her father:

Pappy...Pappy... Niall, don't ever leave me. No one must ever leave me. (HT 67).

These excerpts reveal the agony of loss that Daphne must have felt (but largely concealed) when her father had suddenly died in 1934.

Hodges confirms Daphne's abiding fascination with incest and with the family itself as a multi-generational unit of deep significance. She loved the countryside and animals, too. Some of her short stories were, she said, "a protest at the cruelty and misunderstanding which abound in the world – beneath the surface lurk evil we do not understand, things in ourselves" (HT 37). Daphne, says Hodges, "later came to believe that compassion is the only quality worth praising, and cruelty the only sin" (HT 41). Daphne was, as a writer, a supreme craftsman with "an extraordinarily powerful imagination". After her husband died Daphne wore his shirts, sitting at his desk and using his pen (HT 64). She had, similarly, worn her father's clothes for years after his death.

The final tragedy for Daphne was that she wrote little or nothing in the last thirteen years of her life. *Rule Britannia* had appeared in 1972 (when Daphne was aged sixty-five) and her biography of philosopher Francis Bacon in 1976. Publications after these dates were merely collected memoirs, the completion of a book about Cornwall and some rehashed short stories. Nothing substantial that drew upon her unique fantasy world appeared before her death in 1989 at the age of nearly eighty two. Why was this?

During the latter part of the 1970s Daphne had become depressed and this depression continued until the end of her life. She constantly complained that her creative fires were now extinguished and that she could not write. Her depression seems to have been triggered initially by tax worries and a concatenation of deaths. Almost a dozen relatives and old friends had died in these years, culminating in the death of Ellen in April 1978. All three of the great loves of her life – Gerald, Gertie and Ellen – had died when she had not really expected them to do so. Above all, perhaps, she had lost Menabilly (i.e. her father) in 1969.

Daphne was now dragged down into a vicious cycle of despair: *her depressive illness was making her unable to write and her inability to write was making her depressed.* To make matters worse, Daphne claimed (MF 402) that, in addition to sleeping pills (Mogadon) and anti-depressants (Prothiaden), she was also taking Largactil. She may have acquired this medication illicitly, but whatever its source, this powerful anti-psychotic might have further closed down her access to the boy in the box, to her secret world of fantasy, and to her chances of writing again.

If only the vicious cycle could have been broken. She had averaged half a dozen works of fiction each decade until 1972; subsequently, practically nothing. Perhaps, at its deepest level, her depression was the manifestation of her inevitable failure to right the wrongs of her childhood: her yearning either to resolve her love affair with her extraordinary father or to reverse her mother's rejection or, impossibly, both. Perhaps all the rest – her friendships, her marriage and even the writing itself, had all been desperate, but largely successful, anti-depressant tactics that had now become extinct or inaccessible.

Above all else Daphne had needed to write in order to keep going. Writing gave her catharsis, structure and achievement. It also satisfied her barely conscious desire to continue to please the memory of her father. Writing was by far her most powerful anti-depressant weapon, if only she could break the vicious cycle of depression in order to use it. If her depression could have been lifted sufficiently to allow her to write again, then the cycle could have been reversed: the more writing she could do the more her depression would be vanquished.

Sadly, Daphne seems to have believed that her creativity had withered away due to old age. She never realised that depressive illness itself, regardless of its causes, almost always destroys creativity. Memories of depression can be valuable in providing balance and depth to artistic creation, but depression itself is, above all, a blocker. Nearly all writers need to escape their depression in order to write successfully. Most effectively, they need a few bursts of elevated mood to do this. The raised mood brings back ideas into consciousness, connects these in creative ways, and provides the drive and confidence to express them. Tragically, Daphne's vicious cycle of depression was never to be broken.

What a tortured world of artificiality so many of us lived in during the twentieth century, pretending to be people we really were not!

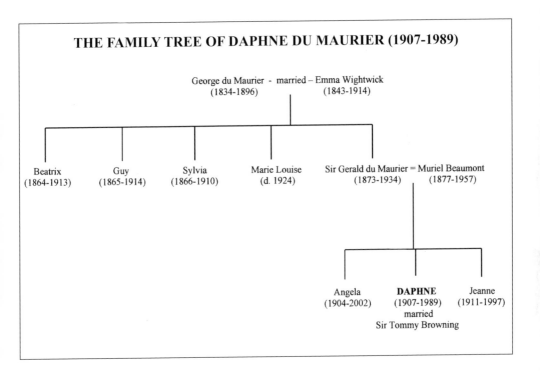

THE FAMILY TREE OF DAPHNE DU MAURIER (1907-1989)

George du Maurier - married – Emma Wightwick
(1834-1896)   (1843-1914)

Beatrix (1864-1913) Guy (1865-1914) Sylvia (1866-1910) Marie Louise (d. 1924) Sir Gerald du Maurier (1873-1934) = Muriel Beaumont (1877-1957)

Angela (1904-2002) **DAPHNE** (1907-1989) married Sir Tommy Browning Jeanne (1911-1997)

SOURCES

Jane Dunn, *Daphne du Maurier and Her Sisters*, William Collins, London, 2013

Margaret Forster, *Daphne du Maurier*, Arrow 1994

Flavia Leng, *Daphne du Maurier: a Daughter's Memoir*, Mainstream Publishing, 1994.

Daphne du Maurier, *Gerald: A Portrait*, Gollanz 1934, Virago 2004

Helen Taylor (ed) *The Daphne du Maurier Companion*, Virago, 2007

6

ISSAC NEWTON (1642-1727),

ALBERT EINSTEIN (1879-1955) and

ALAN TURING (1912-1954)

Great Scientists

 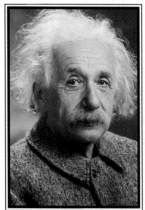 

This chapter just makes one important point and does not go into the full personalities of these three scientists.

What can be said of the three great mathematical geniuses Isaac Newton, Albert Einstein and Alan Turing? What did they have in common? The answer is that, as children, they were all loners who had felt abandoned by their parents. They did not play too well with other children, and especially not with other boys. Instead, they took up thinking as their chief hobby, concentrating upon issues such as time, gravity and light. All three enjoyed just thinking. Of course, they were all intelligent but they also developed the skill of concentration. They would think for hours, often appearing, in consequence, to be absent-minded and forgetful. The young Einstein would sit in his bath for over an hour. They were thinking about matters that were far removed from the everyday events going on around them. When asked how he made his great discoveries Isaac Newton replied: "I keep the subject constantly before me, till the first dawnings open slowly, by little and little, into the full and clear light." None burdened their minds with remembering facts they could get from printed sources. They were far more interested in the ideas that linked facts together. All three were trying to establish general rules that explained specific instances. They were all driven to find the truth. All indulged in thought experiments, and all three became excited when their minds provided sudden answers to the problems they were pondering. But all three were cautious, reluctant to say too much without being certain that everything they said was exactly accurate. None accepted conventional explanations as being necessarily true. Partly for this reason, none were recognised as being brilliant until well into their teens. They were deep and solitary thinkers, who persevered with their thoughts, alone.

In other important respects, however, Newton, Einstein and Turing were significantly different from each other. Einstein and Turing were emotionally far warmer than Newton and, in their later teens, formed several good friendships with other people, usually of their own age, with whom they discussed their ideas. Newton, on the other hand, appeared emotionally cold and had few friends. He kept his ideas to himself, often publishing them with apparent reluctance years after he had formed them. Whereas Newton and Turing sometimes did small scale physical experiments, Einstein rarely did so. Einstein had two marriages and fathered two children while Newton and Turing had none. Indeed, both Newton and Turing were homosexual. Einstein and Turing could laugh and smile, whereas Newton hardly ever showed that he was happy.

So it is the feeling of isolation that is common to all three scientists and it was initiated chiefly by the physical absence of their parents in childhood. Isaac Newton's father died before he was born and his mother remarried and moved away when Isaac was only three. Albert Einstein's family went to Italy when he was fifteen, leaving him alone in Germany and, later, in Switzerland – he never lived long-term with them again. Alan Turing's parents went to work in India when he was only fourteen months of age, leaving Alan with professional foster parents. When his mother returned he was nearly nine, and she remarked that Alan had changed from being "extremely vivacious - even mercurial – making friends with everyone" to being "unsociable and dreamy" (HO 10). All three boys felt deserted by their parents and all three, at various times, subsequently expressed anger towards their mothers for their perceived desertion. The mothers of all three boys were firm, austere and unemotional women. All three probably loved their sons but none of them showed this affection very openly during the boys' childhoods.

All three boys reacted to the absence of their parents, not by becoming openly delinquent (as could have happened) but by turning in upon themselves, narcissistically enjoying their own company and living in their own minds. None of the boys found solace in early childhood friendships and, at school, all three disliked the rough and tumble lives of other boys.

All children who lose their mothers in childhood, whether through death or separation, suffer badly. Some react with anger, revenge and delinquency, others with depression. Many develop compensating fantasies, as in the case of both Horatio Nelson and Adolf Hitler. A few, such as these three scientific geniuses, avoid the despair of their loneliness by cultivating their own worlds of thought, sometimes with earth-shaking consequences. In childhood they were neither talkative nor gregarious, and their thoughts became their companions.

Their lives demonstrate that great creativeness can be provoked by loneliness.

SOURCES

Andrew Hodges: *Alan Turing*, Vintage Books, 2012
Philip Steele: *Isaac Newton: the Scientist who Changed Everything*, National Geographic, Washington, 2013
Frieda Wishinsky: *Albert Einstein,* DK Publishing, 2005

7

RICHARD WAGNER (1813-1883)

Composer

The key to understanding Richard Wagner is to realise that he saw himself as an unloved underdog. He wanted to be exactly the opposite, and it is for this reason that his cravings for love and power dominate in his music.

Richard was born in Leipzig on 22 May 1813, the seventh of eight surviving children of Johanna Rosine Pätz. Before marriage, Johanna had been the mistress of a local prince and her good looks, wry sense of humour, secretiveness and interest in men, make it possible that she continued to live a life of sexual intrigue during the period of her first marriage to police registrar Friedrich Wagner. When Friedrich died of typhus in November 1813, Johanna moved in with his close friend Ludwig Geyer who was an actor and artist. She brought with her her infant son Richard, calling him Richard Geyer – a name he continued to use until he was fourteen, some six years after Geyer's death. Richard referred to Geyer as his step-father although there is evidence that he suspected him to be his biological father. Geyer, a warm and sociable man with a sparkling wit, involved Richard in his stage productions and encouraged the boy's love of the theatre.

Richard adored his mother but found her to be mysterious and remote, bemoaning her lack of motherly affection: "I can hardly ever remember being cuddled by her", he wrote in his memoirs (*Mein Leben*, Munich 1963, pp17-18) "- in fact there were never any displays of tenderness in our family, whereas a certain restless, almost wild, boisterousness appeared very natural."

There is a modernity and insight in Richard's reminiscences, such as this one, that is quite striking. In his childhood, Richard's family moved around in the Leipzig and Dresden areas, his older sisters becoming actresses. After Geyer's death in 1821 Richard was lodged with various pastors and uncles. Hugely impressed by Weber's opera *Der Freischütz*, as well as by other productions, young Richard became fascinated by his sisters' thespian lives:-

It was the more delicate costumes of my sisters, on which I often saw my family working, that exerted a more stirring effect on my imagination; just touching these objects could cause my heart to beat wildly. Despite the fact that, as I have mentioned, there was little tenderness in our family, particularly as expressed in loving hugs, the predominantly feminine environment must have strongly influenced my emotional development.
(Mein Leben p20).

For the love-starved little boy, his sisters' theatrical costumes became tactile substitutes for affection, and his yearning for motherly love probably, at this juncture, became mixed up with his pubescent sexual feelings. He describes his love of the theatre at this age as "an attraction amounting to intoxication". Theatres are, of course, places where people can show off and become noticed and this was probably a further reason for becoming stage-struck.

Richard changed his name to Wagner when he moved back to Leipzig in 1827, aged 14, went to a new school and wrote his first play (*Leubald*) which involved the melodramatic murder of most of its characters. Humorously, Richard later wrote –

The plan was quite stupendous: forty two people died in the course of the play and I found myself obliged to bring most of them back as ghosts, since otherwise I should have run out of characters!
(Autobiographical Sketch, 1843 WDS p11).

Why Richard changed his name at this time is unclear. Was it a bureaucratic requirement or was there a psychological reason? Was he, for example, wanting to feel closer to his siblings who used the name 'Wagner'?

A central problem with Richard Wagner has been his undoubted anti-semitism. It is important to realise, however, that his prejudice was altogether of a different variety from that commonly to be found in the twentieth century. Richard grew up in German cities in which there were large, affluent and easily identifiable Jewish communities. His antagonism against them, therefore, was not a looking down upon a despised minority so much as a resentment of a powerful elite. In his youth Richard felt himself to be an underdog and he disliked the ruling class in all its forms. He became, as we know, a 'left-wing' rebel siding with the down-trodden and oppressed, with animals and the proletariat, against the rich and the powerful. He disliked the French far more than he disliked the Jews. So his anti-semitism was not, initially at least, on racial or religious grounds, but was more analogous to the feelings of a socialist's resentment of the upper classes. In his thirties Richard became actively involved in revolutionary politics, narrowly escaped arrest and fled to Switzerland where he was obliged to live for some eleven years. What was the content of Richard's revolutionary thought? He wanted to dispense with class distinctions, end the aristocracy (although maintain royalty), destroy money and property, and create a society full of freedom and gentleness based upon the 'law of love' (BM 72-73). Money, property and class standing were all things that the young Richard lacked, so their abolition, in a way, would solve his feelings of envy. One of the more idiosyncratic elements in his philosophy was Richard's contempt for finance. This was enduring and sincere and, helps to explain his life-long problems with money, its borrowing, lending and spending, over many decades. He despised not only the love of money but also what he saw as the "superficiality" of materialism – attributing both of these tendencies to Jewish artists and musicians. He was not conventionally religious himself but was philosophical, and constantly thought in terms of lofty abstract principles such as truth, beauty, love and the will. In the German tradition of such thinkers as Hegel, Kant, Schopenhauer and Nietzsche he never worked out these ideas into a clear and coherent theory, but wallowed in their sheer complexity, alluding to them conflictingly in his operas. Such was his hypomanic over-confidence, Richard insisted in writing his own librettos. He believed his operas had an intellectual message of supreme importance, although what it is exactly, is a matter of controversy.

Music, of course, is not a good medium for the exposition of philosophy, although philosophy can often inspire great music – as in the case of Richard Wagner. Art in many forms can thrive in the rich soil of conflicting and ambiguous ideas precisely because they *are* conflicting and ambiguous. Some of the greatest moments in Wagner's music are when such conflicts of ideas reach apparent *emotional* (although rarely *rational*) resolution. Richard entertained Schopenhauer's concept of the will (and the suppression of sexuality) as well as his friend Nietzsche's concerns with the striving after power and the rejection of Christianity, although Nietzsche broke with Richard ostensibly because of the composer's growing nationalism and anti-semitism. Nietzsche, for example, disliked what he saw as the soft Christianity of Wagner's great opera *Parsifal* which deals, among other things, with environmental issues, vegetarianism, a respect for animals and the underlying ethic of compassion. In the 1870s Richard became an active anti-vivisectionist, writing:

Everyone who revolts at the sight of an animal's torment, is prompted solely by compassion, and he who joins with others to protect dumb animals, is moved by naught save pity, of its very nature entirely indifferent to all calculations of utility or the reverse. BUT, THAT WE HAVE NOT THE COURAGE TO SET THIS MOTIVE OF PITY IN THE FOREFRONT OF OUR APPEALS AND ADMONITIONS TO THE PUBLIC IS THE CURSE OF OUR CIVILISATION.

In an open letter to Ernst von Weber in 1879 he said of experimental animals – "the thought of their suffering penetrates with horror and dismay into my bone; and in the sympathy evoked I recognise the strongest impulse of my moral being, and also the probable source of all my art..." (Quoted by John Vyvyan "In Pity and in Anger" (Michael Joseph, 1969) p.125).

These were not just empty words. Richard meant them. His furious sense of justice and compassion for the underdog are the underlying motives for his blaring brass and clashing cymbals. Richard was not a poseur, he spoke from the heart. He cared about women, animals and the disadvantaged generally. As the smallest and youngest boy in his family he had suffered maternal neglect and been farmed out to various other relatives, his mother never showing an interest in him. What comes across in his music is an angry striving for love and power – the love and power that he very much felt he lacked as a child. He wanted to be noticed! Such feelings continued into his later years. To make matters worse Richard never entirely grew up. Even as an adult he was only five foot five inches tall and his emotional growth was similarly stunted. In a sense Richard Wagner always remained a child – an *enfant terrible* rushing around impulsively and angrily upsetting the more staid adult world around him. He was at his worst when he was befriended and hero-worshipped by another permanent child, King Ludwig II of Bavaria. Stupidly, Richard lied to him about his relationship with his mistress Cosima and interfered rashly with the King's political problems. Far from being the true psychopath, Richard was an extraordinarily bad liar. He behaved more like a spoiled child who had been found out.

One of the many outstanding features of Wagner's personality is that his undoubtedly huge narcissism never destroyed his compassion for others. Indeed the reverse is true. He was a far more empathetic, generous and loving person than has usually been realised. He was not simply the power-mad narcissist. Besides, he was a narcissist, not because others had pampered his ego, but because they had not. He had to do his self-pampering for himself.

One key to understanding Richard, as I have said, is that he was compensating for his feeling that he was an unloved child. The other key is realising that he lived much of his life in a state of *raised mood*. Like so many creative giants, and successful people generally, he was, for much of the time, hypomanic. Psychiatrists and psychologists may realise the importance of mood in explaining behaviour, yet other writers and biographers steadfastly refuse to recognise it. We often hear of depression (lowered mood) but far less often about mania (raised mood) and its little sister hypomania, (hypo – meaning 'under' or 'beneath', that is to say, a lesser form of mania). Although far less often encountered than depression, raised mood is still quite common. As a recognised *disorder*, depression is approximately fifteen times more likely to be diagnosed than is a disorder of raised mood. No doubt this is partly because someone with raised mood is enjoying life and does not want to visit a psychiatrist. Only when the mood is raised so high that it begins to cause serious problems for the sufferer or for other people, do such patients, often against their will, receive treatment. Moods often alternate and when such variation becomes pronounced is it labelled as bipolar or manic-depressive disorder. What, then, does chronic hypomania (raised mood) look like? The answer is that it looks remarkably like Richard Wagner! Here is a modern text book description of hypomania:

There is elevation of mood, increased energy, over-activity, pressure of speech, reduced sleep, loss of normal social and sexual inhibitions and poor attention and concentration. The elevated mood may manifest as euphoria, but sometimes patients can instead be irritable and angry. The patient may overspend, start unrealistic projects, be sexually promiscuous and, if irritable or angry, be inappropriately aggressive. (BKP 77-110).

The description continues by mentioning such signs as flamboyant clothing, flight of ideas, extravagance, inflated ideas of self-importance, expansive and grandiose ideas about the significance of the patient's opinions and work, delusions of persecution, hyperacusis, buying sprees, sexual indiscretions and foolish business investments. Characteristically, the hypomanic has charisma and attracts those who agree with him while being short tempered with those who do not. He does not suffer fools gladly.

All this, I would suggest, is a very good description of Richard Wagner's behaviour. He did occasionally show weeks of normal mood and days of depression but, I would submit, that most of the time he was hypomanic. People who met him spoke of his volcanic energy and warmth. (M 135) One person recalled: "As soon as he appeared, he burst forth like a flood tide...one was left dazzled by his exuberance". He has been much criticised by naïve biographers for his sexual freedom, his financial unreliability and his persecutory ideas; yet these are all classic signs of hypomania. Typically, hypomanics show disturbed social relationships, especially characterised by impatience with the much *slower* reactions of those around them. When they meet a similar fast reactor, however, as Richard did when he met Liszt, a lifelong friendship can be born.

Richard, of course, loved women. He had loved his mother from afar, and his sisters. Later, he loved many women he met, particularly singers and actresses. It was all part of his childish craving for maternal love that had become mixed up with his sexual feelings. Sometimes these burst forth a little inappropriately. He simply could not help it. Like so many creative men he tended to fall for much younger women. He had met Cosima Liszt when she was only sixteen and he was forty. (A few months earlier he had met his muse Matilda Wesendonck, when she was twenty three.) There was usually a gap of about twenty years between Richard and the women he adored. With these younger women Richard felt more confident, and especially with the doting Cosima who was, so it seems, masochistically aroused by Richard's dominance. Yet, paradoxically, he also wanted Cosima to be the mother he never really had. Their love was deep and lasting. Living with Cosima he also became quite a good father to their three children. He loved both the children and his dogs.

Psychologists still argue about the causes of hypomania. Clearly there is a genetic component. We know from his own description that Richard came from a family that showed a "restless, almost wild, boisterousness..." In my view, hypomania is a way of coping with stress that some individuals have inherited; others simply lack this hypomanic capacity. There is a tendency in hypomanics to make cognitive and emotional connections that most people do not make, (e.g. puns and clang associations) and there is, I would suggest, a marked tendency in Richard's music to connect ideas with sounds, and to merge sensory modes. Like Liszt he was synaesthetic and, seemingly, could also convert *ideas* into *sound*. As regards this tendency it is interesting to note, as Barry Millington has done, that Richard showed strong fetishistic inclinations, wearing specially designed silk, satin and velvet clothes. Sometimes this behaviour verged upon transvestism. (He died wearing a pink satin dressing gown!). Probably the origins of these fetishes were in his childhood experiences in the theatre dressing-rooms where his early sexual feelings became associated with his admiration for his older sisters, his yearning for their love, and coming into tactile contact with their fascinating theatrical costumes. The smell of grease paint, of human bodies and the sound of music, may have all become connected in his mind at this impressionable age; throughout his life he loved exotic perfumes. Richard was the complete sensualist. The touch of rich textiles and the smell of perfume became, to him, substitutes for maternal love.

I am not, of course, saying that the greatness of Wagner's music itself was caused by his hypomania or by his psycho-dynamics. For every Richard Wagner there are a thousand other maternally-deprived hypomanics who do *not* write great music. The ability to express himself in music was probably in his genes, although without the hypomania it may not have had its glorious expression. There are downsides to such strange personalities: like most narcissists, for example, Richard could not effectively edit his own work and, in consequence, it tends to be far too long – narcissists tend to overvalue everything they create, and hence become unable to throw away their lesser creations.

The heroism in his music has appealed to many underdogs over the years, including the young Adolph Hitler. Richard Wagner and Adolph Hitler were both maternally obsessed narcissists but, unlike Richard, Hitler had both a doting mother and a bullying father, where the latter, fatally for the world, poisoned his son's outlook. Instead of writing great music, Hitler could only make war, in his fantasised eternal *struggle* against his father. (See chapter 11). On the other hand, Richard Wagner was truly the charismatic advocate of compassion. He never really grew up, however, and always felt himself to be the unwanted child.

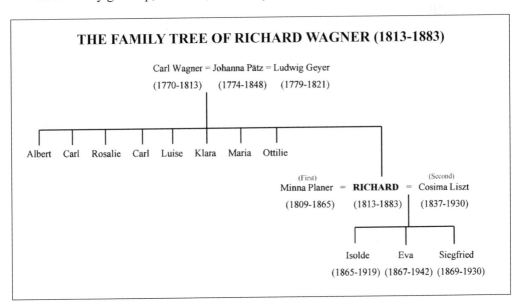

THE FAMILY TREE OF RICHARD WAGNER (1813-1883)

SOURCES

Barry Millington, *Richard Wagner: the Sorcerer of Bayreuth,* Thames & Hudson, 2012.

Basant K. Puri, *Psychiatry,* 2nd edition, W.B. Saunders, 2,000.

Michael Steen, "Wagner" in *The Lives & Times of the Great Composers,* pub. Icon, 2003.

8

GIUSEPPE VERDI (1813 – 1901)

Composer

The psycho-biographer finally meets his match in Giuseppe Verdi. Verdi is easy to describe but almost impossible to explain. We have too little information about his childhood years. Throughout his life Giuseppe appears as a craggy, silent man, grumpy, truculent, and touchy. People feared his bad temper. He held grudges for years and turned against friends if they displeased him. He kept himself to himself and retired to his house in the countryside whenever he could. Yet the wider world loved him. He worked hard, gave instructions to his librettists that they did not ignore, wrote no less than twenty eight operas and yet, when asked about his occupation would describe himself as a farmer. He became closely associated in the public mind with liberal politics, with the expulsion of the Habsburgs and the unification of Italy. He hated priests. He was, above all, a strong and a practical man. He got things done and disliked fuss. In some ways this greatest of all Italian composers was strangely un-Italian. Unlike the stereotyped view of the Italian 'personality', Verdi was taciturn, efficient, undemonstrative, and outwardly cold. Yet his music expresses and arouses every emotion in the book. It is exuberant, explosive and tender. His operas are the ultimate in dramatic effect, and emotion is wrung from every note. Unlike many of the operatic composers, Verdi invests great subtly into his baritone characters, sometimes making them the psychological centres of his stories. They are often the kings, the villains and the father figures. They are needy, confused and ambivalent, and their roles transcend the particulars of time and place. They sometimes express the pointlessness of existence. They are probably Verdi himself.

Verdi also wrote about family relationships in his music. He never spoke about his own relationships and so in his operas are, perhaps, some of the only clues we have. We see a husband dealing with his wife's infidelity, for example, two long lost brothers duelling for the same woman and no less than thirteen versions of the father-daughter relationship. Why?

We know very little about Giuseppe's actual childhood. He grew up in a small village, La Roncole, in the flat plain of Parma. His father Carlo was the local innkeeper and his mother Luigia the daughter of the innkeeper from a neighbouring village. There are only two plausible anecdotes about the little Giuseppe's relations with his parents: his mother allegedly hid with him in the church tower in order to escape marauding French troops, and his father bought him a simple spinet when he was eight, which is now in the La Scala Museum. We also know that Giuseppe had a sister, Giuseppa, three years younger than himself, who died of meningitis when he was aged twenty. Some biographers say that he was close to her, but that is all we know.

At the unusually early age of ten, Giuseppe left home to go to the grammar school (ginnasio) in Busetto, three miles away, lodging with a cobbler, and walking home on Sundays to play the village organ at La Roncole. In Busetto he was more or less adopted by the wine merchant, Antonio Barezzi, who encouraged his musical interests, and from the age of thirteen Giuseppe started to compose marches for brass bands, concertos for the piano (which he played at local concerts), church music and arias, duets and trios for the voice. From 1831 the seventeen year old moved into Barezzi's house to share it with Barezzi's two sons and four daughters, the eldest of whom, Margherita, took singing lessons from Giuseppe, who fell in love with her. In 1833 Giuseppe was sent by Barezzi to the great city of Milan to further his musical studies. He applied to the Milan Conservatory which refused him – a slight that Giuseppe never forgot - and started private music lessons instead, all paid for by Barezzi. After a year, Giuseppe applied for the organist's job in Busetto but the church authorities appointed another candidate, and a huge controversy ensued. Wearied by these musical wars, young Giuseppe applied for a better job in Monza thereby stirring up resentment among his own supporters! Eventually, in April 1836, aged twenty two, he obtained the job of *maestro di musica* in Busetto. He married Margherita the following spring and had a son and a daughter by her, both of whom died aged little more than a year.

In 1839 Giuseppe completed his first opera, *Oberto*, which the famous soprano, Giuseppina Strepponi, persuaded the authorities to put on at the La Scala opera house in Milan. It was a success and led to a commission for three more operas. A few months later, in June 1840, Giuseppe's beautiful young wife, Margherita (Barezzi), suddenly died of encephalitis. Giuseppe was devastated. Forced by his contract to do so, he completed another opera that was a flop, retired to his flat in Milan and decided, in his misery, never to compose again. Fortunately, he was cajoled into writing a further opera by Bartolomeo Merelli, the impresario at La Scala, and *Nabucco* was performed in 1842 to huge acclaim, being hailed as supportive of the Italian Unification movement.

Giuseppe was certainly a good businessman. He invested his earnings in buildings and land, setting up his father and himself as farmers near Busetto. Almost immediately the two men fell out, Carlo managing the land incompetently, and they began to correspond only through lawyers. His father also disapproved of Giuseppe's relationship with Giuseppina Strepponi whose voice had failed, forcing her to retire. Giuseppe had met her again in Paris, and from 1849 at least they were living together, unmarried. She was both a beautiful and a businesslike woman, but had been promiscuous, giving birth to several children out of wedlock by various lovers and having them adopted or taken into orphanages. She was to prove a wonderful lifelong companion for Giuseppe, understanding as no one else did, how to handle this difficult man. Unlike Puccini's wife, she encouraged his composing and Giuseppe Verdi's total of 28 completed operas is remarkably more than Puccini's mere ten. Despite being a rich international celebrity by the 1850s (after his searing successes with *Rigoletto, Il Trovatore* and *La Traviata*), Giuseppe's relationships with his parents and with the local people of his home town, Busetto, worsened. Shy, withdrawn and haughty, he ignored their disapproval of his menage. Poor Strepponi had to live like a prisoner, constantly aware of the provincial gossip and criticism around her. Sometimes she even had to remain on their farm while Giuseppe was off in Milan on business. It seems she was by this time incapable of having further children, for the couple never had any until they happily adopted the seven year old Maria in 1867.

Giuseppe was a workaholic. By the time he was fifty he had composed twenty four operas. In his remaining 38 years he wrote only another four – *Don Carlos, Aida, Otello* and *Falstaff*, but all of them were masterpieces and all, to varying degrees, had been coaxed out of him by Strepponi. He composed often at night and alone, accepting comments only from her. Eventually they married quietly in 1859. Although the couple would sometimes escape together to Paris, London or St Petersburg, when they were back in Italy they were often surrounded by warfare. The forces of King Victor Emmanuel II of Piedmont, assisted by the French, as well as by the irregular forces of Garibaldi, were engaged for some years in expelling the Austrian armies of the Habsburg occupiers of northern Italy. In 1866, while writing *Don Carlos*, for example, Italian forces were only 15 miles away from the Verdi farm. Friends of Giuseppe had joined up with Garibaldi. The absurdly reactionary Pope Pius IX was eventually stripped of all his Roman territories except for the Vatican City, and Italy was joyously proclaimed a unified state, although Verdi would have liked the revolutionary reforms to have gone further, by removing all political powers from the Pope. His music said it all and was everywhere acclaimed as inspiration by the patriotic forces. Yet Giuseppe carefully kept out of actual politics. He said he was no good at that sort of thing, although eventually, albeit briefly, agreeing to become an inactive senator. During the last three decades of their life together, Giuseppe and Giuseppina were busy expanding their gardens, endowing hospitals and a retirement home, and adoring their dogs as well as their married adopted daughter Maria.

In 1869, aged fifty six, Giuseppe fell in love with the thirty-five year old Teresa Stolz, a soprano from Prague who was singing in a production of *Don Carlos*. Aware of what had happened, Giuseppina Strepponi exercised consummate tact in diffusing what might have become a disaster. She wrote clever and friendly letters to her rival and put carefully calculated pressure upon Giuseppe. Within a few years, and after several rows, a genuinely friendly menage a trois emerged which endured peacefully for thirty years until Giuseppina's death in 1897. For the last four years of Giuseppe's life, Teresa Stolz was always at his side.

Conclusions

So we can see what Giuseppe Verdi was like. He was truculent, bad tempered and aloof. He did not suffer fools gladly, but found many about him. He was demanding in his relationships, and especially with women. He was immensely self-centered and yet, despite appearances, was a liberal and a modernist in his beliefs. He was not, like some other composers (for example Wagner and Puccini), a mood swinger who composed while his mood was high. For most of the time Giuseppe Verdi's mood was depressed, sometimes markedly so. Like Wagner (unlike Puccini) his music is full of anger as well as love. Unlike Wagner, Giuseppe had strong self-discipline, composed succinctly and so maintained the dramatic tension in his music at all times. Like both other great composers considered here, he despised the theories of musicologists and critics, writing only to thrill and entertain his audiences. He never indulged himself as Wagner did in long-winded fantasies nor ever considered the stories of his operas to be of supreme importance. Yet, unlike Puccini, he had a deep interest in political ideas and the complexities of character. If Wagner and Puccini remained children all their lives, Verdi was the permanent stroppy teenager.

Once again we have the feeling that the music emerged from another world.

Yet events around Giuseppe Verdi must have influenced his work. Indeed, in mid-life the wars of Italian unification may have given his music its often defiant, patriotic and rebellious qualities. The enemies of reform and compassion are, as with Wagner, his ultimate villains, and his music darkens dramatically when he is dealing with them. But is there any way in which we can link the early situations of Giuseppe Verdi's personal life with the character of his music?

What early experiences may be significant? There are seven obvious ones:
1. The lack of evidence of his early relationships with his parents may itself be an indication of a coldness or inadequacy on their parts. In particular we hardly hear anything of his mother. Yet he was her only son and, after he was twenty, her only child.
2. At the early age of ten he was made to leave home and go away to school, staying in lodgings in Busetto three miles away. Was this usual practice for the times or does it suggest parental ambition, spartanism, or rejection?
3. At sixteen Giuseppe moved into the household of Antonio Barezzi and fell in love with Barezzi's daughter Margherita. Had he adopted the Barezzi family because his own was unsatisfactory?
4. At the age of twenty Giuseppe lost his only sibling, his sister Giuseppa, aged seventeen. We know nothing convincing of this relationship or of his reaction to her death. (There is a strange similarity in the names Giuseppe and Giuseppa. Why did his parents choose these names?)
5. Aged twenty three, Giuseppe married Margherita. She gave birth to two children who died when they were just over a year old. Again, we are unsure as to how Giuseppe reacted to this double loss. Does the loss of his baby daughter account for his recurrent treatment of the father-daughter relationship in his operas?
6. In June 1840, Giuseppe's first wife died of encephalitis. He is said to have been "heart-broken" and years later recalled the death of his wife and children as occurring more or less simultaneously, when in fact they were about a year apart. Brain infections killed both his sister and his wife.
7. In August 1840 his opera *Un Giorna di Regno* was a disaster and Giuseppe resolved to give up composing entirely. This, and the rejection by the Milan Conservatory, were early and hurtful experiences of failure.

All one can say with certainty is that Giuseppe's first twenty seven years of life were hard and bitter. Hardly surprisingly, perhaps, he appears at this age to have been a shy, withdrawn and humourless man. He was to remain bitter and depressed for years.

While the flamboyant Wagner did not conform to the German stereotype, the dour Verdi did not seem typically Italian. Both sympathized with the revolutions of 1848, both were rebels, male chauvinists and, in their own ways, egotists. They could be equally ungracious. Yet Giuseppe made some good friends over the years, although most were connected with his later celebrity. Unlike Puccini he even made friends with some of his librettists who recognized in him a seriousness of mind which was not so obvious in Puccini's case. It seems that from childhood there was a tough and spikey quality to Giuseppe's personality that predated the loss of his first wife and children. Maybe he felt himself to be on a higher plane than many of the naïve and superstitious country people around him. Maybe he was right.

There was clearly something unsatisfactory about Giuseppe's parents. Did alcohol play a part? Both of them were from innkeeping families, where alcohol abuse can often be a problem. Dutifully, Giuseppe set them up with a house and a little land, but they fell out with him. Giuseppe had found alternative parents for himself: Barezzi as a surrogate father whose death in 1867 he mourned, and Countess Maffei as an occasional mother. Then, in 1848, he fell in love with Giussepina Strepponi who was to become his lifelong lover, business partner and adviser. She encouraged his composing and was hugely tactful and long suffering. He treated her demandingly and with bad temper, giving us a clue, perhaps, as to what had been wrong in his relationship with his mother. Had Luiga spoiled her son and neglected him at the same time? This can happen. Maybe she had given in to his will while not providing her boy with much warmth or understanding. Strepponi gave him all these things. When his mother Luigia died in 1851, Giuseppe did not seem to be devastated. Maybe Luigia had been a bit of a slave to Giuseppe's father and, for a while, that is how Giuseppe treated Strepponi.

Like many male artists Giuseppe ended up surrounded by women, among them his two ageing lovers, Giuseppina Strepponi and Teresa Stolz, and his sweet-natured adopted daughter Maria.

Above all, Giuseppe Verdi's music remained largely independent of his life, arousing and expressing universal feelings ranging from grief, anger and revenge, to joy and love. It reveals all the emotions that the composer concealed. Above all it is about musical perfection and not the demands of any time or place. Giuseppe was not interested in musical systems that were merely fashionable. As he himself once said, testily, no doubt: "the point is not to know whether [Don Carlos] belongs to this or that system, but whether the music is good or bad." (PSS. 112) It was almost always gloriously good.

THE FAMILY TREE OF GIUSEPPE VERDI (1813-1901)

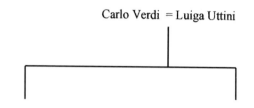

Carlo Verdi = Luiga Uttini

GIUSEPPE (1813-1901)   Giuseppa (1815-1833)

Married: 1st Margherita (1814-1840).

Their son and daughter died in infancy,

Virginia aged seventeen months.

Married 2nd: Giuseppina Strepponi (1815-1897)

Partner: Teresa Stoltz (1834-1902)

SOURCES

William Berger: *Verdi with a Vengeance*, Vintage Books, New York, 2000

Peter Southwell-Sander: *Verdi*, Omnibus Press, London, 1978

Michael Steen: *Verdi* in The Lives & Times of the Great Composers, Icon Books, London, 2003

9

GIACOMO PUCCINI (1858 – 1924)

Composer

hat can a psychologist have to say about Giacomo Puccini? The origins of musical skills are not yet well understood but are, surely, genetically inherited to a large extent. As with his two great operatic predecessors, Verdi and Wagner, the brilliance of Puccini's music was, I suspect, largely the product of his genes. The scion of a long line of professional musicians on both sides of his family, (e.g. Puccini's father, both grandfathers, great grandfather, great grandmother, and great great grandfather) Puccini's gift for melody distinguished him from many of his contemporaries who worked harder at music school and college than he did but lacked his innate genius.

Giacomo was also lucky to have a forceful middle class mother who constantly promoted his interests, as well as the help of several powerful promoters, such as the publisher Giulo Ricordi and teacher Amilcare Ponchielli, who provided funds and support during Giacomo's early years of failure. They were right to persevere, for once his slight waywardness had been tamed, Giacomo's special gifts would deliver half a dozen of the most musically glorious operas ever to be written.

Giacomo Puccini was born in the slightly out of the way city of Lucca on December 22nd 1858 to Michele Puccini and Albina Magi. Michele died when Giacomo was five and his mother, eighteen years younger than her husband, applied to relatives for assistance in caring for herself and her eight children of which Giacomo, her eldest boy, was her fifth child. So little Giacomo grew up surrounded by women, two of his sisters dying in infancy. His only brother was the youngest in the family. Giacomo loved his siblings, especially his sister Ramelde and his little brother Michele.

How is a little boy affected by such circumstances? First, he grows up feeling at home with women, secondly he feels a lot of pressure from his widowed mother to help provide for his family financially, and finally, he escapes the usual controls on his behaviour that are imposed by the average father. In consequence, young Giacomo turned into a rather naughty and lazy boy who disliked schoolwork and discipline. He became a prankster, had sexual relations with girls from an early age, and was fascinated by the usual boyish things such as guns, machines and gadgets. He might have been forgotten like a million other such boys if it had not been for two things: his forceful mother, determined that he should train to continue the family's musical tradition, and his own extraordinary musical talent. That he had the latter is evident from the way he composed, as well as the fact that several great teachers remarked upon it. Typical reactions to his earliest compositions stress their fluency and inventiveness. The teenager seemed "totally in command of his material" and already sounded like "an experienced composer". (JB 9-11). At the age of seventeen Giacomo saw a performance of Verdi's *Aida* and vowed to become a composer of operas himself.

Like Wagner and Mozart, Giacomo Puccini never quite grew up. He always remained a bit of a boy. In his case this meant endless sexual affairs with pretty girls, crawling around his childhood swamps shooting at birds, and driving cars as fast as he could. He was not, however, a total tearaway. He was shy, often depressed and frequently alone. He loved beautiful things, not just women, but also ships, flowers, clothes and paintings. Culturally, he was utterly Italian. Like Verdi, he composed at night, at his own piano, and sometimes encouraged the presence of a few drinking companions with whom he would break off composing in order to play cards. He enjoyed doggerel and word-play. Above all he was a romantic whose constant addiction to adventures with new and younger women is celebrated in his music.

Giacomo Puccini is one of the last of the great musicians whose innate ability to express and arouse a range of emotions through his music, marks him out from the twentieth century's herd. His death marked the end of an era. (After him came musicians who had little gift for melody, painters who could not draw and writers who found it hard to tell a story. Skills that were hard to perfect were abandoned.) In fact, like Richard Strauss (another supremely gifted composer), Giacomo was made to feel ashamed of his own melodic talent by the untalented critic-vandals of the beginning of the century. Sadly, he tried to agree with them that his music was, as he said, a bit "sugary". Yet it was this very quality, unacceptable as it was to his critics, with their insecure sense of masculinity, that marked his brilliance. He could create not only sugar but the auditory equivalents of cream, honey and chocolate as well! Moreover, two of his operas – *Tosca* and *Turandot* – were far from being lightweight, both dealing with love's conquest of political tyranny. They were not sugary at all, but strong meat.

Giacomo loved his mother Albina but he was also a little afraid of her. She was a powerful and determined woman, and he felt guilty that he had not worked hard enough to come up to her expectations. He often wrote fond letters to his mother. In one he said: "You can't imagine how much I want to see you again – and if I have made you angry so often, it's not because I don't love you; it's because I am an animal and a rascal…" (P-M.27). The women he chose for his early affairs seem to have been with similarly overpowering characters and, in 1884, at the age of 26, while mourning the death of his mother, he took up with one such strong-minded woman, Elvira Gemignani and, a year later, made her pregnant. Giacomo, never a fighter and afraid of Elvira's husband's fury, eloped with Elvira to be near his sisters in Monza, where his son Antonio was born in 1886. For the next twenty-five years Giacomo and Elvira would live together intermittently in a stormy and quarrelsome relationship, getting married eventually in 1904 after a fight in which they had come to blows. Elvira's main complaint was Giacomo's relationships with other women. Paradoxically, the more she complained the more Giacomo searched for the love of others. Unlike her, many of his lovers were gentle and kind, indeed some were beautiful and intelligent women with interesting careers of their own. Many became good friends with him. Yet Giacomo could never bring himself to break from Elvira entirely. The nearest they came to separation was after Elvira's paranoid persecution of their teenage maid, Doria Manfredi, in 1908. Elvira accused Doria of seducing Giacomo, called her a whore and fired her. Giacomo was distraught, denied the accusation, wrote apologetic letters to Doria and her parents, and fled to live in Rome. After weeks of further persecution by Elvira the poor girl swallowed disinfectant and died in agony. Her suicide note protested her innocence (her virginity was confirmed post-mortem), begged her family to take revenge on Elvira but specifically exonerated Giacomo who had, she said, never done anything wrong. Elvira was convicted of libel and threatening to kill, and sentenced to five months in prison. Giacomo's friends urged him to seize the opportunity to split from her, but he could not bring himself to do so. Elvira, clearly mentally disturbed, continued to poison Giacomo's life for the remainder of his days. She is an interesting example of a negative muse. In some ways she reminded Giacomo of his mother, yet appeared to be an entirely uninspiring and anti-creative influence. He had fallen in love with her in November 1884, only four months after his beloved mother's death, almost certainly as a rebound, and it is possible that he felt, perhaps unconsciously, a filial loyalty to her. Giacomo had told his sister that he was always thinking of his mother and would have little happiness without her. (JB 46) His dying mother had, after all, placed her wedding ring on his finger on her death-bed, and he wore it all his life. Elvira, however, was not an accurate mother substitute, she did not appreciate any sort of music, and sneered whenever Giacomo mentioned his own. Stupidly, she saw music as simply another rival for his attentions.

Surprisingly, Giacomo nevertheless managed to write eight successful operas, although some people have thought he could have written twice that number if it hadn't been for Elvira's constant nagging. But perhaps his operas were written precisely because he had to escape from her. They are all about beautiful women! Indeed, seven out of his eight outstanding operas are themselves named after their heroines. It is the women and not the men who are the principal characters. Each opera deals with a central (and sometimes also a secondary) love story and each heroine is a slightly different sort of woman. Two are psychologically powerful (Tosca and Turandot), three are gentle and loyal (Liu, Butterfly and Mimi), one or two are wild (Musetta), and one is mysterious (Suor Angelica). Yet all these soprano figures are sexually attractive. Giacomo was obsessed with women and loved many of them. They were his escape from Elvira. He called his affairs his 'little gardens' in which grew his music. They were what he lived for.

Giacomo was hardly an intellectual. He was most happy with friends, good food and fast cars. He was a boy who never grew up. He was not religious, saying "If God exists, he is very cruel". Nor was he interested in deep philosophical or political issues. This is one reason why he constantly fell out with his librettists. Giacomo wanted to write beautiful music, that is all. Where it came from he didn't know, nor did anybody else. As with all the great composers, the beauty of his music derived not from the conscious world of reason but, seemingly, from the ether itself. He was merely the lightening conductor that picked up the heavenly charge and converted it into sound. This is why he could never really *explain* to his librettists what it was that he wanted from them, other than making pleas to them for more "poetry". He was not very interested in their plots nor in their characters. This does not mean that the stories and characters don't, nevertheless, reflect something to do with the composer. They do. But Giacomo's main concern was with his music, and he wanted to fit the libretto to the music and not the other way around.

Budden reports that Giacomo's publisher, Guilio Ricordi, had to find a go-between to smooth out Giacomo's relationship with his librettist Luigi Illica. Highly successfully he appointed Giuseppe Giacoso, an older man and one of the outstanding literary figures of the day. It seems Giacoso understood Giacomo's cravings for love and for poetry, and he not only acted as a diplomat but added some of the verse that Giacomo needed. The trio successfully created Giacomo's three best-loved operas – *La Bohème* (1896), *Tosca* (1900) and *Madame Butterfly* (1904). When Giacosa died in 1906, Puccini and Illica effectively separated. (B.134) Both Giacosa, and Ricordi himself, were father figures for Giacomo.

The *meaning* of the words was only of secondary interest to Giacomo, it was their rhythm and sound that mattered to him. As Giacomo's sometimes literal-minded work-a-day librettists could not grasp what he was looking for, he composed little snatches of nonsense verse that illustrated the sounds and rhythms that he needed in order to enhance his music. Because these words literally were nonsense his librettists sometimes thought he was stupid. One excellent example of this nonsense doggerel was preserved by Luigi Illica. When Giacomo had written some music expressing "something about love" (as Illica says dismissively), Giacomo wrote under it the words:

> *Topi – trabanti – sogliole*
> *Sego - bilance – pargoli*
> *Son figli dell'amor!* (Quoted by Mary Jane Phillips-Matz.p84)

The first two lines are clearly dactyls (one stressed syllable followed by two short ones), and consist of rollicking delicious vowel sounds ending in, more or less, a rhyme. The third line is declamatory. That, I think, is what Giacomo wanted from the exasperated Illica. Unfortunately the librettist could not (or would not) see past the literal meaning of the words, which is:

> *Rats – satellites – fish*
> *Tallow – weighing scales – infants*
> *Are children of love!*

The constant failures to communicate between the inspired musician and his pedestrian librettists delayed Giacomo's operas for months. It was a struggle of wills. Which came first, the words or the music? Thankfully for us, Giacomo usually won this one. The trouble was that he was neither articulate with words himself, nor particularly assertive, and so these battles became unnecessarily prolonged. Verdi would not have tolerated such nonsense from his writers for more than a few moments! But then Verdi was also far more interested in ideas. We know, incidentally, that the old master approved of Puccini's sense of 'the symphonic' and of his melodies too. (JB 45)

One can only feel sorry for Giacomo. He had the magic gift for melody yet many in his environment tried to stifle it: Elvira demanding his attention, critics demanding priority for their ugly modernism and librettists for their words. These pressures led Giacomo Puccini to cut himself off in the countryside with only the company of his dogs and his card-playing friends, or to seek the love and understanding of intelligent young women. Depressed, he wrote to one such, the Hungarian writer, Margit Vészi, in 1913:

> ...and for my art, which comes so much from the soul, I really need a guide, a spirit who will understand me.

Giacomo yearned for love and understanding for himself and his music, and he had said as much to Toscanini's wife, Carla, two years earlier:

> I feel alone in the world, and I am always sad of that, and yet I have always tried to love people; but no one has ever understood me, that is, people have always taken me wrong. (PM.208)

What were they misunderstanding? They saw him as a rather superficial sentimentalist, and missed the depressed and complicated genius whose music expressed the love for which he yearned. Part of the trouble was that he was vain about his appearance and posed for publicity photographs looking grandiose and pompous. He presented to the world the misleading appearance of a well-dressed dandy, lazy, supercilious and over-confident. He was none of these things. In fact he was a shy and lonely man longing for a strong mother figure with whom he could enjoy a romantic and caring relationship. The young son of one of Giacomo's girlfriends, Vincent Seligman, later recalled "the look of indulgent affection in his large brown eyes and the rare sweetness of his frank smile – and yet even when he was in his happiest and jolliest mood there always seemed to lurk at the corner of his mouth a hint of melancholy". (J.B. 284)

When Giacomo died in 1924 there was an outpouring of affection. He had made friends in all sections of society, and had been an amusing, affable, polite and charming man. He had adored the music of both of his great predecessors, Verdi and Wagner, but, unlike them, he had been easy to get along with. Indeed, his weakness was that he had gone along with others all too easily, tolerating and acceding to the pettiness of critics and the manipulations of Elvira.

Too much time is spent, perhaps, trying to determine the meaning of operas, and too much effort is made by critics in analysing plots, acting performances and librettos. If you want a good play or a great acting performance you should go to a playhouse and watch actors. In the opera house you get music. Those macho critics over the years who have castigated Giacomo Puccini's music as "sentimental" or "superficial", are merely revealing to the world their own lack of sexual sophistication. His music is all emotion, celebrating romance, and for all those who have felt the magic of love, Puccini's music just brings it all back again.

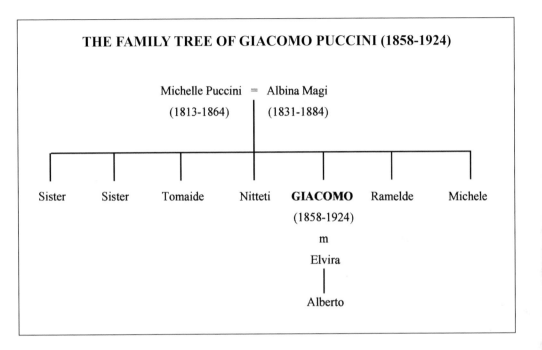

THE FAMILY TREE OF GIACOMO PUCCINI (1858-1924)

Michelle Puccini = Albina Magi
(1813-1864)   (1831-1884)

Sister   Sister   Tomaide   Nitteti   **GIACOMO**   Ramelde   Michele
(1858-1924)

m

Elvira

Alberto

SOURCES

Julian Budden. *Puccini: His Life and Works,* OUP. 2002

Mary Jane Phillips – Matz. *Puccini: A Biography.* Northeastern Univ. Press. 2002

Michael Steen. 'Puccini' in *The Lives & Times of the Great Composers* Icon Books, 2003

10

MARGARET THATCHER (1925 – 2013)

Politician

Probably one of the most misunderstood celebrities of modern times, Margaret Thatcher has been eulogised as a powerful, intellectual, radical and patriotic reformer, while her critics have seen her as heartless, divisive and dogmatic.

At Oxford, the head of her college, Dame Janet Vaughan, described her as an "empty-headed" ambitious student of "limited intellectual ability", and years later Thatcher's special adviser Sir Anthony Parsons testified to her "intellectual naivety" and the narrowness of her vision. Both these people, who knew Thatcher well, emphasised the limits of her intelligence *(Personal Communications)*. At university she was found to be a poor student academically-speaking and, initially, had few friends. Then she joined the Oxford University Conservative Association and became an ardent party-goer attending numerous Conservative balls and cocktail parties. Her good looks guaranteed her male attention although she took some time to find the right man. She wrote incessantly to her sister about her clothes, ballroom dancing and social life, revealing a very calculating attitude towards her courtships, passing on one of her unwanted suitors to her sister. She was clearly determined to rise socially and this meant finding a rich husband. She was not interested in feelings nor ideas, only in what she called 'facts', and her aim was neither to help others, nor to understand, only to forward her own career. After Oxford she moved almost entirely in Conservative Party circles, gradually cutting herself off from her father whose class attributes had become embarrassing to her. When he died, she was hardly in touch with him. Her continuing letters to her sister lack any serious intellectual content and consist chiefly of unreflective trivia. She had few social or cultural interests outside those that affected her career. On his departure as her Special Adviser on Foreign Affairs, Parsons had told Thatcher that in retirement he was going to research the literary influence of Joseph Conrad on D.H. Lawrence. He remarked that "she had clearly heard of neither of these men".

Thatcher became Prime Minister in 1979 but within two years she had become one of the least popular Prime Ministers of the century. On the eve of the Falklands War in 1982 she was attacked by Enoch Powell and other Conservative MPs for being weak and indecisive. They made it clear that if she did not show her metal against Argentina she would be replaced. Over the next few weeks her remarkable team of spin doctors and voice coaches transformed her public image from an apparent ditherer into the decisive and deep-voiced Iron Lady of history. The image makeover was very much assisted by the victory of the British armed forces in the Falklands, for which Thatcher took much credit in the public mind.

The 1970s had been a period of economic recession and unemployment, social chaos and trade union stridency. After 1982 Thatcher accepted the advice of her coaches that a large section of the electorate was looking for a strong leader with clear principles who would stand up to the unions and arrest the nation's apparent decline. For several years she now acted the part of the Iron Lady in the manner that her advisors had prescribed. She lacked, however, any genuine political philosophy. In order to counteract the view that she had no intellectual depth her spin doctors put it about that she had been impressed by the doctrines of Friedrich Hayek and Milton Friedman while at Oxford, and that she was herself a pioneering monetarist. In fact, as Kenneth Clarke has emphasised, she was far more cautious and pragmatic than she appeared to be. Now required by her advisers to show firm opinions in public on almost every subject, she often fell back on declaring her shopkeeper father's naïve principles of thrift, self-sufficiency and patriotism, although such attitudes were sometimes dressed up as being based upon academic theory. Not fully aware of the effects of her decisions upon the lives of ordinary people, she showed little sympathy for the victims of her policies, misconstruing their protests as unprovoked socialist hostility, or even communist conspiracy. In fact her policies sometimes had effects opposite to those she proclaimed, including damage to national treasures such as the BBC and the NHS, and the near destruction of Britain's manufacturing industry. On retirement she left England divided into a predominantly Tory South and a Labour North. In Scotland she stirred up an intense hatred for Conservatism, and for many things English, that lasted for several decades, and helped to drive Scotland towards independence.

By 1985 Thatcher had discovered that she enjoyed playing the part of the strong-willed termagant and the role became habitual. She had no interest in feminism and, indeed, preferred to be the only woman in her team, reflecting perhaps her childhood rivalry with her older sister Muriel. She used her looks, however, to sexually attract and manipulate older males such as William Whitelaw, François Mitterand, Ronald Reagan and Augusto Pinochet. After her third election victory in 1987 power finally went to her head and she became convinced that she was always right. This familiar political hubris syndrome caused her to ignore advice and to follow extreme policies as regards the Poll Tax and Europe. Late in the day, and understandably, her Cabinet colleagues eventually ousted her.

By curtailing the power of the over-mighty Trade Unions, privatising some badly run state industries, and encouraging patriotic entrepreneurialism, Margaret Thatcher almost certainly helped to stop Britain's post war decline. But the governments of other countries in Europe had dealt with similar economic problems without being confrontational, cruel or divisive. Nevertheless Thatcher certainly encouraged a more aggressive attitude that helped British business generally. Thatcher's brazen manner, however, and lack of intellectual subtlety, probably also encouraged the culture of greed and selfishness in British financial circles that promoted the collapses of 2008 onwards. Her failure to formulate policies of recovery for those she put out of work, and, for example, her callous closure of many psychiatric hospitals, are evidence of her genuine lack of public compassion. Psychiatric care in England took over forty years to recover. Anxious to prove that she was not a weak woman she eschewed all such shows of tenderness. To some she seemed to be a fake, to others a reversion to the old-fashioned values that the social revolution of the 1960s had seemingly rejected. One of her advisers, Sir John Hoskyns, described her as 'incompetent', and 'a bully' who rarely praised the successes of her colleagues, blaming others for her own failures.

How, then, did Margaret Thatcher win three General Elections (albeit without increasing her overall support in the country) and govern for eleven years? The answer is that she had extraordinary luck. In the first place she had been aided by the belief of certain senior Conservatives such as Airey Neave,that their then elitist party needed, in order to maintain its popular appeal, a non-elitist leader. Furthermore, Neave could see that the extreme conservatism of his party at that time could be disguised by the mould-breaking, indeed almost revolutionary, choice of a woman as leader. So, without Neave and his colleagues Thatcher never would have become party leader in the first place. Secondly, she came to power at a time when Britain was enjoying unprecedented wealth due to North Sea oil (which she is said to have squandered). Thirdly, her political opposition was in total disarray due to the disintegration of the Labour Party and the formation of the Social Democratic Party. Fourthly, she was given, by the bravery of her armed forces and the stupidity of General Galtieri, the gift of the Falklands victory. Fifthly, and most importantly, she received the enthusiastic support of the new Murdoch press. Sixthly, she experienced increased public sympathy after the determined IRA attempt on her life at Brighton in 1984. At home she was fortunate enough to have the steady support of her wealthy husband Denis while, internationally, her decade in power happily coincided almost exactly with that of an American soul-mate, President Ronald Reagan, with whom she enjoyed an unprecedentedly flirtatious and congenial relationship. It was extremely lucky, too, for both of them, that their old enemy, the Soviet Union, was taken over at this time by the uniquely enlightened Russian leader, Mikhail Gorbachev, with whom they could do business. Finally, Thatcher was also most fortunate in the quality of nearly all her advisers, and especially her publicity team. Without these extraordinary strokes of good fortune, it is doubtful that her premiership would have survived 1982. She was, surely, the luckiest British politician of the twentieth century.

Are there any psychodynamic features of importance? Yes. As in the case of Tony Blair, Thatcher seems to have entered politics partly in order to complete the disrupted political career and social ascent of her father. In Blair's father's case the disruption was due to severe illness whereas in the case of the career of the ambitious Alderman Roberts the disruption was caused by Labour politicians. Both Margaret Roberts and her older sister had competed for their father's approval and both probably knew, albeit barely consciously, that he yearned for a son who would take up his fight against Socialism, thus continuing his career. Before she scraped into Oxford, Thatcher had resolved that she would fill this role. Seeking social and class advancement, she proceeded to take elocution lessons in order to lose her lower middle-class Lincolnshire accent and to acquire, initially at least, a pastiche of received pronunciation that caused irritation to some listeners. After the Falklands crisis of 1982 she underwent a further overhaul of her image, and took advice on how to transform herself in order to appeal to the British electorate. She was told to appear to be indifferent to popularity and to become the forceful exponent of the apparently principled, no-nonsense, down to earth, self-help materialism that had for decades been a strand in British culture, and especially among libertarian shopkeepers and small business interests. She was introduced by Sir Keith Joseph (whose publicity role it was to provide the appearance of intellectual gravitas to her regime), to various economists whose monetarist theories approximately coincided with this position. Unsteeped in these theories, however, Margaret Thatcher increasingly reverted to using her father's opinions as the core of her political outlook. He had believed in sound money, hard work, hostility to public spending and traditional Victorian values. This regression to her childhood culture gave her easy access to instant conclusions and simplistic views on almost every subject. She admitted some of this on the day she first became Prime Minister in 1979 – "I just owe almost everything to my own father. I really do," she said.

Margaret Thatcher, more than any other British Prime Minister, was the successful creation of her spin doctors. She was a hard worker but, in truth, she lacked any real substance or originality. After a few years she was gripped by hubris, repeating the same simple messages over and over again, and displaying the simplicity and obstinacy of an unsubtle mind. Her advisers' main achievement was to replace her earlier attempts to appear forceful, when she had adopted a stagy and irritating stridency, with the more convincing husky and contralto qualities of the Iron Lady. In fact, all these attributes were superficial performances that helped to mask the intellectual, moral and emotional emptiness within.

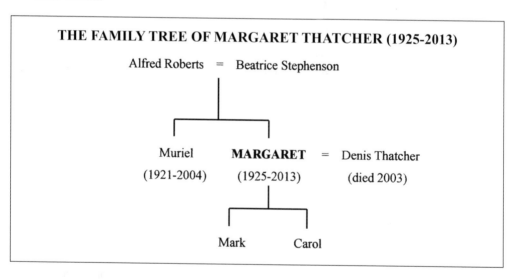

THE FAMILY TREE OF MARGARET THATCHER (1925-2013)

Alfred Roberts = Beatrice Stephenson

Muriel   **MARGARET** = Denis Thatcher
(1921-2004)   (1925-2013)   (died 2003)

Mark   Carol

SOURCES

John Campbell: *The Iron Lady. Margaret Thatcher, from Grocer's Daughter to Iron Lady,* Vintage Books, 2012
Charles Moore: *Margaret Thatcher: The Authorised Biography* (Penguin 2013)
Margaret Thatcher: *The Autobiography* (Harper Press 2013)

11

ADOLF HITLER (1889 – 1945)

Dictator

"No one claims to understand Hitler". Martin Amis.
BBC Today 27/8/14

Adolf Hitler was born in Austria in 1889 but lived with his mother Klara just over the border in Germany, in the town of Passau, from 1892 to 1894. So, for nearly three years, during some of the most formative years of his life (aged three to six), Adolf lived in Germany. For much of the time mother and son led an undisturbed life together but, on occasions, their peace was disrupted by visits from Adolf's father Alois. He was working as a Customs officer just over the Austrian border, and every few days, would return home, wearing an Austrian uniform, and often the worse for drink. He would beat his wife, his dog and, especially, his little son Adolf.

I believe these were the experiences that led to the Second World War and all its attendant miseries. It was the beginning, in little Adolf's mind, of a life-long hatred of his Austrian father and the start of the gradual building of his belief that Germany meant his mother and all that was good, while the rest of the world meant his father and all that was bad. It was the start of Adolf's life-long *struggle* (as he put it) against his father and what he stood for. Adolf always wanted to be German rather than Austrian and, in 1925, he actually renounced his Austrian citizenship. Furthermore, local people said that his father, Alois, was partly Jewish, and Adolf grew to believe that it was indeed the Jews who were responsible for Germany's defeat in the First World War and for so many other things that he saw as being rotten and bad. Alois mistreated his wife and moved the family from one small lodging to another, and young Adolf could see that Alois did not give Klara the life, or accommodation, that she deserved. (Adolf was not against Austria itself but considered that Austria had been swamped by Jewish immigrants, mainly from the East.)

As soon as Adolf gained some power in 1930 he commissioned a top secret investigation into his father's possible Jewish paternity. He did not receive from his investigator, the lawyer Hans Frank, the sort of whitewash he may have wanted. There was the obvious possibility that Alois' father might have been Jewish as his unmarried mother, Maria Anna, had worked as a servant for several families that either were Jewish, or at least sounded as though they were Jewish, at about the time that she fell pregnant. Some said she had been employed by Baron Rothschild in Vienna and later, as a cook, by a family called Frankenberger in Graz. Furthermore, the Frankenberger family had reputedly paid regular support to Maria Anna for the upkeep of Alois until he was fourteen. According to the historian Ian Kershaw all this is without reliable foundation as there were 'no Jews in Graz' at the time and the name Frankenberger is not necessarily Jewish. Yet Adolf certainly heard these stories, and rumours of his alleged Jewish descent circulated openly in the 1920s and 1930s. Of course, even if the Frankenbergers were, despite their name, not Jewish, Adolf could still have *believed* that they were, and so could others. Furthermore, Adolf was not against Jews because they observed a particular religion but because of their race, so it is impossible to be sure that there were "no Jews in Graz", in that sense.

Adolf himself had been born in Braunau Am Inn in Austria on 20 April 1889. His mother Klara (from whom Adolf inherited his extraordinary blue eyes) was aged twenty-nine when Adolf was born and he was her fourth child, her three eldest having died in infancy. Already being cared for by Klara were her husband Alois' two children by a previous marriage – Alois (Junior) born in 1882 and Angela born in 1883. They addressed Klara as 'mother'. So, until the age of five, the infant Adolf found himself the youngest in a family of three and, because he was his mother's only surviving child, after three infant deaths, he was, naturally, very much her favourite. At the age of five, in 1894, Adolf's privileged position was challenged when a brother, Edmund, was born, to be followed when Adolf was seven by a sister, Paula, in 1896. In the same year Adolf's older half-brother Alois (Junior) left home for good. So Adolf was, from the age of seven, the oldest boy in the home, with 'jolly' older half-sister (Angela), younger brother (Edmund) and 'quiet' baby sister (Paula). This situation continued until Edmund's death through illness in 1900 when Adolf was eleven. Adolf then became the only boy in the house again. (Adolf would support his sister Paula financially until his death in 1945.) As Klara had lost four of her children, it was not surprising that she made her only surviving son, Adolf, feel so special.

Both of Adolf's parents had come from peasant stock. They were cousins, and for this reason they had had to seek authority to marry. His mother addressed his father as 'Uncle' and had been his maid before they married, setting the tone for their sado-masochistic marital relationship. Adolf's father Alois, clearly an ambitious and hard-working man, had climbed the social ladder successfully. Work colleagues described Alois as 'very strict, exact, even pedantic at work and a very unapproachable person'. He was also said to be humourless, pompous, and unpredictably bad-tempered. At home Alois was a stern, distant and punitive father who frequently beat his children, especially Adolf. When Paula Hitler, Adolf's little sister, was interviewed on 5 June 1946 at Berchtesgaden she recalled a family of

...very lively children who were perhaps somewhat difficult to train. If there were ever quarrels or differences of opinion between my parents it was always on account of the children. It was especially my brother Adolf who challenged my father to extreme harshness and got his thrashing every day.'

Angela, his half-sister, also spoke of these regular beatings, and Adolf himself described his father to Joseph Goebbels in 1932 as a *haustyrann* or 'domestic tyrant'. William Patrick Hitler (Adolf's half-brother's son) claimed that on several occasions both his father and Adolf were beaten unconscious by Alois, Adolf once being left for dead. Alois drank regularly and smoked heavily and was, so it seems, more interested in bee-keeping than in his family.

Adolf was, as he said, "forced into opposition" with his father, not least over Adolf's ambition to become an artist, which appalled Alois – "he opposed it with all the determination of his nature". Adolf recalled this in his autobiographical *Mein Kampf*, which literally, and highly significantly, means "my struggle". Adolf and his father argued about everything and the little Adolf took pride in the development of his powers of argument – "my father, for understandable reasons, proved unable to appreciate the oratorical talents of his pugnacious boy…". So Adolf's oratory, which was the weapon he used eventually to seduce the German people, and to win power, had been forged as a weapon he used successfully in his struggle with his father.

On 3 January 1903, when the abused Adolf was thirteen years old, his father collapsed and died while drinking in the local pub. At one level Adolf had won. Throughout his 'very painful' teens, as he later described them, he was now the only man about the house. Central to his adolescent development, says Kershaw, had been his conflict with his aggressive father. Adolf now turned into 'an idle, resentful, rebellious, sullen, stubborn and purposeless teenager'. He was, however, cosseted by his doting mother who believed he could 'do anything'. After his father's death, Kershaw says, Adolf 'lived a life of parasitic idleness… during the days drawing, painting, reading or writing 'poetry'; the evenings were for going to the theatre or opera; and the whole time he daydreamed and fantasised about his future as a great artist'. Adolf loved Wagner's operas. The skinny little school dropout found in Wagner all the magnificence he lacked. In general, Wagner's overall theme is that of the Germanic hero overcoming the forces of evil. Adolf certainly identified himself with this. To the embarrassment of some Nazi ideologues, Adolf especially loved *Parsifal* with its soft environmental motifs, mystical sense of union with nature and its ambiguous disapproval of sexuality. More publicly, Adolf's favourite was *Rienzi* where the hero rescues a female relative from abduction. The parallel with Adolf's core personal fantasy is obvious. Moreover, the heroes, Parsifal and Rienzi, are eventually killed by their enemies, the latter dying and being consumed by flames, just as Siegfried and Brünnhilde are in *Götterdämmerung (The Twilight of the Gods)*. The kingdom of the gods is destroyed around them just as the Third Reich was. Did Adolf, ordering his own cremation in Berlin's ruins, see himself in this way? Almost certainly. This raises the possibility that Adolf was always drawn to suicide, and could help to explain the succession of suicidally inept military decisions he took in the years 1940 to 1945, and to provide the reason why he opted to die in the conflagration of Berlin rather than retreat to the South of Germany and give himself up, tamely, to the Americans.

Adolf's military mistakes are mostly characterised by an obstinate refusal to retreat, and by his reckless creation of new enemies such as Russia and America. What was the origin of this stupidity? Was it simply suicidal or was there another reason? Remember that for ten years, as a child, Adolf had fought his father and had eventually won: when he was thirteen, Adolf's father had died! Unconsciously, therefore, he may also have assumed that such obdurate tactics were bound to be successful again. In the world of unreason, these two motives – romantic suicide and heroic obstinacy – are not necessarily in conflict. However, I feel that suicide was never his main intention; it was merely a romantic fall-back position. Adolf's original premise was that wilful obstinacy would again be victorious, as it had been in his childhood. His early military successes in France in 1940 merely confirmed and encouraged this view. So Adolf recklessly opposed his generals, treating them as he had treated his father. Adolf believed in the magical power of his own will. As a child this had manifested as reckless obstinacy and a refusal to submit to his father's wishes. Fatally for Germany this wilfulness was reapplied as Hitler's overall military strategy. What had appeared to work as a child, and in 1940, however, turned out to be a total failure in the longer term.

As far as Adolf's later childhood is concerned there is one remarkable witness – his only boyhood friend, August Kubizek – whose memoirs confirm much of what Adolf describes. Kubizek pictures a solitary, self-obsessed, lazy and angry boy, inhibited, shy, yet brilliantly articulate, dogmatic and bursting with ideas; in many ways Adolf appeared to be the classic "spoiled brat". By the time Kubizek first met him he was already essentially the Adolf Hitler of adulthood. Kubizek remarks that Adolf's dead father "was still ever present to his family", adding with crucial insight:

...the authority of his father still remained, even after his death, the force in the struggle with which Adolf developed his own powers. His father's attitude had provoked him first to secret, then to open, rebellion.

Kubizek rightly emphasises Adolf's continuing "struggle" (*kampf*) as being with his dead father. Alois had never settled and during his period of service in Braunau recorded twelve changes of address, often accommodating his family in small inns.

Kubizek says of the young Adolf –

He just had to talk and needed someone who would listen to him", adding –"everything aroused his (Adolf's) interest...(he) had to find an outlet for his tempestuous feelings...(he) seemed to be like a volcano erupting... something strange, other-worldly, was bursting out of him...such rapture...this was not acting, not exaggeration, this was really felt...how vividly he managed to convey his feelings, how easily the words flowed from his mouth.

This could be a classic description of *hypomania* – the psychiatric label used to describe abnormally elevated mood. Such a label would also fit with Adolf's outbursts of temper whenever thwarted or disagreed with, as well as with his sense of self-importance. Adolf, so Kubizek implies, was usually in this raised mood during his middle teens. The textbook criteria for a diagnosis of hypomania are a persistently elevated, expansive or irritable mood (for four or more days), decreased need for sleep, pressure of talk, inflated self-esteem or grandiosity, flight of ideas, distractibility, increased goal-directed behaviour and excessive involvement in pleasurable activities. Most of these traits fit the young Adolf Hitler very well, especially if one takes into account the exceptionally goal-directed behaviour of his later political career and the "pleasurable activities" he was obsessed with – art, architecture, opera and music generally. He was always a poor sleeper, often staying awake until the early hours, and rising late. There is also a possible genetic correlation between mood disturbances and those, like Adolf, who sleep late and work best in the evenings.

Perhaps an even better label for Adolf would be *cyclothymic* – a term used to describe persistent mood abnormality involving periods of both mild elation *and* mild depression – because depression later became an additional feature in Adolf's life. Whichever label is chosen, I am fairly certain that Adolf Hitler, by the age that Kubizek describes him, is already showing clear signs of a mild *bipolar mood disorder* of this sort. Any such condition is typically accompanied by marked impairments in social, occupational and sexual functioning – all of which also apply in Adolf's case. Adolf tended to be shy with individuals but at ease with a crowd. Studies show that an adolescent onset of bipolar disorder is associated with a family history of the condition – in Adolf's case, his father was probably also affected.

Adolf states in *Mein Kampf* – "I had honoured my father, but my mother I loved", and when we turn to consider Klara Hitler, Adolf's mother, the contrast with Alois is considerable. She was, in many ways, the opposite of her husband. Born Klara Pölzl in 1860 she was twenty-three years younger than Alois, and his second cousin. In 1876, aged sixteen, Klara had left the family farm and joined Uncle Alois in Braunau as his maid. Alois separated from his first wife in 1880 and his second died in 1884, by which time Klara was already pregnant by him. After receiving special dispensation on grounds of incest, the couple were married in January 1885. As we have seen, three children were born in rapid succession but, by January 1888, all had died through illness. Then, on 20 April 1889, in a Gasthof where they were then living, Klara gave birth to Adolf, her first surviving child. Kubizek, who met Klara Hitler often between 1904 and 1907 describes her as: "– a beautiful woman to the day of her death… submissive and accommodating…she told me once that Adolf was a very weak child and that she always lived in fear of losing him." This fits with Paula Hitler's description of her mother as "a very soft and tender person, the compensatory element between the almost too harsh father and the very lively children…" Adolf's mother was, said Kubizek:

…the only person on earth to whom he felt really close…I was always surprised by the sympathetic understanding and patience with which Adolf

tried to convince his mother of his artistic vocation. Contrary to his habit, he never became cross or violent on these occasions.

Klara remained anxious about Adolf, realising that he was lazy, unrealistic in his plans and without solid qualifications for a job or proper financial means of support. Early in 1907 she became ill and had an operation. Adolf visited her daily in hospital. When she had recovered Adolf finally left for Vienna intending to enter the Academy of Arts. Almost immediately his mother's breast cancer returned and Adolf came home to care for her, under the direction of the family's doctor, Dr Eduard Bloch. Kubizek recalls seeing Adolf shortly after the doctor had broken the news to him of the seriousness of his mother's condition:

> *He looked terrible. His face was so pale as to be almost transparent, his eyes were dull and his voice hoarse...'Incurable, the doctor says' – this was all he could utter...his eyes blazed, his temper flared up. 'Incurable – what do they mean by that?' he screamed. 'Not that the malady is incurable, but that the doctors aren't capable of curing it. My mother isn't even old. Forty-seven isn't an age where you give up hope. But as soon as the doctors can't do anything, they call it incurable.'*

The young Adolf now took over the running of his mother's cramped little household. Kubizek records:

> *One day on my arrival at the Blütengasse I found Adolf kneeling on the floor. He was wearing a blue apron and scrubbing out the kitchen, which had not been cleaned for a long time. I was really immensely surprised and I must have shown it, for Frau Klara smiled in spite of her pain and said to me: 'There, you see, Adolf can do anything.' (My emphasis.) Then I noticed that Adolf had changed the furniture around. His mother's bed now stood in the kitchen because that was heated during the day. The kitchen cupboard had been moved into the living room, and in its place was the couch, on which Adolf slept, so that he could be near her during the night as well.*

For the remaining weeks of his mother's life, eighteen-year-old Adolf, wearing his apron, did everything he could for her:

> *Adolf anticipated her every wish and took the most tender care of her. I had never before seen in him such loving tenderness. I did not trust my*

own eyes and ears. Not a cross word, not an impatient remark, no violent insistence on having his own way. He forgot himself entirely in those weeks and lived only for his mother. Kubizek records.

When Klara died just before Christmas (21 December) Adolf "could hardly speak" yet made all the arrangements with the undertakers. The doctor said he had never seen anyone so devastated by bereavement. Four days later it was Christmas Day but Adolf refused to visit either the Kubizeks or his half-sister Angela Raubal (he detested her civil servant husband), apparently spending it alone at the now empty home. In future years Christmas would always be a difficult season for Adolf, and in 1941, 1942 and 1944 he would make war-losing decisions at that time.

After his mother's death in December 1907 Adolf eventually returned to Vienna. He tried again to enter the Academy of Arts but again failed. He had not told his dying mother of his first failure and now, initially at least, he concealed both rejections from his only friend August Kubizek, with whom he was sharing his lodgings. Kubizek says:

Nothing more terrible could have happened to him. But he was too proud to talk about it, and so concealed from me what had occurred...he did not mention it at all...There was neither revolt nor rebellion, instead came a radical withdrawal into himself.

So Adolf had suffered two huge losses within twelve months – the death of his beloved mother and the double failure to be accepted by the Academy of Arts. For such a youth – romantic, narcissistic, lonely and self-important – these blows must have been psychologically devastating. Biographers often describe the next seven years of degradation as if they had no explanation, yet I think they indicate, quite simply, that Adolf became significantly depressed as a reaction to these blows. The directors of the Academy had said that Adolf might be better suited to become an architect, and Adolf seems to have taken comfort from this. Already there are hints that he saw his vocation as being the designer of new and spacious houses and towns. Even on the eve of his suicide in 1945 he was still studying designs for his mother's home town. While in Vienna Adolf became obsessed with buildings and was constantly planning new living spaces, bridges, stations and museums. He began to detest property speculators, exploitative landlords and the squalid housing of the Viennese working class. He started to plan gardens, playgrounds for children, railways, better water supplies, drains, bathrooms, and light and airy houses. "I am working on the solution of the housing problem in Vienna" he announced. Houses had become more real to him than people. With his usual insight Kubizek remarks: "No doubt this ardent desire for a total reorganisation of life was his personal response to his own fate." He was certainly trying to reorganise and re-plan himself but was he also, unconsciously, planning a better living space for his dead mother? It was what she had always wanted.

In 1913 Adolf moved to Munich, registering himself as stateless and, after months of evading conscription, eventually enlisted, probably illegally, in the German (rather than the Austrian) army in August 1914 on the eve of the Great War. In the four years that followed, Adolf at last found some sense of purpose and structure in his life. He even won a medal, on the recommendation of a Jewish officer, for rescuing a wounded comrade. When the war ended, the gassed and wounded Adolf felt betrayed. No sooner had he found a meaning to his life than it had been dashed from him! He had been stationed on parts of the front that had not seen many German defeats and he could hardly believe that the Allies deserved their victory. Angry and rebellious, he became increasingly politicised, nationalistic and, apparently for the first time, anti-semitic. In October 1918, just before the armistice, Adolf had been blinded after an Allied gas attack and was admitted for treatment at Pasework where, according to the British psychologist David Lewis writing in 2003, a German neurologist, Dr Edmund Forster, had secretly diagnosed the blindness as being hysterical in origin. At the time, such a diagnosis would have been highly dangerous and could have been seen as tantamount to cowardice, a charge on which hundreds of German soldiers had already been shot. Forster, however, in order to avoid such problems, assured Adolf that the cause of the blindness was physical and told him that he (Adolf) was an exceptional man, chosen by God, who could use his extraordinary and heaven-sent will-power as a cure. This treatment worked but, according to Lewis, it also confirmed and intensified Adolf's already established belief in his messianic specialness. This account, so it seems to me, also suggests an additional reason for Adolf's strange insistence upon waging an apparently unnecessary war in 1939; it was as if he was still continuing the Great War of 1918 in an effort to reverse its result and "cancel out" his own unconscious, hysterically denied, cowardice. He may still have felt narcissistically exaggerated guilt for Germany's defeat some twenty years earlier. Germany had "died" in 1918 just as his mother had died in 1907, and he had failed to save either of them.

Adolf had found the First World War "like a redemption from the vexatious experiences of my youth". During these years Adolf went out of his way to be subservient to his superior officers and was not popular with the other men who regarded him as odd. His closest friend was his dog, Foxl, which had come over from the English lines. Adolf was bitterly upset when this animal was later stolen from him. Dogs and Adolf were always friends, probably because both had been victims of his father's beatings. After the war Adolf suffered from nightmares. These were possibly signs of post-traumatic stress and would have been found in many survivors from the trenches. Yet, according to Walter Langer, one of his witnesses had heard that, on one occasion, the half-asleep Adolf had been found

...swaying in his room, looking wildly about him. 'He! He! He's been here!' he gasped. His lips were blue. Sweat streamed down his face... then suddenly he broke out 'There, there! In the corner! Who's that?'

These are not typical of the nightmares of war and suggest a deep fear of an individual – perhaps, in Adolf's case, his father. (Langer, a well-established New York psychoanalyst, had been ordered to make a psychological report on Hitler, for military purposes, in 1943.)

Adolf writes in *Mein Kampf*:

Let us imagine the following: in a basement apartment of two stuffy rooms live a worker's family...Among the five children there is a boy, let us say, of three. The smallness and overcrowding of the rooms do not create favourable conditions. Quarrelling and nagging often arise because of this. When the parents fight almost daily, their brutality leaves nothing to the imagination...especially when the mutual differences express themselves in the form of brutal attacks on the part of the father towards the mother or to assaults due to drunkenness. The poor little boy, at the age of six, senses things which would make even a grown-up shudder. Morally infected, the young 'citizen' wanders off to elementary school.

I agree with Langer that, however it is disguised, these highly significant passages are Adolf recalling his own childhood. Although Adolf's father would, while sober, appear to be "the soul of dignity", when drunk he became "brutal, unjust and inconsiderate", hitting his wife, his children and his dog. As we have seen, Adolf later hints at witnessing "with disgust and indignation" lower-class families where "the wife, for the sake of the children, stands up against... (the) drunk and brutal (husband)". Klara had stood up for Adolf and tried to prevent the beatings he received.

Although Langer, in my opinion, rightly recognises Adolf's great anger towards his father he does not go on, as I do, to see Adolf's hatred of the Jews and, indeed, the waging of the war itself, as expressions of this anger. Adolf was, says Langer, so afraid of his aggressive fantasies being discovered by his father that he repressed them. But I believe that these feelings re-emerged in 1939 as his crazy determination to wage war. Why did Adolf, after the Great War, begin to construct his devastating anti-Jewish delusional system? For me, there is one outstanding probable cause – and that is *Adolf's belief, conscious or half-conscious, that his sadistic father was partly Jewish, and his fervent desire to protect the memory of his mother from this man.*

What is the evidence to support this hypothesis? Well we first have to accept that the unconscious mind operates on a network of loose associations that are not, strictly speaking, rational. In Adolf's case there was an association in his mind of a number of issues that, to the sane onlooker, appear to be unconnected. Furthermore, in the unconscious mind, dead figures can remain alive and active. We have already noted that Adolf heard the rumours of Alois' Jewish paternity that were rife in the 1920s, and we know that he had commissioned research into this possibility in 1930 that apparently tended to confirm this. In other words, Adolf had reasonable grounds to believe in his father's part-Jewishness. We also know that Adolf would rave repeatedly about Jewish men raping and defiling Aryan women, and there is that well known piece in *Mein Kampf* which we have already examined, where Adolf speaks of a boy witnessing attacks by his father on his mother – "things which would make even a grown-up shudder". Once, when asked why he suspected the Jews of being responsible for so many ills in his Reich, Hitler merely said, instead of his usual ranting – "personal reasons". Maybe as a little boy, he had indeed seen his ogre of a father hitting or sexually assaulting his mother. We know that his father could be violent, drunken and libidinous. Furthermore, Adolf was never able fully to express his hatred and fear of his father and so these feelings could have become spread onto Jews in general. This sort of displacement does happen. The strange phrase "morally infected" in the famous quote from *Mein Kampf*, echoes the words in the passages where he is describing prostitution and the mysterious sexual dangers of Viennese life, and it does seem likely that sexuality in general became associated in Adolf's mind with his father. So I think it is at least probable, that when attacking Jews, Adolf was in fact unconsciously attacking his father. Certainly the Jews became the general scapegoats for all ills, including his own failures. Just as his father had indirectly sabotaged Adolf's education, scorned his oratory and opposed his artistic career, so the Jews were responsible, in his eyes, for everything else that went wrong, including the loss of the Great War, their own destruction and the 1939-45 War itself. But for Adolf the Jews were far more than mere scapegoats relieving him of any sense of guilt or failure. Remember that the insightful Kubizek tells us that "the authority of his father still remained, even after his (Alois') death, the force in the struggle with which Adolf developed his own powers", and Adolf himself admits in *Mein Kampf* that his father had unwittingly "sown the seed" for his (Adolf's) future career. So for Adolf, the war *was,* psychologically speaking, his unfinished battle or "struggle" with his father that had been interrupted by his father's premature death. By what is known as the Zeigarnik effect, such "unfinished business" tends to persist far more tenaciously than do conflicts that are concluded.

Much of Adolf's political career, as well as the day-to-day decisions it entailed, were based upon a sound grasp of realities and common sense. Increasingly, however, patterns and peculiarities emerge that have a deeper and pathological origin. The *intensity* of Adolf's hatreds may have been augmented by his sexual frustration and by his fears of impotence, but their *direction* was surely dictated by his all-consuming central fantasy. The ultimately unnecessary attacks upon France, Poland, Britain, Russia and other nations followed. How far were these attacks all expressions of "the struggle" he confusedly and unconsciously believed he was waging to rescue his mother from his (Jewish) father? Adolf certainly accused Britain, Poland, France and Russia, dominated as they all were, in his opinion, by the Jews, of traits he remembered and hated in his father, accusing them of "cruelty", "lack of moral restraint" and "the brutality of the violent egoist". Later, he even depicted Churchill as the "undisciplined swine who is drunk for eight hours of every twenty-four". This, too, sounds very much like Alois, his father.

Adolf's series of land-grabs in Europe became progressively more irrational and riskier as the years went by. To start with Adolf had simply reclaimed territories taken from Germany after the loss of the First World War. Then came the Germanification of a willing Austria. These were decisions taken in summer months and made some sort of political sense. But Adolf could not stop. He then marched into Czechoslovakia and Poland thus rashly and prematurely forcing France and Britain to declare war. Adolf reacted to opposition from Poland and the West with childish tantrums. Increasingly, his decisions revealed the pressures of his internal personal "spoiled child" psychopathology. On 20 April 1939 he had celebrated his fiftieth birthday and suddenly it seemed to him that time was short – "the problems must be solved by *me*, and I can wait no longer". What exactly Adolf thought that "the problems" were, is unstated. Almost certainly he did not understand that his insatiable need to continue fighting was being driven largely by his unconscious desire to defeat his father. In his mind the Jews were everywhere – in every country – and he had to overcome them before it was too late. It was now or never.

So one can speculate that Adolf transferred onto the Jews the hatred he really felt for his father, while for Germany and her 'Aryan' culture, he expressed the love he had for his brilliantly blue-eyed mother. By winning the war (against

Thomas Hardy's mother, Jemima (1813-1904), whose deprived early life provided the main substance for his novels. Bookish yet impoverished, Jemima inspired Thomas to become a novelist and thereby to right the wrongs she felt she had endured.

Verdi in old age surrounded by the women in his life. From left: his adopted daughter Maria, his wife Barberina Strepponi, and, behind, his mistress Teresa Stolz. Verdi's menage lasted thirty years. (Many creative males have surrounded themselves in this way with much younger women.)

Philadelphia Austen Hancock

Jane Austen's adventurous
Aunt Phila (1730-1792)
became the mistress of the
great Warren Hastings in
India. She and her enter-
prising daughter Eliza
both intrigued Jane. Yet
Jane mostly ignored such
lives of international
melodrama in her novels,
as she did the Napoleonic
Wars.

Wellington's brother
Richard Wellesley (1760-
1842), the eldest of five successful brothers, held the
family together when they
faced financial difficulties.
Richard described his own
parents as "frivolous and
careless personages" and it
was probably in reaction to
these qualities that Wellington turned himself into the
perfect general.

Emma, Lady Hamilton (1765-1815), not only provided Nelson with some sexual love but, more importantly, became a replacement for his lost mother. A strong and competent woman, with her husband Sir William, she supplied Nelson with his fantasised perfect family.

Richard Wagner's mother Johanna Rosine Pätz (1774-1848), beautiful and interested in men, neglected her son Richard. Much of his life and his music expressed his yearning for love.

The future Kaiser Wilhelm (1859-1941) with his beloved mother Viktoria who found his malformed arm repulsive. Her rejection of her son was one of the several reasons why Wilhelm grew up to become such an irritating and bombastic person.

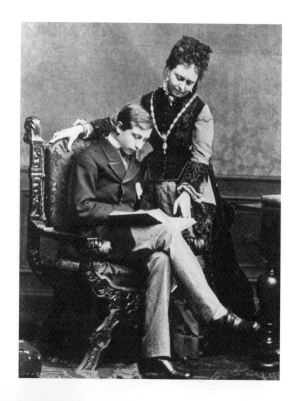

Sir John Conroy (1786-1854) was the person who ensured that the headstrong Princess Victoria received a modern education. He has been accorded no thanks for this from historians. He was crushed between the manipulations of the Coburgs on one hand and the British Royals on the other. Victoria hated him and later confused Gladstone with him. Yet Conroy remains one of the main influences in forming those aspects of Victoria's personality that influenced British culture for over a hundred years.

If one man caused the Second World War it was Adolf Hitler's father, Alois (1837-1903), who beat and abused his son vigorously. The war itself can be seen as an enlarged version of Adolf's lifelong fantasised '*struggle*' with his father.

The original Oedipus Complex. The handsome young Sigmund Freud (aged 20) stands rather possessively behind his mother Amalia (1835-1930) (aged 40), whom he found to be intensely sexually attractive. She adored her "Golden Siggie" and encouraged his ambitions.

Puccini (centre) with car and women – two of his main fascinations in life. Always a boy at heart he had a lot of trouble with both interests.

Wagner's wife Cosima Liszt (1837-1930) was 24 years younger than her husband. It was said she "submitted herself body and soul to the Master". Cosima ensured the growth of the Wagner legend after his death.

Winston's supposed mother, Jennie Churchill (1854-1921). An adventuress and libertine, Jennie was famous for her dark good looks which in no way resembled young Winston's red hair and pale blue eyes. She ignored Winston until he began to make some money as a newspaper reporter during the Boer War.

Sir Gerald du Maurier (1873-1934) adored his daughter Daphne who reciprocated the infatuation. She saw herself as a boy and became a writer largely to please him. Throughout her life she remained enthralled by the idea of incest.

Margaret Thatcher's father Alderman Alfred Roberts (1892-1970). Margaret strove to fulfil his thwarted ambitions and acted out his simple political beliefs.

Perhaps the most influential person in Agatha Christie's life – her much older sister Margaret (called 'Madge' or 'Punkie') (1879-1950). Talented and attractive, Punkie not only inspired Agatha to write detective fiction and plays for the theatre, but also supplied Agatha with her characteristic fascination with intellectual puzzles and disguises. Punkie was Agatha's model, rival and muse.

his father) he would gain the beautifully redesigned 'living space' ('*leben-sraum*') his mother had always needed, getting her away from "the smallness and overcrowding of the rooms" (as cited in the famous excerpt from *Mein Kampf*) where, so he believes, violence, infection and rape occur. 'Lebensraum' – the theory that Germans needed more territory in which to live – was the chief reason given by the Nazis to justify the Second World War. Hitler was obsessed with *lebensraum*. But it was, of course, utter nonsense. There was already plenty of room in Germany for the Germans. Whenever one is faced with such a patently absurd reason for something so serious one must, as a psychologist, begin to wonder whether the real reason is pathological. 'Lebensraum' was another of those notions that Adolf had picked up in the early 1920s. It had been around for years. Adolf subtly changed it, however, by tying it in with his anti-semitism. Lebensraum was now to be sought in the East, he said, and not the West. The Reich would expand into Russia, thus destroying Bolshevism, a system that was, according to Adolf, created and controlled by Jews. *If my speculation is correct, then Adolf was unconsciously seeking living space for Aryans (his mother) by ousting the Jews (his father)*. In his childhood, the Hitlers had never had a fixed home, and Adolf had been fascinated with large living spaces and architectural designs for years. As Junge reports, he had a great liking for huge rooms, and whatever Adolf built or designed reflected this craving for spaciousness. Was this all an expression of his unconscious concern for his mother's proper accommodation and health?

Fairly typically for a political narcissist, the claustrophobic Adolf was identifying himself with his nation. (Louis XIV, de Gaulle and Henry VIII did likewise.) But, like Nelson, he also identified his nation with his mother. Although Germans themselves called Germany the "Fatherland", Adolf frequently refers to it as the "Motherland". Walter Langer also noticed Adolf's clear identification of Germany with his mother – "all the emotions he had once felt for his mother became transferred to Germany", he says. As if trying to bring his mother back from the dead Adolf would, in some of his speeches, shout "Germany must live! Germany must live!" It was one of his most obsessive slogans. *Lebensraum* was, he said, about "the survival of the German people" (i.e. *his mother*) If the Bolsheviks were to win the war then – "the German woman would be fair game for these beasts". In *Mein Kampf* various phrases support the dynamic of secret maternal love and separation, for example:

An unnatural separation from the great common Motherland...
I appeal to those who, severed from the Motherland..."
(They) long for the hour that will allow them to return to the arms of the beloved mother...

The longing grew stronger to go there (Germany) where, since my early youth, I had been drawn by secret wishes and secret love.

Other phrases are compatible with his obsession with the abuse of his mother:

It must be possible that the German nation can live its life…without being constantly molested.

His fantasy of maternal submission to Jewish influences is also expressed:

The state… crawled on its belly before Marxism.

The word 'rape' is scattered through the pages of *Mein Kampf* as if recalling the infant Adolf's vision of his mother being ravaged by his drunken father. Langer suggests that Adolf also identified Austria (and the "depraved" Vienna with its large immigrant Jewish population) with his father, who had proudly worn an Austrian uniform. Adolf had, after all, gone out of his way to enlist illegally in the German army, and not the Austrian, in 1914. Germany (i.e. *his mother*) was "fighting for her existence" Adolf said. In the 1920s he had wanted to end any alliance with "the debauched dynasty" of Austria (i.e. *his father*) – "the quicker the better for the German nation" (i.e. *his mother*). All this seems to support the view that Adolf's career was being driven by his unresolved hatred of his father – "if a people (i.e. *Adolf and his mother*) is to become free it needs pride and willpower, defiance, hate, hate and once again, hate!" Adolf also praised the battle of Königgrätz, where Prussia (Germany) had defeated Austria (i.e. *his father*), seeing it as the true foundation of the German Reich. The Reich emerged, Adolf said, from "a conscious and sometimes unconscious struggle for hegemony, from which struggle Prussia ultimately issued victorious". Again the word "struggle".

In general, he had shown his anger to men and his softness to women, as he had with his parents years earlier. In the bunker he wanted his women (Eva Braun and the secretaries such as Traudl Junge) near him at all times, especially at night. Was this to protect him from the demon of his father that tormented him in his nightmares? Adolf would appear the dictator to male strangers but the kindly uncle to his friends and to women in general. Throughout his life Adolf was driven by intense but half-concealed, hatred. But hatred of what or whom exactly? The Jews? The Bolsheviks? The Slavs? What was the real target and origin of his hatred? Where did it all come from? Once, when fulminating against "the uncivilised brutes" of Bolshevism, he had said – "one day the world will understand what this struggle was about!" But did Adolf, himself, ever really understand what his struggle was about? Could he ever admit, even to himself, that it was all about his unfinished struggle with his father?

Famously, Adolf never related well to his generals because they were, for him, reminiscent of his father. Just as he had feared his father, so he feared his generals would one day kill him – which is precisely what some of them eventually tried to do. On the other hand, his secretaries, such as Traudl Junge, reminded him of his sweet and unselfish mother. This is why he treated his female staff so well, seeking their company at mealtimes and sitting around the fire in the evenings with them.

Not only did Adolf make sharp distinctions between the way he behaved in the presence of men and women, and between his treatment of strangers and friends, but there was also a world of difference between his external social life and his inner world of fantasy. It was the latter that was always the most real to him. The world of ordinary social intercourse, of daily life, was a mere charade of secondary importance. As an amateur actor he could go through the motions and act the part of an ordinary politician or an avuncular friend. But he always knew that his "true" self, the genius Adolf, was entirely separate and, to him, more real. Always behind the soft feminine side he showed to women (his mother in him) and the harsh side he showed to men (his father in him) stood the messianic genius. Yet somehow, all these Adolfs were both real and acted. He was an actor whose medium of power was always his rhetoric. He was brilliantly eloquent but not deeply intelligent.

Conclusions:

In diagnostics terms, Adolf Hitler was a Narcissistic Personality Disorder with mild Bipolar Disorder (mood swings). In the last decade of his life the mood swings became less publically visible. Having gained power, his depressions of earlier years faded or were patched over by the use of amphetamines prescribed by his doctor, but his hypomanic pressure of talk continued.

A standard text book description of Narcissistic Personality Disorder is as follows:

A pervasive pattern of grandiosity (in fantasy or behaviour), need for admiration, and lack of empathy, beginning by early adulthood and present in a variety of contexts, as indicated by five (or more) of the following:

(1) has a grandiose sense of self-importance (e.g. exaggerates achievements and talents, expects to be recognized as superior without commensurate achievements);

(2) is preoccupied with fantasies of unlimited success, power, brilliance, beauty, or ideal love;

(3) believes that he or she is "special" and unique and can only be understood by, or should associate with, other special or high-status people (or institutions);

(4) requires excessive admiration;

(5) has a sense of entitlement, i.e. unreasonable expectations of especially favourable treatment or automatic compliance with his or her expectations;

(6) is interpersonally exploitative, i.e. takes advantage of other to achieve his or her own ends;

(7) lacks empathy: is unwilling to recognize or identify with the feelings and needs of others;

(8) Is often envious of others or believes that others are envious of him or her;

(9) shows arrogant, haughty behaviours or attitudes.

Adolf certainly exhibited items 1, 2, 3 and 5 in the above definition but, to qualify technically, he requires an additional item. This is more questionable. Adolf did not excessively demand admiration, or lack empathy with those he knew personally, or appear envious of others, nor was he particularly haughty. He utterly lacked empathy (item 7), however, with all his many real or imagined adversaries, and especially with those he never, or rarely, met. For him, such groups as "Slavs" and "Jews" did not exist as real people; they had become mere ideas in his head. I suppose we could also characterise Adolf as arrogant, but that is borderline. More probably we could accurately accuse Adolf of item (6) – he was "interpersonally exploitative", at least as far as his enemies were concerned. To his friends he could be remarkably loyal, but to huge numbers of those with whom he was personally unacquainted, especially to groups of persons in the abstract, (e.g. gypsies, the mentally handicapped, non-Germans generally, Bolsheviks, Slavs and, of course, Jews) he was indeed ruthlessly exploitative and destructive. Adolf showed a clear and narcissistic tendency to treat those whom he had met quite differently from those he had not. Once someone had had tea with Adolf, his visitor's life was a great deal safer than it would be have been had he had a drink with Stalin. Adolf did not usually destroy his "friends" – whereas Stalin certainly did. Adolf's justification for his ruthless exploitation of others was, of course, not on the basis of material gain but because of the "specialness" of his goals, which is another peculiarly narcissistic feature. What was strange and rather unusual about Adolf was that his narcissism was tempered by a sort of personal mildness; the kindly Adolf he showed to women. He was a sensitive and obsessional kind of narcissist, living with his fantasies. There were few compromises in Adolf's fantasy world; almost everything was either black or white. On one side were the forces of good with himself at their head: mother, Germany, Aryans, Wagner, women, grand and spacious architecture and nature. On the other side were his father, Jews, foreigners, Marxism, men and racial impurity. He was locked up within himself.

Many attempts have been made to analyse Adolf's sex life, but to what avail? He liked the company of women but was not strongly drawn to them sexually. Lacking confidence in this area of his life, he was attracted by much younger girls whom he could control and impress. He probably had some sort of sexual experiences with only three of these, and some of these experiences, according to Langer, may have included undinism, where he asked the girls to urinate on him. He then tended to lose interest in the girls and neglect them, precipitating several attempted and successful suicides. He was inclined to avoid sex, seeing it as something associated with his hated father, and deployed all his energy into his mission instead. The only woman he had ever really loved was his mother, which is probably why he lusted after his niece Geli – she had been born just as his mother died. When Geli killed herself, Adolf was devastated. Perhaps the incest unconsciously resonated with his own Oedipal longings, and was a repetition of his mother's own experience of being sadistically seduced by *her* 'uncle' Alois. (Geli was thus associated with his mother because she was a relative and born at this traumatic time. Furthermore she was in almost the same relationship as a living-in servant as his mother had been with his father.) Incest is sometimes an Oedipal relationship by proxy. The child does not actually have sex with the *parent* but with a close relative instead, thus avoiding much of the feeling of guilt. Eva Braun's loyalty, however, undoubtedly touched him. Adolf had rescued her from the oppressive control of her strict father, so their relationship was bathed in the light of Adolf being the 'knight in shining armour' who had ridden to her rescue. Rescuing a woman from an overpowering father was, as we have seen, an important part of his central fantasy.

Adolf was not an original philosopher. He was, however, an effective propagandist for ideas that had been in circulation for decades – the romantic nationalism, expansionism and anti-semitism of the old *Völkisch* movement.

Nazism was just a new name for all this. It was Adolf's emotive oratory that persuaded the masses to support these ideas, and the success of his oratory was in large part due to the fanatical sincerity of his own commitment as well as to his hypomanic charisma. This sincerity turned him into a religious leader for millions of Germans who were seeking certainty. Where did his fanaticism originate? It came from Adolf's personal psychopathology. Unconsciously he had injected his own psychodynamics – his Oedipal narcissism, his love of his mother and hatred of his father – into the existing framework of the *Völkisch* (Nazi) ideology. Narcissists can do this; they project themselves onto the world and see links between themselves and big external events. For Adolf, *Völkisch* ideas happened to fit around his personal emotions like a gauntlet. It was his own private frustrations and hatreds, shoe-horned into this iron fist that powered the whole Reich. *His struggle with his father drove not only his anti-Semitism but turned into the Second World War itself. His 'kampf' became the War.*

It is difficult sometimes to convince non-psychologists that many of the reasons why we do things can be unconscious and irrational. Yet many artistic people and fantasists can accept this, perhaps because they are especially prone. Adolf was one of these. As a youth he lived in his own fantasy world. Most of his compensatory fantasies were to do with his own future greatness and the greatness of Germany. The irrationality of our hidden motives lies in the way that ideas become associated and identities disguised. Such mechanisms also dictate the content of our dreams. Ideas, for example, may be linked not logically but according to symbolic similarities or similarities in sound. Such irrational constructions are often driven on huge tides of emotion based upon personal experiences. As we have seen, in Adolf's case these searing personal experiences were his terror and hatred of his father, his adoration of his mother and his devastation when she died, as well as his desperate yearning to protect his mother from his father. The irrational and unconscious side of his adult thinking overlooked the fact that his parents were dead and that nothing could be done to alter the past traumas of his childhood. The irrational side also linked his blue-eyed mother with Germany itself (and the blue-eyed Aryan race), and associated his brutal father with Jews in general. The irrational solution to the need to help his abused mother was to find her spacious accommodation so that she would not be raped or infected with disease. (He believed that "the smallness and overcrowding of the rooms" caused infection.) This idea then became joined irrationally, and probably unconsciously, with the idea of *lebensraum* for the German nation. In conclusion, it was all linked with the unconscious idea of trying to bring his mother back from the dead. She had been for him, after all, by far the most important person in his life other than himself. I believe that Adolf's insistence on the need for a new war was as a continuation of World

War 1, and that he unconsciously identified both world wars with his personal *struggle* to protect his mother from his 'Jewish' father's attacks, just as it had been way back in Passau in his early years.

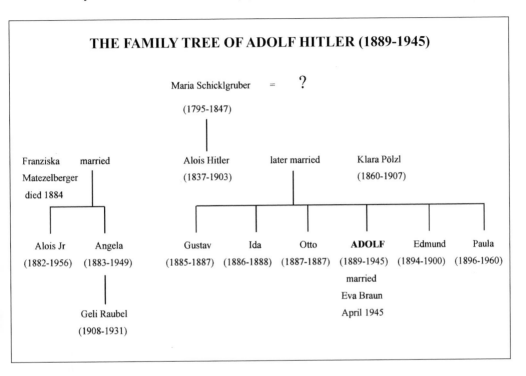

THE FAMILY TREE OF ADOLF HITLER (1889-1945)

Maria Schicklgruber = ?
(1795-1847)

Franziska Matezelberger married / Alois Hitler (1837-1903) / later married / Klara Pölzl (1860-1907)
died 1884

Alois Jr (1882-1956) / Angela (1883-1949) / Gustav (1885-1887) / Ida (1886-1888) / Otto (1887-1887) / **ADOLF** (1889-1945) married Eva Braun April 1945 / Edmund (1894-1900) / Paula (1896-1960)

Geli Raubel (1908-1931)

SOURCES

Bullock, Alan: *A Study in Tyranny*, revised edition, Harmondsworth: Penguin, 1962.

Hitler, Adolf: *Mein Kampf* (1924), translated by Ralph Manheim, Pimlico, London, 1992.

Junge, Traudl: *Until the Final Hour – Hitler's Last Secretary*, Ed Melissa Müller, Ullstein Heyne, Munich, 2002, English Translation by Anthea Bell, Weidenfeld & Nicolson, 2003.

Kershaw, Ian: *Hitler 1889 - 1936 : Hubris*, Harmondsworth: Penguin, London, 1998.

Kershaw, Ian: *Hitler 1836 - 1945 : Nemesis*, Harmondsworth: Penguin, London, 2000.

Kubizek, August: *The Young Hitler I knew. Introduction* by Ian Kershaw, Greenhill, London, 2006. (First published in Germany in 1953).

Langer, Walter: *The Mind of Adolf Hitler*, Basic Books, New York, 1943.

Lewis, David: *The Man who Invented Hitler*, Headline, 2003.

Ryder, Richard: *Nelson, Hitler & Diana: Studies in Trauma and Celebrity*, Imprint Academic, 2009.

12

WINSTON CHURCHILL (1874 - 1965)

Statesman

Winston Churchill is a special case – not just historically but psychologically. He is difficult to understand. It is easy to describe his behaviour because it is extremely well documented, but to understand it is another matter. As a boy he behaved like a spoiled child – but he was not spoiled by his parents. In truth, he was one of the most complex and contradictory of characters, and it is hardly surprising that none of his biographers have quite succeeded in getting under his skin.

After some years of studying him I conclude that there were just three things that really mattered to the young Winston: his parents, his nanny and himself. He had a massive ego but it was very insecure. So he spent his life trying to do what would attract the approval of his parents. Both of these, however, behaved like psychopaths. I need to explain what I mean by that word. It is no longer, if ever it was, a respectable scientific term. By 'psychopath' in this case I mean that the Churchills, Winston's parents, were both desperately ambitious people who were capable of acting ruthlessly and recklessly to achieve their ends. Jennie was stunningly beautiful and sexually promiscuous, while Randolph was a political firebrand who knew he was dying of syphilis. This condition affected his brain and probably made his criticisms of Winston even more withering and disinhibited than they might have been. The little Winston admired his gorgeous mother from afar but felt, rightly, that she showed little interest in him. His father also had little time for Winston and made it clear that he considered his son lacked the qualities necessary to become anything other than a soldier.

> *'Do not think'*, [Randolph wrote to Winston in August 1893], *'that I am going to take the trouble of writing you long letters after every folly or failure you commit and undergo. I shall not write again on these matters and you need not trouble to write any answer to this part of my letter, because I no longer attach the slightest weight to anything you may say about your own achievements and exploits.'* (Richard Holmes, *In the Footsteps of Churchill*, BBC Books 2005, p.37).

Desperate to gain his father's approval Winston proceeded to become a cavalryman, and excelled as an intrepid military risk-taker. In order to make the world (and his parents) aware of his military prowess, he reported his adventures through the press. Just like Nelson, Winston wanted the world to know of his bravery and made sure that the media publicised it.

Social class, when Winston was born, was by far the most usual criterion for one Englishman to use when judging another. Winston was not only born an aristocrat, which put him in the top tiny fraction of one per cent of society, but he was the grandson of one of less than twenty English dukes – the most senior rank of the aristocracy. Yet the Churchills (the Dukes of Marlborough) were not rolling in money. They lived in a palace that cost them thousands of pounds a year to look after and employed over seventy staff to run the place. To live like a ducal family was supposed to live in the nineteenth century, was highly costly. To make matters worse, the opportunities for a career for an aristocrat were extremely limited. Only the eldest son would inherit the title and estates, and Winston's father (Randolph) was the old duke's second son. There were really only four career possibilities open for such a man and his sons to pursue: the Church, the Army (less so the Navy), the law or politics. If the family had been extremely cash rich, as some ducal families were, then they could afford to tolerate a few wastrels, gamblers or playboys within the family. The unemployed offspring of such wealthy families often had sufficient funds to become lifelong collectors, explorers or harmless eccentrics. A few might become connoisseurs or amateur scientists. But if the family lacked large quantities of ready cash, as the Churchills did, then the opportunities were few indeed. Most professions, and even banking, were regarded as middle-class and so beneath them. Trade and commerce were considered to be even worse. As for Academia, it was still regarded as the offspring of, or as a preparation for, the Church.

The upper classes, on the whole, remained 'cultured' but anti-intellectual. 'Brains' were naively considered to be an inherited trait that was neither fully manly nor respectable.

As Winston never showed any real interest in religion, and perhaps because of his difficulties with maths and spelling, his private schools branded him (wrongly as it proved) as being not a scholar, and this description would stick to him throughout his life. Yet he was to become an accomplished writer and speaker and an almost constant fountain of new ideas and creativity.

The emphasis on manly sports at British private schools (confusingly called "public schools") towards the end of the nineteenth century had become a heavy one. One reason was the idea that such exhausting activities would help to curb a boy's burgeoning sexuality. But by far the most important rationale was that the upper classes of Britain needed to supply the British Army and Navy with mentally and physically tough officers to organise and control the absurdly huge British Empire that occupied about one quarter of the surface area of the globe. Large, strong and especially athletic boys were thus at an advantage in the culture of such schools. Sadly, this was also an area where Winston failed to qualify. He was small for his age (only five foot six inches tall at 18) and of a spindly and slightly roly-poly physique. The sports at school were mostly violent and dangerous activities like boxing, rugby football, cricket and horse-riding. Injuries were frequent and smaller boys suffered especially. This was also partly intentional as far as the school authorities were concerned. It was a way of weeding out the weaker specimens. Such qualities as leadership, team work and personal bravery could compensate for physical weakness, however, and were to be encouraged. Here Winston was later to excel. Consciously building the character of the British gentleman on Spartan prototypes, the British 'public' schools of the period (and, to a lesser extent up until the latter part of the 20th century) also inculcated attitudes of physical toughness, discipline, promptness, self-reliance, reliability and mental stamina. These regimes went on to produce a country divided by two quite different sub-cultures: that of the five per cent who were privately educated (the officer class or gentry) and the remainder. Phrases such as "officers and men" or "gentlemen and players" would typify British society for over a hundred years. Foreigners would sometimes be surprised by how different were the attitudes, values and customs of Britain's ordinary ninety five per cent compared with the brisk and stiff upper-lipped stereotype of its upper classes. They found they were dealing not with one nation but two quite different peoples. But the stereotypes could also miss the point. Many of the starchy upper classes, on closer inspection, turned out to be streaked by unexpected traits of liberality, rebelliousness, creativity and compassion.

Characteristically, having been educated at single sex public schools, such well-bred men showed a fascination with sex which was sometimes excessive or frankly weird. Over more than a hundred years, however, the public schools of Britain were careful not to record their failures. But many failures there were – boys who had breakdowns and disappeared, some who withdrew from society in general, others who stuttered their way into solitude and loneliness, or surrounded themselves with protective shells of affectation or eccentricity. Many became depressed or unable to earn a living, others committed suicide. Every year boys at public schools went into anxiety states or developed conversion or dissociative hysterias, obsessive rituals or tics. Wracked by nightmares, anger and fear, scores would suffer for years from undiagnosed states akin to post-traumatic stress disorder. What proportion of public-school boys became such 'failures'? Five per cent? Fifty? Nobody has ever tried to count them. They kept themselves to themselves, broken and unstudied. They were considered to be the price worth paying for the system's triumphs – the great empire builders, military heroes and dignified statesmen of the late Victorian era.

This gives a glimpse of the strange and frightening world in which the young Winston had to grow up: callousness at home and cruelty at school. Not content with hardening up the boys on their playing fields, the 'public' schools accustomed them to cold baths every morning, a strict regime of time-keeping and tidiness, hard academic tests, a military training in the school's cadet force, physical fitness exercises and barbaric punishments for even minor disciplinary offences. These usually took the form of physical beatings with a three foot cane, usually ranging from four to twenty strokes to the backside, each one able to draw blood and capable of leaving bruises and scars that took weeks and sometimes months to heal physically, and a lifetime mentally. Over the course of a twelve week term even obedient boys would inevitably accumulate the three or four cautions that earned a beating, often administered with maximum force by a six foot, muscular prefect four or five years older than themselves. So, for much of the term, boys would anxiously strive to avoid their final caution which could be awarded at any time (without appeal) for an untied shoelace, being a few seconds late for chapel, for stepping on a forbidden lawn or for untidy hair. All boys from the age of twelve were "broken in" in this way. In their first few terms at a public school every boy would experience at least one beating a term, perhaps two or three or, in the case of a really disorganised little boy, maybe ten or more. It was a form of universal torture not abolished by law until 1999. What made this brutalising process particularly damaging was that boys were constantly under the fear of beatings and other tests of physical endurance regardless as to whether or not they were true delinquents. This constant stress led to physical as well as psychological disorders, stomach pains, headaches, skin disorders and sleeplessness. The unspoken intention was to produce hardened men who showed no fear and were able to withstand hardships of any sort without complaint. The young Winston suffered from a stream of minor and apparently physical disorders as a schoolboy, and I expect these were often stress-related.

Also prevalent, of course, was the common system of so-called 'fagging', where younger boys were made to work for the older boys, unpaid – cleaning rooms and shoes, making food for them or running errands. This, no doubt, was intended to breed a respect for authority. It also encouraged the widespread manifestation of homosexuality between the boys.

Like the best products of such a para-military training, Winston emerged from it as a tough and courageous military adventurer but always with streaks of questioning rebelliousness, compassion and creativity in his make-up. He was very much the product of this extraordinary system.

Winston's mother, Jennie, was an American, and so probably failed to understand the hidden brutality in British private education. His father, like most upper class fathers of the period, probably understood the brutality but thought it was good for his son. What had been good enough for him would be good enough for Winston. At Winston's first 'prep' school there was a sadistic headmaster who beat the little boys with particular vigour. But it was not Winston's parents who noticed this. It was Winston's beloved nanny, Elizabeth Everest, who saw his bruises and persuaded his reluctant parents to remove their little son to another school. Winston himself reacted to beatings with anger but did not complain openly about them. He did, however, write a constant stream of manipulative letters to his mother beseeching her to visit or, at least, to write to him at school. She hardly ever did so. She was, it seems, far too busy with her love affairs and with the general social whirl of hunt balls, shooting parties and country house week-ends. Meanwhile her son suffered at school; not only from the harshness of the disciplinary regime and the roughness of the sports but, according at least to some of his biographers, from bullying from the other, usually physically larger, boys. On one occasion, according to Johnson, they hurled cricket balls at the little Winston. In terror, he ran away and hid from his persecutors. This was a sensible thing to do as cricket balls can kill, but it may also have aggravated his fear – every boy's fear – that he was a coward. Ten years later Winston would take reckless steps to disprove this in his own and other minds by volunteering to take appalling risks upon various battle-fields.

How did Winston react to this almost total lack of parental love or understanding – and to the ordeals at school? He could have given up and become one of the public schools' many failures. Or he might have succumbed to almost permanent depression. Or he could have joined the thugs and bullies and become a cad. Indeed he did get caught up in two unsavoury instances of bullying while at Sandhurst (training to become an Army officer) but he seems to have regretted this quite quickly. By the time he was twenty-one he had three careers in mind – soldiering, journalism and politics. One way or another he was determined to make a success of his life, and he became aware that he would have a public reputation to care for and protect. So from being quite an averagely nasty and bumptious young man at military college he gradually developed into the sparkling, complicated and sensitive adult of his later years.

Why did Winston fail academically? Was it lack of general intelligence? This is unlikely. Was it due to a form of dyslexia? Bearing in mind his later verbal and written fluency this seems improbable. Was it sheer obstinacy – a refusal to try at subjects he found were initially difficult? Possibly. He had been happy with his lead soldiers and other toys and could not quite see the point of such subjects as Algebra and Latin. Was it delayed maturity? He certainly was a late developer in some ways and it seems he went on growing physically and intellectually until well into his twenties. Or was it some other, unidentified reason, such as a failure to understand the purpose of the questions he was being asked at school – possibly a feature of some highly creative individuals who constantly need to go back to basics in every subject. They cannot accept any proposition unless they feel they have understood it fully. So statements such as "Let x equal 3" or "Mensa is 'Oh Table'" have to be fully deconstructed, explained and understood before progress can be made. This may have been his problem, although the self-reports of his academic difficulties were written to be humorous, and so remain unhelpful for the diagnostician.

Winston was a romantic. He used fantasies about himself as his chief defence. He fantasised that one day he would be some kind of a hero, like his revered ancestor the first Duke of Marlborough. These messianic fantasies were his way to gain the very *conditional* love of both of his unsympathetic parents. By the time his father died in 1895 Winston had already started to prove to Randolph that he was a successful soldier. In the next few years, in the Boer Wars, he also began to win over the attention of his mercenary mother by earning large sums of money as a journalist. As soon as he started to receive big cheques as a war correspondent his mother suddenly, and for the first time, began to show an interest in Winston. They formed a money-spinning team of two. Jennie would chat up the generals, who allowed Winston his extraordinary double career as soldier and reporter, and once he had been paid, Jennie would proceed to blow the money on parties, clothes and jewellery. Winston had become her cash cow. Furthermore she treated him almost like one of her many far younger lovers. For the first time in his life Winston found himself on con-spiratorially intimate terms with her.

Jennie, hardly surprisingly, has had a bad press for her callous treatment of Winston until he began to earn big money in his early twenties. It is almost as though Winston, not a man who later showed much interest in money for its own sake, made money especially to buy his mother's love. So, he had become a soldier in order to attract his father's approval and a money-spinner in order to gain his mother's. He ran both careers simultaneously. His mother was also a sucker for celebrity and, as soon as Winston began to become a bit of a war hero, due to his own newspaper reports of his adventures in escaping from the Boers in South Africa, she enjoyed sharing the limelight with him. Prior to this success, however, Jennie had ignored him. Indeed, some of her critics have re-marked that she had treated Winston, when a baby and a child, as if she was not his mother at all. Certainly, as a psychologist, I feel there was something deeply strange about Jennie's relationship with Winston. For twenty years she shows profound indifference towards him, then starts sponging off him and even flirting with him. Was she a total psychopath or is there another reason for this?

As I have previously explained, being a psychotherapist should entail build-ing a number of hypotheses to explain one's client's behaviours. There is often a range of possible ways in which to explain things. These have to be then tested by the facts and when disproved, discarded. Well, I have done this with the very strange relationship between Winston and Jennie Churchill. Why was she so unmotherly towards Winston? Had a difficult birth estranged her from him? No, the birth, although allegedly painful, was not extreme. Was she over-burdened with other duties? No, she was a woman of leisure. Did she herself come from a cold, dysfunctional family background? No, she had apparently good relationships with her sisters and her caring parents. Was she suffering from depression or other serious mental disorder? No, there are simply no re-ports of this. Was her un-maternal behaviour culturally normal for the time? No, she went far beyond the normal arms-length attitude of some Victorian mothers. Was she separated geographically from her child as some empire-builders' wives were? No, absolutely not.

My most outlandish hypothesis to explain her behaviour is that Jennie was not actually Winston's mother at all. Although this appears startlingly unlikely, it has proved strangely hard to debunk and, when trying to do so, I have en-countered a lot of minor, but supporting, evidence to the effect that this might have been the case. So, because it is an intriguing story in its own right, re-sembling a Victorian who-dunnit of the Sherlock Holmes era, I will go into fur-ther detail.

Elizabeth Everest   Young Winston Churchil

THE CASE FOR ANOTHER MOTHER

The Main Events Surrounding the Alleged Birth

Lord Randolph Churchill (1849 – 1895), the second surviving son of John, 7th Duke of Marlborough (1822 - 1883), first met the American Jeanette "Jennie" Jerome (1854 – 1921) at a Cowes regatta shipboard party on 12 August 1873, and they became engaged to be married only three days later. He was aged twenty-five and she was nineteen. It is likely that doctors had already told Randolph that he had syphilis. (WM 96)

After a delay while the two families negotiated financial terms, Randolph and Jennie were duly married at the British Embassy in Paris on 15 April 1874, at what was an unexpectedly quiet wedding. The groom's parents did not attend. The newly-weds took up residence in London, leasing 48 Charles Street, off Berkeley Square.

Only seven and a half months after the wedding Jennie and Randolph travelled to Oxfordshire and, on Saturday 28 November 1874, chose to attend a ball at Blenheim Palace, Woodstock, the home of the Churchill family. During the course of the evening Jennie reported pains and withdrew to a downstairs room where, after approximately twenty-four hours, she supposedly gave birth to a healthy boy at 1.30 am on the morning of Monday 30 November. Nobody, other than Jennie, is reported as being present at the birth.

This apparently premature confinement occurred over a weekend so that neither of the couple's usual London nor Oxford doctors could, according to Randolph, be present. Only the local doctor from Woodstock, Dr Frederic [sic] Taylor, was consulted. The London specialist arrived at approximately 9.00 am on the Monday – seven and a half hours after the reported delivery. Seemingly, he found that all was well with mother and child, and no special care was prescribed although it was later claimed that Jennie had been encouraged not to breastfeed[2]. The doctor apparently left at around lunchtime on the same day.

Sometime shortly after the birth, Mrs Elizabeth Ann Everest was appointed to be the baby's nurse. Anne Sebba reports that Mrs Everest had certainly been engaged by 27 December, the date of Winston's christening at Blenheim, but her employment could have commenced on the same day as the birth itself. (AS 74)

The Evidence

The primary evidence for the circumstances surrounding the birth itself is to be found in two letters, the first from Lord Randolph to his mother-in-law, Mrs Jerome, in Paris. It is dated "Monday 30, 12.30 pm" (i.e. the day of the birth) and reads as follows:- (RC 3)

> *Dear Mrs Jerome,*
> *I have just time to write a line, to send by the London Dr to tell you that all has up to now thank God gone off very well with my darling Jennie. She had a fall on Tuesday walking with the shooters & a rather imprudent & rough drive in a pony carriage brought on the pains on Saturday night. We tried to stop them, but it was no use. They went on all Sunday. Of course the Oxford physician cld not come. We telegraphed for the London man Dr Hope but he did not arrive till this morning. The country Dr is however a clever man, & the baby was safely born at 1.30 this morning after about 8 hrs labour. She suffered a good deal poor darling, but was vy plucky & had no chloroform. The boy is wonderfully pretty so every-body says dark eyes and hair & vy healthy considering its prematureness. My mother and Clementine have been everything to Jennie, & she cld not be more comfortable. We have just got a most excellent nurse & wet nurse coming down this afternoon, & please God all will go vy well with both. I telegraphed to Mr Jerome; I thought he wld like to hear. I am sure you will be delighted at this good news and dear Clara also I will write again tonight. Love to Clara. Yrs affty RANDOLPH S.C.*
>
> *I hope the baby things will come with all speed. We have to borrow some from the Woodstock Solicitor's wife.*

The other pertinent letter was from Lord Randolph's mother, Duchess Fanny. She wrote to Mrs Jerome, also on 30 November, as follows:-

> *My dear Mrs Jerome*
> *Randolph's Telegram* [which has not survived] *will already have informed*

you of dear Jennie's safe confinement & of the Birth of her Boy. I am most thankful to confirm the good new & to assure you of her satisfactory Progress. So far indeed she could not be doing better. She was in some degree of Pain Saturday night & all Sunday & towards evg of that day we began to see that all the remedies for warding off the Event were useless. Abt 6 of P.M. the Pains began in earnest.

Dr Hope only arrived at 9 of this Morg to find dear Jennie comfortably settled in bed & the baby washed and dressed! She could not have been more skilfully treated though had he been here than she was by our little local doctor. She had a somewhat tedious but perfectly safe & satisfactory Time. She is very thankful to have it over & indeed nothing could be more prosperous.

We had neither cradle nor baby linen nor any thing ready but fortunately <u>every</u> thing went well & all difficulties were overcome. Lady Camden, Lady Blandford & I were with her by turns & really think she could not have had more care. She has had an anxious Time and dear Randolph and I are much thankful it is over. I will be sure to see you receive a Bulletin every day. We expect today a 1st Rate Nurse. Best love to Clara & Believe me, Yrs sincerely F.Marlborough

There are a number of interesting features of these letters: The mentioning of Jennie Churchill's two alleged physical traumas is usually interpreted by historians as an attempt by Lord Randolph to make what was really a full-term birth appear to be a premature one, since the baby's condition rather suggests he was full-term. (Lord Randolph sites a "rough ride" *and* "a fall" as the causes of the allegedly premature labour. Giving more than one excuse for something is, according to some theorists, often a sign that neither is true). As Randolph himself admits, the baby was "very healthy considering the prematureness". Certainly, there is no mention of the baby's birth-weight and this is a significant omission. A low birth-weight at thirty-three weeks gestation would be expected, and would be the obvious way to substantiate the claim of prematurity. Furthermore, unlike this one is reported to have been, premature labours are usually brief and relatively painless. Charles Higham asserts that, at birth, Winston appeared "fully formed, of good weight, with no health problems and even with a tuft of red hair, all extremely unlikely if he were two months premature". (CH 52)

Pains were first reported during the St Andrews' Ball on the Saturday/Sunday night and Randolph claims they "went on all Sunday". Duchess Fanny says that the pains only began "in earnest" at about 6.00 pm on

the Sunday night. Why, then, did Jennie remain in the bleak little down-
stairs room that has variously been described as little more than a "cloak-
room" or a "passage"? It seems there was plenty of time to move her
somewhere more comfortable.

Lord Randolph's entirely inaccurate description of the baby as having "dark
eyes and hair" is striking. Was this intended to confirm the likeness of the baby
to a very dark haired Jennie?

According to Duchess Fanny, the London doctor (Dr William Hope) only arrived at 9.00 am on 30 November and found Jennie already "comfortably settled" and "the baby washed and dressed". Lord Randolph's letter implies that
Dr Hope would return to London around lunchtime of the same day, after only
a brief visit.

Although the Duchess, Lady Camden and Lady Blandford are reported to
have attended Jennie during her confinement, there is no clear indication that
any were present at 1.30 am when the baby was delivered. Nobody is named
as witnessing the actual birth.

Lord Randolph writes at 12.30 pm on Monday 30 November, a few hours
after the alleged birth – "we have just got a most excellent nurse and wet nurse
coming down this afternoon". To whom was he alluding? Was one of these
Elizabeth Everest? The Duchess confirms that "we expect today a 1st Rate
Nurse". The words "coming down" suggest the nurses were coming down from
London. But in the days before telephones or emails, how had Randolph secured their services so quickly, and especially over a weekend?

Lord Randolph says "Of course the Oxford physician cld not come". Why
"of course"? Why does he say this? Oxford is only six miles from Blenheim.
Surely there was some well qualified Oxford doctor who could make the journey to the palace and receive an appropriate ducal fee? The incentives would
have been strong.

The Characters of Lord and Lady Randolph (Jennie) Churchill

No historian could describe either spouse as being naïve in the ways of the
world. Both were rebellious, ambitious, high-spirited and reckless. By 1873
the intensely physically attractive and headstrong Jennie had been living, on
and off, in Paris for the best part of six years, unchaperoned by any male relative, at a time when Paris was notorious for being the social and erotic capital
of the world. (Her womanising father was mostly in America.) It is therefore
highly likely that Jennie, by the time the couple met, was already the experienced and enthusiastic libertine that she proved to be as an adult. During the
remainder of her life she would continue in this style, constantly partying, play-

ing practical jokes, taking numerous lovers and always spending beyond her means. It is known that while still a teenager she had already, innocently or not, caused at least one violent marital storm in Paris.

Lord Randolph had lived a similarly wild life of parties, gambling, prostitutes and mistresses. He was friends with notorious lechers such as Frank Harris, Francis Bertie and the Prince of Wales. When he died in January 1895 it would almost certainly be due to syphilis which he had contracted in Oxford in the 1860s. During his relatively brief political career he would reveal himself to be eloquent, unscrupulous and erratic, and, above all, a risk-taker.

Biographers have commented on the speed with which Randolph and Jennie had become close. Immediately they met in Cowes they seemed to reach an understanding and to enter into a personal conspiracy together. Both were determined to be the centre of attention and to get ahead, despising the stuffy conventions of respectable Victorian life. Randolph's roguishness undoubtedly reminded Jennie of her adored father: both men were gamblers, not only with money but in their lives generally.

The central tragedy in Randolph's life was his illness, and there is now some consensus that he knew about his diagnosis by the time he married. It was common practice in Victorian medical circles for doctors to impress upon their syphilitic patients the need for stringent care in their sexual relationships, so as to reduce the chances of spreading the infection, especially to spouses and offspring. Many doctors advised total celibacy (AS 96). Jennie was not, however, a naïve English bride. She was probably already familiar with the dangers of syphilis and with safe methods of sexual gratification that fell short of full intercourse. Maybe these were further reasons why the pair bonded. They were birds of a feather. It might also explain Randolph's surprising tolerance of Jennie's later love affairs. We will never know if Randolph told Jennie of his illness or whether she had somehow found out about it. Someone, such as Randolph's older brother George, may have ensured that she knew. (It was certainly in her interest to be told).

Jennie and Randolph's relationship was one based upon shared secrets about love-affairs, health, politics and finance. They enjoyed a life of intrigue and excitement. Randolph, in particular, always appeared to be in a hurry, perhaps because he knew his days were numbered. Both Jennie and Randolph, however, were short of the large sums of money they required in order to live the high-life that both craved. Jennie's father had recently lost money on the New York Stock Exchange and Randolph had just become the unsalaried Member of Parliament for Woodstock. His private means were limited and he was frequently in debt.

The Dukedom of Marlborough

Lord Randolph was the second surviving son of the 7th Duke of Marlborough. During his childhood, therefore, he was second in line to inherit the title, the palace of Blenheim and all its estates. As David Cannadine has pointed out, in the 1870s "primogeniture ruled", not only as regards titles but also wealth (DC12). Most titles could only be inherited by the eldest eligible male. Although Randolph enjoyed being his parents' favourite son, he had a relationship of intense rivalry with his rakish older brother George, the Marquis of Blandford, who was heir apparent to the dukedom. When his brother was publicly attacked, Randolph stood up for him, but otherwise not much love was lost between them. At the time of Randolph's marriage to Jennie, George's marriage was already on the rocks and his only son (Charles) was a sickly two year old. Quite a few nineteenth century members of the Churchill family, including several of Randolph's siblings and two of George's previous children, had already died in infancy (CH 51 & WM 92). So this child's (Charles) survival was manifestly uncertain.

Thus, if George and his infant son predeceased Randolph, Randolph would inherit everything and there would no longer be any shortage of funds for the two big spenders. If Randolph died before a childless George, however, Randolph's legitimate son would still eventually inherit. (In the event, George did die before Randolph but the former's son, Charles, survived. For two years, however, Winston did, in fact, become second in line to the title.)

Was it, therefore, just out of brotherly concern that George opposed Randolph's marriage to Jennie? Ten days after Randolph's engagement to Jennie, George sent to his brother an overbearing letter, dated 25 August 1873, in the following terms:

> I tell you that you are mad simply mad. I don't care if **la demoiselle** was the incarnation of all moral excellences and physical beauties on God's earth." If Randolph wanted to run off with a married woman, George said, that would be alright. "But my friend, **le marriage**! (The emphasis is George's). (RC 11)

It is important to note here that George is not opposing his brother having an affair. He is only opposing his *marriage*. Without marriage, of course, Randolph could not produce a rival heir to the dukedom. Was it possible that, at the heart of the rivalry between the two brothers, there existed a fierce contest as to which of them would continue the Marlborough ducal line, and enjoy its material benefits?

The Aylesford Affair

Shortly after George tried to stop his brother marrying, Randolph tried to stop George divorcing. In 1875, a few months after Winston's birth, Randolph caused a huge scandal by trying to stop George's divorce from his estranged wife, Albertha. (George and Albertha were no longer sleeping together). The reason for Randolph aggravating this national scandal has never been explained by historians. He had no religious scruples about divorce, so perhaps Randolph's recklessness can be explained by his urgent desire to prevent George from producing any further legitimate heirs. Why else should Randolph become so involved in trying to stop the divorce that his brother wanted? (RC 30) On the face of things it really was not any of Randolph's business! (George wanted to marry his lover Lady Aylesford who later did indeed bear him a child illegitimately.) Yet Randolph clearly felt so strongly that he rashly tried to blackmail no less a personage than the Prince of Wales into stopping George's divorce (and Aylesford's), by threatening to publish the Prince's love letters. This rocked the throne itself. Understandably, the Prince reacted furiously and the Churchills were informally banished to Dublin for nearly four years, as personae non gratae. There must have been some very strong reason why Randolph and Jennie took this extraordinary social risk and lost. Could it have been because Randolph and Jennie had just taken a very great deal of trouble to legitimise Winston?

What did George's poor wife, Albertha, think of her husband's infidelity? Famously, she reacted by placing a pink baby doll under the silver dome of one of her husband's breakfast dishes instead of the expected poached eggs! What did she mean by this? The usual explanation is that she mistakenly believed that George had already impregnated Edith Aylesford. A more subtle explanation, however, could be that it was a reference to the succession issue generally and to George's need to stay with her in order to produce further *legitimate* babies. Perhaps the doll even represented the threat posed by the baby Winston himself. It was to remind George that there was a "baby race" going on between the two brothers and that George should start sleeping with his wife again.

Other than the social ostracism, the upshot of Randolph's reckless behaviour during the Aylesford affair (solved eventually by the intervention of Queen Victoria and Disraeli) was that Randolph's relationship with George, not surprisingly, deteriorated even further.

The Physical Appearance of Winston

Several historians have commented, in passing, that Winston did not much resemble his mother Jennie in physical appearance. She was famous for her flashing brown eyes and raven hair, while Winston's hair was reddish and his eyes a pale blue. Charles Higham describes Jennie as having "black hair" and "brown incandescent eyes" (CH 51), Anne Sebba sees her as "dark and fiery" with "deep-set eyes, black brows, dark hair and naturally coloured lips" and as "a beautiful dark haired lady …with raven hair (AS 161)", while William Manchester quotes a contemporary description (by Viscount D'Abernon) of her "dark lithe figure… radiant, translucent, intense… the flashing glory of her eyes. More of the panther than of the woman…" (WM 116).

The baby Winston, however, is described by Manchester in the following terms:- *"He had an upturned nose, red curls, and what his daughter Sarah later called "strange pallid eyes""*. As a child he appeared *"freckled, redheaded and pug-nosed"* and was described by a teacher as *"a small red-haired pupil"* (WM 127). By the age of eighteen Winston was only five feet six inches tall (considerably shorter than either of his supposed grandfathers) and was a little later depicted by a contemporary as *"a slight, red-headed, freckled, snub-nosed young subaltern…(NYT 87)"*. The luxurious locks taken from the five year old Winston are still displayed at Blenheim and are still unmistakably reddish. Paintings of the young Winston also confirm this.

An examination of the surviving photographs reveal other marked differences in appearance between Jennie and Winston. They not only have dissimilar hair and eyes, but also their mouths, noses, eyebrows, and ears are also clearly different. Whereas one can imagine some likeness between Winston and Lord Randolph Churchill (and, more particularly, with the latter's parents), there is none whatever with Jennie, nor with either of her parents. Even more strange, one or two of the well-known photographs of the infant Winston clearly show that attempts have been made to touch them up so as to blacken the appearance of the infant's hair, and, possibly, his eyes. Was someone desperately trying to enforce a likeness with Jennie? The truth is that Winston looked very much like his nanny, Elizabeth Everest.

As Winston's own grandson and namesake would later write, in another context:- *"for me physical features speak louder than any entry in a register of births"* (Quoted by Martin Gilbert).

Conclusions about the birth

Is it possible that Winston Churchill was a changeling smuggled into Jennie's bed at Blenheim Palace in the early hours of 30 November 1874? Although Jennie had apparently told a few people of her alleged pregnancy by July, she had not shown any reported signs of it, attending balls and horse-races frenetically throughout the summer. (Some of her relevant letters are, tantalisingly, undated, and could have been written much later). Only three people within Blenheim needed to know the full truth: Jennie and Randolph themselves, and the real mother. The usual doctors were conveniently absent. Only "our little local doctor" from Woodstock was in the offing and, as a member of Randolph's parliamentary constituency and living almost at the gates of Blenheim, he probably could have been prevailed upon not to rock the boat with unwanted questions and examinations of his patient. The Woodstock of the period was described by a political rival as "a town corrupted by (Churchill) influence" (CH 36). In the event, Dr Taylor's career prospered and he took his practice to London. (A receipt exists for twenty-five guineas being paid to Dr Taylor by Randolph. This refers to advice concerning the "confinement", but it does not mention his attendance at the actual delivery.)

What would have been Jennie and Randolph's motives? To provide an heir to the dukedom, and thus a solution to their chronic financial difficulties, besides enhanced social status and a victory in their fierce rivalry with Randolph's unspeakable brother George. Besides, by providing a son, Randolph might have been able to request more immediate financial support from his father, the Duke. Randolph might be dying but after both brothers (George and Randolph) were dead, and if sickly little Charlie did not survive, the dukedom would pass to Winston (to be enjoyed by Jennie).

Why could Jennie not have waited for her own legitimate pregnancy? Because both Jennie and Randolph knew of his syphilis. They probably never fully consummated their marriage at all. If so, Jennie's only child was 'Jack' Churchill who was born in 1880, and he is usually reckoned to have been fathered by one of Jennie's many lovers. (Roy Jenkins proposes the Earl of Roden as the father while others have favoured Count Charles Kinsky or Viscount Falmouth) (RJ 7). Artificial means of insemination were unknown. But could not Randolph and Jennie have waited for Jennie to fall pregnant by a lover? Yes, but this might have been more than Randolph could have tolerated at that time. The couple were in love. However much Randolph may have wanted to produce an heir to the dukedom, he would not, at that early stage in his marriage, have found it easy to encourage his wife's deliberate infidelity.

If, however, it turned out that Randolph had impregnated a mistress in say, February 1874, then the obvious opportunity presented itself. Instead of having to pay off the mother in the usual way, Randolph could offer her a job as its nurse and the Churchills could "adopt" the baby themselves. Furthermore, Randolph could thus produce an heir who really was of his own blood, and without risking Jennie's health. Jennie's forgiveness of his infidelity during their engagement could be another possible reason why Randolph later forgave Jennie her own many subsequent lapses.

Who, then, provided the baby Winston? Almost certainly Elizabeth Everest. Judging by the extraordinary similarity in appearance between herself at about the age of fifty and Winston at a similar age, they were, in fact, close blood re-lations. Winston was probably either her son, grandson or nephew. Winston and Elizabeth shared the same fair colouring, the same fine hair, the same rounded features, the same small build, the same ears, the same chin, the same nose, the same eyes and the same thin-lipped smiling mouth. In short, their faces in middle age were almost identical. So Elizabeth (or a near female rela-tion of hers) may have been one of Randolph's many mistresses. Although the Churchill family always stressed her respectable previous job of working for a kindly vicar (the Rev Thompson Phillips), near Carlisle, one may ask why a girl from Chatham, should have been offered a job by a philanthropist so far from home? Had Elizabeth already been in trouble? Allegedly she had a child to care for in Carlisle called Ella. In any event, it is perfectly possible that when Randolph says, on the morning of the supposed birth, "we have just got a most excellent nurse and wet nurse coming down this afternoon" that one of these was Elizabeth Everest, who had already smuggled the baby Winston into Jen-nie's conveniently located ground floor room the night before.

It is in itself strange that Jennie and Randolph had chosen, not Jennie's bed-room, but a small and gloomy downstairs room in the almost unused West wing of the palace in which to endure an apparently prolonged labour of some twenty four hours. The palace contained 187 rooms, many of which were warm and comfortable and had pleasant views of the palace grounds. Instead, they chose a room with windows overlooking the kitchen yard, and two entrance doors in op-posite walls giving it the function of a passageway linking the two principal ground-floor corridors of the palace. This room was, however, about as far away as possible from the Churchill family's bedrooms which were on the first floor of the East wing. Indeed, the family's living quarters were on the far side of the palace's main staircase and Great Hall from the alleged birth-room. The latter was, in fact, in a part of the building that had hardly ever been actively occupied by the family. At one thirty in the morning Jennie and Randolph could have done almost anything in the alleged birth-room without the rest of the family being made aware of it. Furthermore, the room was easily accessed by a servants' stair-case as well as by the West Stair up which a baby could have been carried from the Water Terrace of the garden to Jennie's bed in less than sixty seconds.

It is also strange that, before the days of telephones or emails, Randolph could, within only a few hours of the supposedly unexpected birth, announce with con-fidence that a nurse and wet nurse had already been engaged to arrive on the same day. Although the telegram system existed, there would have been no time for advertising in the newspapers, nor interviews. Randolph and Jennie, who apparently had not even had time to obtain a cradle, baby linen nor other "baby things", nevertheless had managed to engage two "excellent" nursery nurses remarkably quickly. By saying the nurses were "coming down" Randolph may have wanted to give the impression that they were coming from London. Was this feasible? If Randolph could not get a doctor from Oxford only six miles away, how did he manage to arrange for two excellent nurses to come from London sixty miles away? Was there enough time for all this to have been arranged? Or had the two nurses, in fact, been engaged long before the weekend? Were one or both already lurking in the neighbourhood? Had their apparent competence already convinced Dr Taylor that they could care for his patient if he was absent during the night, as he seems to have been? Among the seventy or so palace servants they probably would not even have been noticed as strangers by members of the family. The wet nurse might have been the child's actual mother. The couple were probably Elizabeth Everest and her sister.

The rest, as they say, is history. All biographers have recorded the marked psychological distance between the young Winston and his supposed parents. Randolph was chronically ill, as well as busy with his political career, but what reason did Jennie have to be so neglectful of her alleged first born? She would later turn out to be far more interested in her Jack when he was a baby than she had been in Winston. As a child Winston admired Jennie as "a fairy princess… I loved her dearly… but at a distance." Indeed, he constantly complained of his supposed mother's indifference towards him, while praising his "dearest and most intimate friend" Elizabeth Everest (WC 73) who "tended all my wants" (MG 2). Egged on by Elizabeth, the little Winston used to call her "Woom", and she continued to encourage this name for herself into her old age. (Was hers in fact the womb from which he sprang?) Elizabeth clearly adored Winston and considerably indulged him. When she wrote to him at school she addressed him not as "Winston" nor "Master Winston", as might have been correct for a Victorian ducal nanny, and as she referred to him in letters to Jennie, but as "my Precious boy" and, even more remarkably, "my own darling boy". Is Elizabeth Everest here trying to tell us something? Maybe the truth is being spoken and we have, hitherto, ignored it.

Did Winston have any conscious inkling that he might not be Jennie's child? Probably not. He did, however, make jokes about his birth and he was certainly very proud of his Churchill ancestry and researched it. He also marvelled, in print, at how Elizabeth could give him so much love when he was *not* her child.

If this outrageous 'changeling theory' is true it also helps to explain why Elizabeth Everest continued to be employed by the Churchills. She knew too much. Neither Jennie nor Duchess Fanny liked her. They thought (rightly) that she had spoiled Winston. But they kept her on far longer than her duties as a nanny required. Such situations were not especially unusual although, in the Churchills' case, they could hardly financially afford to do this. Winston was eighteen by the time Elizabeth was finally retired in early 1893. He reacted angrily when he discovered her removal, and continued to support Elizabeth in every way he could until her death. It is interesting that Elizabeth died in the same year as Randolph, although no historian has suggested that they shared the same infection. (A family rumour however, had it that Randolph contracted his syphilis from a Blenheim servant around the time of his marriage.) (AS 96)

This changeling hypothesis would also help to explain Randolph's motivation for trying to blackmail the Prince of Wales during the Aylesford Affair – extraordinary behaviour that has, hitherto, not been satisfactorily explained by historians. The Aylesford business, no less than the tragi-comic affair of "the pink doll", and the letter from George to Randolph opposing the latter's marriage, are all compatible with the existence of fierce rivalry between the two brothers over the succession to the ducal title and estates. Death, especially due to infectious illness, and particularly in children, was far more likely in Victorian times than it is today. An heir (like the sickly little Charlie) might disappear overnight.

To some who are not professional historians the idea of the changeling may seem to be outlandish and improbable. Yet historians will know that such cases of doubtful maternity have been far from uncommon in British history, especially in families threatened by infertility, and where high fortunes or great titles have been at stake. Before the days of genetic testing, evidence was rarely certain, but historians have sometimes doubted, for example, the exact parentage of such outstanding figures as James 1 of England, Mary Queen of Scots, or John of Gaunt. Mothers of great dynasties who suffered still-births were sometimes under secret "adoptive" pressures and Randolph Churchill, himself a bit of an amateur historian, would have heard of such cases. We have become used to the idea that biological fathers may not be who they are supposed to be, but we must also bear in mind that mothers too can differ in identity.

Are there any other similarities, other than physical ones, between Elizabeth Everest and Winston? Roy Jenkins, although not suggesting a blood relationship, nevertheless remarks upon how they both showed "great descriptive power" (RJ 9). Others have noted their shared volubility and sensitivity. Their common love of Kent was not genetic so much as taught or inspired by Elizabeth, as Winston himself relates. (WC5)

So who was Elizabeth Everest? Little has been discovered with certainty. She is believed to have been one of four children of a grocer, born around 1840 at Chatham in Kent. There is no record of her marriage or children. She certainly had a (probably younger) sister who, by the time Winston was four, had married a prison warder on the Isle of Wight. (RT 20) Unusually for ducals of the period, Elizabeth would take the young Winston to meet her working class sister and brother-in-law at Ventnor. The latter would take Winston for walks, regaling him with stirring tales of mutiny and adventure. (WC 32) Such visits, which entailed overnight stays, might not be considered too unusual today. But in the 1870s, ducal families stood apart as pinnacles of Victorian society, at a time when class divisions were rigid. Was Elizabeth perhaps introducing the unwitting Winston to his aunt or even his natural mother?

In 1895 Winston rushed to Elizabeth's bedside as she lay dying of "peritonitis" at her sister's house in North London. She died easily, he said (WC 73). Winston paid for her grave and managed to persuade the Rev Thompson Phillips from Carlisle to attend the funeral. He failed, however, to coax Elizabeth's alleged previous ward, Ella, to also attend. As far as we know, Winston was never to meet Ella, about whom he had heard so much from Elizabeth and whom he had come to regard almost as his absent sister. Perhaps she was just that.

Elizabeth had remained a "partisan" supporter of Randolph, Winston reports, and Randolph had taken the trouble to have a meeting with Lord Rothschild, no less, in order to secure Elizabeth's finances for her retirement. Even for a good employer (not Lord Randolph's most accurate description) consulting at such a high level showed remarkable concern for an old retainer. Such solicitude would, perhaps, be less of a surprise if Randolph and Elizabeth were, indeed, old lovers and especially if Randolph needed to secure Elizabeth's continued silence (WC 32).

Winston himself described Elizabeth as his "foster-mother" and biographers have sometimes called her Winston's "mother-surrogate" (RH 32). I am only suggesting that it may be necessary to drop the words "surrogate" and "foster". This would not only help to explain and excuse Jennie's extraordinary lack of maternal feeling for the young Winston, but Elizabeth's oft-remarked-upon, over-abundance of the same quality. Why should Jennie bond emotionally with a baby that was not hers and was, indeed, her husband's love-child by another woman? It would be quite natural for her not to do so.

Conclusions

If Elizabeth Everest was Winston's mother, then this lets Jennie off the hook. We no longer have to see her as a cold-hearted rejecting psychopath of a mother. We can see her instead as a very naughty lady who deceived the world while conniving with her dying husband in gambling for a dukedom. Jennie was certainly very mercenary. As Boris Johnson points out, Winston once had to sue her for the return of some of his money. She remained interested in both money and men throughout her life, eventually marrying a husband who was considerably younger than her son.

Winston was constantly haunted by his so-called 'black dog' of depression.

Unlike many mood-swingers, however, he seems to have had some control over his moods and could stave off his depression by keeping active. For decades he was immensely active writing, painting, building brick walls in his garden and politicking. All these can be seen as anti-depressant activities that helped maintain the levels of dopamine and serotonin in his brain. They were also part of his constant need to prove to himself that he was not, as his father had asserted, a failure as a human being. One could invent the term '*achievement neurosis*' for people with this common problem. Winston had to keep achieving and, in his eighties, hated retirement. The lack of love he had received from his parents in childhood continued to rankle with him and he had to continue to prove that his achievements made him a man worthy of their approval. He also sought the constant 'oral' gratifications of food, drink and cigars – a substitute, some would say, for the parental affection he had never received as a boy.

Yet he received wonderful love and support from his wife, Clementine, who treated him as a sensitive but wayward child. Terrified, perhaps, that it had been his father's lechery that had caused Randolph's decline and death, Winston kept clear of extra-marital sex and there are no convincing reports of affairs. Perhaps deliberately he tried to redirect his libido into all the other activities of his life. It was a popular idea in Edwardian England (simplifying Freud) that sexual energy could be transmuted into other things. Clementine also played a valuable role in restraining Winston's impatience with subordinates. Once Winston was on a high as Prime Minister he expected his staff to put his orders into effect immediately and he could become irritable and explosive if they did not react with sufficient alacrity. In the early months of his premiership in 1940 he had become unpopular in Downing Street, being seen by some of his staff as high-handed and tyrannical. Clementine had to intervene gently but firmly, telling Winston to calm down and to show some patience. It worked. Indeed this event illustrates one of the marked differences between Winston and his arch enemy Adolf Hitler. Winston continued to learn from his mistakes, whereas Hitler did not. (Although Hitler was very popular with his female staff.)

Strangely though, there are many similarities with Hitler; so many perhaps that, precisely for this reason, Winston found it easy to understand and predict the dangerous course of Adolf's career. Winston had suppressed the Adolf in himself. Although they had, in many ways, opposite values and their effects upon history would be entirely different, in their personalities there are some strange coincidences: both Hitler and Churchill were outstanding and painstaking orators, both were artists, both were proud of their medal-winning military service and (when young) both were fascinated by war, both were great patriots and imperialists, indeed both greatly esteemed the British Empire, both adored their mothers and had lost their fathers when young, both loved nature and animals (although Winston preferred cats to subservient dogs while Adolf was vice versa), both were charismatic, both had rages, both were afraid of female sexuality, both believed themselves to be 'men of destiny', both revered history, both were successful leaders, both were narcissistic and bipolar (although Churchill's depressions were more severe than Hitler's), and both blamed a conspiracy for most of the world's problems – the Jews in Hitler's case and the Nazis in Churchill's. What, then, made the difference? Churchill was certainly the more thorough historian and had the better sense of humour but, far more importantly, he was part of a culture that highly valued decency, moderation, fair-play, compromise and peace. He was also an aristocrat whose background had equipped him with knowledge of the dangers of power and fanaticism, whereas Hitler's recent peasant background gave him no such warnings. Churchill thus corrected the inevitable political hubris whereas Hitler failed to. Churchill's psychology contained little hatred and permitted him to have warm and admiring relationships with other men. (His rejecting father had never beaten him nor openly fought with him.) Churchill was never the loner that Adolf had been and, unlike Hitler, he had never cultivated his inner world of messianic fantasy, although the messianism was certainly present. Whereas Churchill learned not to overrule his generals, Hitler, showing a rigidity typical of a personality disorder, continued to do so. Churchill may have been unconsciously trying to complete his father's interrupted political career whereas Hitler was determined to destroy his father. Churchill was not surrounded by sycophants as Hitler was, and had a wife, Clementine, who could if necessary bring him down to earth. Whereas Hitler rejected any form of weakness, Churchill was a compassionate man who would fight to *protect* the weak. Above all, Churchill did not have an adoring mother. Both men worshipped their mothers but Churchill's never really reciprocated this love. Whereas Adolf traumatically lost his mother when he was eighteen, Jennie Churchill continued to live until Winston was in his late forties. Adolf continued to fight the fantasy of his father and all he stood for (Jewishness in particular) whereas Winston never got over his need to live up to his father's expectations, and to achieve successes of which his father would have approved.

There was a moral content, too, to Winston's character that Adolf's lacked. It would be easy to say that Winston as a child had absorbed from his family all the Christian decencies of the British way of life. But the Blenheim subculture at the time was not notably decent. So where did Winston's basic decency come from? Where did he acquire his adult compassion, his concern for animals, his fierce defences of democracy, liberty and justice? Neither of his parents showed much genuine interest in such things. The answer, I believe, lies in his relationship with Elizabeth Everest – a stout defender of low-church

Christian values and certainly someone who constantly concerned herself with the moral character of her charge. Later, Clementine kept hubris at bay.

After leaving school without much academic success, Winston proceeded to try to catch up by privately reading history, economics and philosophy (rather as Wellington had done). After repeatedly risking his life in the Boer War, Winston became less bumptious and more thoughtful generally. Once elected to Parliament he even crossed the House and became, for several years, a Liberal, and a strong supporter of Lloyd George's social reforms.

Winston's father had said some very hard things to him, making Winston feel that he had to achieve some sort of glory in order to win his father's love. Randolph could be scathing and contemptuous of Winston. Yet Winston never turned against him nor, at the time, understood that his father's increasingly garbled cruelties were the effects of illness. Tertiary syphilis attacks the brain and, as in Randolph's case, can cause insanity. The teenage Winston never appears to have been told that this might be the reason why his father ignored him and treated him with apparent disdain. It seems that Elizabeth Everest never explained this to Winston. She continued to revere Randolph to the end.

Winston was, in effect, the product of three subcultures – the spartanism of Harrow, the daring hedonism and relentless ambition of his parents, and the very ordinary warmth and kindness of Elizabeth Everest. His parents had made him feel inadequate while Elizabeth had made him feel special. In order to reconcile these two opposing views of himself he had to become a hero. The result was a restlessly ambitious man, a dashing soldier, a bold innovator, a romantic traditionalist, a risk-taker, a champion of freedom and justice, a political reformer, a patriot who sought world peace, a supporter of the weak, someone who could see the big picture both globally and historically, a lover of fame and excitement, a creative thinker, an exponent of mischievous wit and impish humour, an impatient doer, an endurer of hardships who nevertheless enjoyed endless cigars, champagne and food. He was an artist, a builder and a permanent child. These characteristics flowed naturally when his mood was high, and when he was depressed he tried to force himself to continue with the same ebullience. In company he was always the centre of attention, but when he was solitary he thought and wrote. Alone in bed in Downing Street, during the War, he would discuss military strategy with his beloved cat, Nelson, whom he addressed as "Nelson Darling". Winston loved all animals and spoke to them constantly in the same tone of voice as he would to human friends. Few animals on his home farm were ever slaughtered as he believed it was wrong to kill any animal to whom he had said 'Good Morning'. Always a part of Winston was stuck in his childhood, basking in his memories of the nursery or trying, in his mind, to put right his disappointments with his parents.

I once looked down on Winston from an Admiralty building that used to exist at Hyde Park corner. He passed almost directly below in an open Coronation carriage, and looking up, smiled and waved at me. Lying back in his barouche he looked very much like a big pink baby.

Final Thoughts

So what made Winston the man he was? It seems to me that he was the product of two strangely conflicting forces: the wholly unconditional love of his nanny, Elizabeth Everest, and the thoroughly conditional disapproval of his parents. Elizabeth may or may not have been his real biological mother (DNA testing could disprove this) but she treated him with such fondness and solicitude that she produced a little boy who was convinced that he was a person of some merit and importance. Indeed he showed some of the signs of the classic 'spoiled child' in consequence: wilfulness, obstinacy, and bumptiousness.

When sent away to Spartan boarding schools from the age of seven, Winston found himself not to be so special. He did not excel at the rough sports that such schools encouraged, nor did he do well at mathematics, classics and the other subjects they esteemed. At school he felt lonely and unvisited by his parents. Was he actually bullied by the other boys? Boris Johnson (one of the best of his most recent biographers) has claimed that Winston *was* so bullied. Either way, Winston was physically small for his age – often sufficient reason in itself to instigate peer group indifference, if not actual bullying. Certainly his painful experiences at boarding school intensified his angry determination to prove himself a hero.

Jennie was a frenetic socialite and his father Randolph an ambitious Tory minister. So Winston saw very little of either of them when he was at school. Nevertheless Winston revered both of them. The only possible career that Randolph thought Winston capable of following, was the military one which Winston then took up. Surviving his rash adventures in the Boer War (motivated in part by Winston's desire to win medals) Winston created a simultaneous career as a newspaper reporter. This earned him so much money that his spendthrift and neglectful mother at long last started to show an interest in him. After his father's death in 1895 Winston then took up politics – as if to complete his father's unfinished work. Extremely ambitious, bubbling over with ideas and apparent confidence, Winston was quickly promoted to Cabinet office during the First World War, then held responsible for the catastrophic failure of the Gallipoli Campaign and demoted. He rejoined the Army and served some months at the Front in an act of self-inflicted punishment and contrition.

Yet his experiences of being a young Cabinet Minister in the First War stood him in good stead for the Second World War. Unusual perhaps among narcissists, Winston nearly always learned from his mistakes. So the 1914-18 War acted, for Winston, as a huge dress rehearsal for the war of 1939-45 when he was Prime Minister.

People remarked upon Winston's extraordinary levels of energy. Even as a man in his sixties he would often work into the early hours of the morning – writing, reading and dictating. His use of wordplay and colourful language was often dramatic and exciting and frequently he would erupt with a score of original ideas, some practicable and some not, as to how to deal with the constant stream of political and military problems facing the country. His enthusiastic support for new and unorthodox solutions (from the first ever tanks and aircraft in the First War to SOE, Enigma, and Mulberry Harbour in the Second) often proved of huge value to the country's war effort. Once again we see the importance of raised mood, or hypomania, as a feature in the lives of great men like Churchill. His eloquence, energy, flight of ideas, puns, quips, charisma and creativity are typical.

If he had received only his nanny's exceptional affection on its own, Winston might have turned into a lazy and perhaps artistic loafer. With only the disapproving apathy of his parents he could have either given up and become depressed, or rebelled, or become quite a nasty military bully. It was the combination of Elizabeth Everest's maternalistic kindness with the challenges produced by Lord Randolph Churchill in particular, that produced that extraordinary man, the Winston Churchill that is known to history.

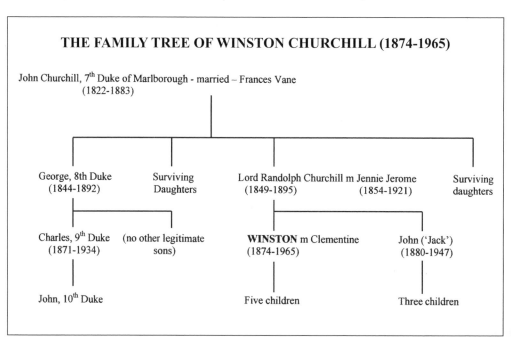

THE FAMILY TREE OF WINSTON CHURCHILL (1874-1965)

John Churchill, 7th Duke of Marlborough - married – Frances Vane
(1822-1883)

George, 8th Duke (1844-1892) — Surviving Daughters — Lord Randolph Churchill m Jennie Jerome (1849-1895) (1854-1921) — Surviving daughters

Charles, 9th Duke (1871-1934) — (no other legitimate sons) — WINSTON m Clementine (1874-1965) — John ('Jack') (1880-1947)

John, 10th Duke — Five children — Three children

SOURCES

David Cannadine: *The Decline and Fall of the British Aristocracy*, Yale University Press, 1990.

Randolph S Churchill: *Winston Churchill*, Volume 1 *Youth*, 1874-1900, Heinemann, London 1966.

Randolph S Churchill: *Winston S. Churchill*, Volume 1 Companion, Part I, 1874-1896, Heinemann, London 1967.

Randolph S. Churchill: *Youth*, 1874-1900

Winston Churchill: *My Early Life*, (1930), Eland, London, 2000.

Winston Spencer Churchill, quoted by Martin Gilbert in *Churchill & America*, pub *The Free Press*, 2005

Martin Gilbert: *Churchill* (1991), pub Pimlico, London, 2000.

Frank Harris: *My Life and Loves*, New York, 1963; Julian Osgood Field: Uncensored Recollections, E. Nash, 1924

Charles Higham: *Dark Lady : Winston Churchill's Mother and Her World*, Virgin Books, London, 2006.

Richard Holmes: *In the Footsteps of Churchill*, BBC Books, London 2005.

Roy Jenkins: *Churchill* (2001), Pan Books, London, 2002.

William Manchester: *Winston Churchill : Visions of Glory*, Little, Brown & Co., Boston, 1983;

New York Times, *Memoriam*, p 87

Anna Sebba: *Jennie Churchill : Winston's American Mother and Her World*, Virgin Books, London, 2006.

Richard Toye: *Churchill's Empire*, Macmillan 2010; Winston Churchill: *My Early Life*, 1930

13

KAISER WILHELM II (1859 – 1941)

Emperor of Germany

The eldest grandson of Queen Victoria, Wilhelm, was crowned in Germany in 1888. Within two years he had dismissed his forebears' famous Chancellor, Otto von Bismarck, and launched Germany on a bellicose trajectory that culminated in the First World War (1914-1918). Bombastic and tactless, Wilhelm lost the support of the Army and abdicated in 1918, dying in exile in the Netherlands in 1941.

A traumatic breech birth had left Wilhelm with a paralysed and shortened left arm which he took pains to conceal throughout his life. He was the first child of the intelligent and beautiful Princess Victoria (Vicky) of Britain, the eldest daughter of Queen Victoria, who was obsessed by his damaged arm and instigated years of painful and futile treatments for it. Attempts to mobilise his arm were unsuccessful although, despite his handicap, the boy was subjected to rigorous lessons on how to ride a horse, the weeping little prince enduring repeated falls in the process. Vicky, repelled by her son's deformity and unable to accept Wilhelm as a cripple, gave her love to her younger children instead. At first, Wilhelm reacted by becoming obsessed with his mother, repeatedly having dreams of being in affectionate situations with her and of kissing her left hand. Later, he became distanced from her and this distance was encouraged by Bismarck after Wilhelm joined the Army, where he found friends and became fascinated by military matters generally. After his father died he succeeded to the crown and, in an angry outburst in 1889, said "an English doctor killed my father and an English doctor crippled my arm – which is the fault of my mother". (By this he may have meant that she had allowed only English doctors to attend her family). Clearly his ambivalent attitude towards England itself was being coloured by his ambivalent anger towards his English mother.

We can see two simple dynamics at work here:

1. His physical handicap is prompting him to compensate by acting in a hyper-masculine and militaristic manner.
2. His rejection by his English mother is provoking great anger towards her and, by association, against England itself.

Wilhelm, however, still continued to be fond of his grandmother Queen Victoria who showed him some kindness, calling him "a clever, dear, good little child". Later, in 1901, he claimed that the old Queen had died in his arms. After this time, however, his antagonism towards England and his rivalry towards his Uncle Edward and cousin (the future King George V) intensified. He built up Germany's Naval and Armed forces, keenly competed against King Edward in the annual yachting races at Cowes, and envied Edward's colonial possessions. In exile after the War this fierce love-hate attitude towards England continued until Wilhelm's death in 1941. Wilhelm's handicap, Erb's Palsy, made his left arm about 6 inches shorter than his right and in most photographs he goes to some trouble to conceal this by holding a stick or a sword-hilt or a pair of gloves. It is clear that he was constantly aware of his deformity and deeply ashamed of it. When Wilhelm was first taken to visit his relations in England, aged four, he attended the wedding of his Uncle Bertie (the future King Edward VII) and was made to wear a Scottish costume. His eighteen year old Uncle Alfred, Duke of Edinburgh, was charged with his care and, during the ceremony, told the fidgety little boy to be quiet, whereupon Wilhelm drew his dirk and threatened him.

Wilhelm, unloved by his mother, turned to the Prussian militaristic culture around him for support, immersing himself in macho companionship. For years, he was seldom seen out of uniform. "In the Guards", Wilhelm later said, "I really found my family". Bismark had ruthlessly separated him from his parents' liberal influence. Nevertheless, once he became Kaiser in 1888, Wilhelm opposed Bismark's foreign policy, urging a more aggressive expansionism. Two years later Wilhelm and Bismark further fell out over the latter's wish to violently suppress the socialists and, because of Wilhelm's intemperate determination to be closely involved in all aspects of government, Bismark resigned. Wilhelm proceeded to devote his and the state's time and resources to the massive expansion of the German fleet in order to rival England's.

Obviously, Wilhelm was not of sufficient calibre to run any country. He was hasty, restless, unable to relax and constantly searching for public applause, probably as a substitute for maternal love. He appeared arrogant and liked to show off his achievements, clearly compensating for his feeling that he was handicapped and a failure. Historians have aptly commentated: "From the outset, the half-German side of him was at war with the half-English side." (F.20). Wilhelm lacked clear objectives and seemed primarily concerned with asserting his power. Yet, despite his swagger, he felt insecure, was often depressed, and still craved acceptance by his English cousins who, however, found his manners less than attractive. Indeed, most of his European royal relatives, including the British and the Russian, disliked him. By the eve of the Great War, Wilhelm had become paranoid and panicky. He had convinced himself that "England, France and Russia have conspired themselves together to fight an annihilation war against us" (W47).

Margaret MacMillan gives us a very good impression of Kaiser Bill's irritating behaviour. Intensely aware of his own physical handicap, he nevertheless made fun of the physical oddities of others, teasing, for example, the representative of the state of Baden about his bald head. Wilhelm's childish sense of humour prompted him to indulge in crude horseplay, pushing people over from behind, digging them in the ribs or pulling their ears. Smacking kings on the bottom (as happened to the King of Bulgaria) was not, perhaps, the most sophisticated nor successful of his diplomatic tactics. Wilhelm was, as MacMillan says, "both lazy and incapable of concentrating on anything for long…he refused to read newspapers and tossed long documents aside in irritation…he wanted the power and the glory and the applause without the hard work" (MM, 70). His cousin King George V called him William the Fidgety. Wilhelm was distractible, rarely sitting still, his mind leaping rapidly from one topic to another. He was often agitated and prone to outbursts of temper. Friends and acquaintances would ask whether he had "a screw loose".

Attention Deficit and Hyperactivity Disorder (ADHD) is characterised by chronic inattention, hyperactivity, impulsivity, fidgeting, restlessness and impatience. Such traits typically first appear in childhood and adversely affect both home and school life. They can continue into adulthood and are more common in males than females. Unfortunately, the causes of ADHD are not well understood although various forms of brain damage have been mooted. There is some evidence to suggest correlations between ADHD symptoms and the presence of widespread brain dysfunction in, for example, prefrontal cortex, caudate, pallidum, corpus callosum and cerebellum. Such dysfunctions could be caused by birth traumas or perinatal asphyxia. Wilhelm's mother, Vicky, had been only eighteen when he was born and the birth was extremely prolonged and traumatic, endangering the lives of both child and mother. Not only were some of the nerves of Wilhelm's arm severed but it is quite possible that the child's brain was also damaged, either by reduced oxygen or by direct trauma (e.g. by the use of forceps), or both.

So did Wilhelm become the self-important and strutting figure that he was because of head-injury or upbringing? The answer is that both influences probably played their part. The brain damage (if it happened) had made him inattentive, hyperactive and impulsive, while his damaged arm and the consequent maternal rejection had made him angry, competitive and vainglorious. In fact Wilhelm did not want a war but the violence of his language gave the opposite impression – as did his boyish insistence upon building up the German navy. The world concluded that Germany sought to dominate the world. Wilhelm was, as MacMillan says, a "man trying to show a forceful dominance which did not come naturally." (p.60) Behind all the swagger and bravado there was still a damaged child looking for the parental love and approval he would never receive. His handsome mother was fussy towards him but remained unloving. (Mothers can react in at least three ways to a child born in a prolonged and painful delivery – as fellow victim, as the victim of their own maternal failure, or as the cause of the problem. Vicky seems to have done the latter, although sometimes blaming herself. Wilhelm blamed his mother not so much for his handicap – for which he largely blamed the doctors from England – as for her rejection. Nevertheless he felt chronic anger on both counts).

In one way or another Wilhelm lacked most of the skills necessary for a successful statesman. He was without patience, imagination, intelligence, calmness, tact, perseverance or firmness. He was a shining example of what is wrong with the hereditary principle. Did he start the Great War? No. But he did not stop it. A strong and balanced ruler of Germany would have been in the unique position of being able, not only to restrain his own military machine, but also to have stopped Austria's overreaction to the Serbian provocation. If Wilhelm had had the skills of Bismark he could have stopped the War. But there were no great men in control in 1914, just little ones, and Willy was probably the littlest of them all.

We can see that Wilhelm's personality accentuated the tensions between Germany and the other great states. As with many rulers, he confused his own needs with those of his nation, thus striving to increase Germany's power and prestige internationally. The causes of the First World War are complex but it is certain that an Emperor with competitive, jealous and militaristic personality traits was ill-equipped to avoid the nearly inevitable conflagration.

At the end of the war the Kaiser blamed Germany's defeat on a conspiracy of Jews and Communists. But having made himself the supreme power in Germany by 1914, in charge of all senior appointments, he was as responsible as anyone for allowing the War to proceed, and for Germany's ultimate defeat. Before the end of his life, while in exile, Wilhelm had grown violently anti-Semitic and absurdly anti-English, believing that England had become the land of the Anti-Christ and Satan – their ruling classes were, he once said, "Freemasons thoroughly infected by Juda".

The case of Kaiser Wilhelm is one of the clearest examples of where childhood psychodynamics and birth traumas have had catastrophic consequences – the deaths of millions in an unnecessary World War that he should have been able to prevent.

The following factors stand out:

An accident of birth put Wilhelm in the supremely dangerous position, psychologically speaking, of being the Emperor of Germany, and those around him did not take sufficient steps to counteract the natural arrogance and narcissism that such a position engendered.

To make matters far worse Wilhelm had been born with a crippled arm. His own mother's horror at the condition made the child feel deeply ashamed, weak and unwanted. He reacted strongly by becoming bombastic and, outwardly at least, bellicose.

Perhaps his extremely traumatic birth also left him with ADHD, and its characteristic triad of symptoms – impulsivity, hyperactivity and inattention.

It so happened that the young Wilhelm looked for acceptance and comradeship among fellow soldiers in what was already an extraordinarily militaristic culture. In this way, Wilhelm became separated from the relatively progressive and liberal values of his mother and her relations.

Conclusions

What emerges is a picture of an exceptionally impatient and belligerent man, who tended to look for military solutions to political problems. Furthermore, his rejection by his English mother focussed Wilhelm's anger not only on her but onto the country of her birth, England. His strongly ambivalent feelings of love and anger towards his mother were, by association, projected onto England itself. As with his mother, he longed for the love and approval of his English relatives. His touchy self-importance, however, did not go down well with them and he felt increasingly resentful towards the British royal family's rejection of his advances. Identifying himself with Germany, the kin rivalry became nation against nation. Wilhelm envied Britain's navy and its empire, and took steps to compete. He also resisted the gradual democratisation of German politics, reasserting the rights of the monarchy.

We cannot justly claim that Wilhelm brought about the Great War by himself, but we can suspect that if he had been less abnormally competitive, less aggressive and less militaristic he could, as Kaiser, have stopped German involvement in 1914. So, in this case, we have someone without whose abnormal personality there might have been no Great War.

In fact Wilhelm was not all delinquent. Throughout the war he tried to maintain 'gentlemanly' standards, intermittently opposing, for example, the use of unrestricted submarine warfare against Britain (B.137) and resisting unrestricted air attacks on London - insisting that bombs only be dropped on London to the east of the Tower (and thus away from the palaces of his relatives.) (B.165). In fact, Wilhelm disliked intensely his two hawkish generals – the aristocratic Hindenburg and the middle-class Ludendorff but, because of their popularity, he felt he could not dismiss them. If he had felt really strong and secure, he might have done so. His childhood traumas, however, had ensured that beneath his swagger there remained essential weakness.

The distorted personality of Wilhelm II can be understood most simply using the terms of Adlerian Theory. Alfred Adler (1870-1937), a Viennese contemporary of both Sigmund Freud and the Kaiser, had postulated that all people are driven by the central desire to feel significant. When this desire is thwarted (as it was partially in young Wilhelm's case) we react by becoming competitive and trying to compensate. Children need to feel valued. In Wilhelm's case his physical deformity, and his mother's reaction to this, gave him, in Adler's words, an *inferiority complex* that made him compensate by becoming abnormally assertive and aggressive. The crucial trauma, psychologically-speaking, was not that his arm was damaged, but that his mother had reacted with grief and disgust to this deformity.

SOURCES:
Ian F.W. Beckett: *The Making of the First World War*, Yale Univ. Press, 2014.
David Fromkin: *The King and the Cowboy*, Penguin, 2008.
Margaret MacMillan: *The War that Ended Peace*, Profile Books, 2014.
H.P. Wilmott: *The First World War*, Dorling-Kindersley, 2003.

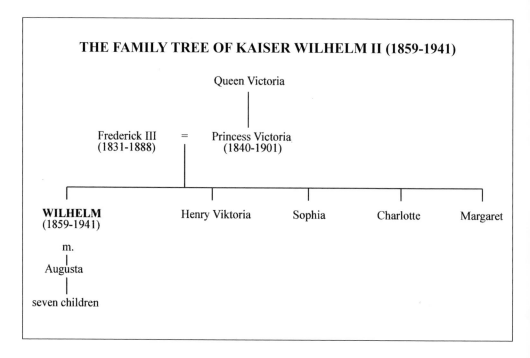

THE FAMILY TREE OF KAISER WILHELM II (1859-1941)

Queen Victoria

Frederick III   =   Princess Victoria
(1831-1888)   (1840-1901)

WILHELM   Henry Viktoria   Sophia   Charlotte   Margaret
(1859-1941)

m.

Augusta

seven children

14

ALFRED THE GREAT (849 – 899)

King and Statesman

Not enough is recorded of the childhood of Alfred to be absolutely sure what happened but it is known that this extraordinary man had an unusual early life. We know he was the youngest child of Aethelwulf, the successful king of Wessex who was, in turn, the son of the equally competent King Ecgberht, the founder of the dynasty. In the ninth century, Wessex stretched along the south coast of England all the way from Devon to Kent. Before he was seven years old little Alfred had twice travelled to Rome, first with an entourage in 853 and then with his father two years later. The purpose of these trips was not merely pilgrimage but was also political. On the first occasion Pope Leo IV had blessed the little boy and given him the title of Roman Consul and made him his godson, thus creating a link of kinship between Wessex and Rome. Alfred was born at a dangerous time when several of the other Saxon kingdoms of England were being destroyed both by internal civil wars and, simultaneously, by external Viking invasions. To the north of Wessex both Mercia and Northumberland had fallen into anarchy and Vikings had settled over much of East Anglia.

King Aethelwulf of Wessex is known to have had at least five legitimate sons and several daughters. His two eldest boys were probably already in their twenties when Alfred was born in Wantage, on the northern borders of Wessex, in 849. Alfred's mother was Osburh, Aethelwulf's second wife, who probably died before Alfred reached the age of six. There is a story about her encouraging little Alfred to learn verses by heart and rewarding him by giving him a book. Alfred's eldest half-brother Aethelstan (who died by 855) had been made sub-king of Kent, Surrey, Essex and Sussex by their father when the latter became King of Wessex in 839. Alfred's other half-brothers were Aethelbald and Aethelberht, while his only full brother was Aethelred. It seems that Aethelwulf had these four tough sons who were interested in military matters and his youngest, Alfred, who was more intellectual. Being a soldier was probably the psychological equivalent of being a keen sportsman today. Aethelwulf may have underestimated the danger posed by the Vikings, who had been raiding Wessex for about fifty years without ever really threatening conquest. So Aethelwulf had put his military sons in charge of fending off the constant marauders while he went off on his long mission abroad, confident that his sons were more than a match for the Scandinavians. He had underestimated the raiders, and while he was away the Vikings threatened the very foundations of his kingdom.

We are told by Alfred's Saxon biographer, Asser, that Alfred was his father's favourite and that, unusually for the period, the little boy was not sent away to be fostered by relatives or nobles but remained with his parents at Court. There is little evidence with which to build up pictures of the personalities of Alfred's parents, yet we can see that his mother may have encouraged her son's education and that his father, Aethelwulf, was a ruler who was, despite the constant Viking threats, determined to visit the courts of the descendents of Charlemagne in France, as well as the Pope in Rome, perhaps partly in order to build alliances with powerful Frankish rulers who were coping, but not always successfully, with the same Viking problem. Maybe Aethelwulf was seen by some of the Saxons as being too interested in travel, culture and religion, and not sufficiently in the urgent defence of his realm. This may have been why, in his absence of about twelve months, his battle-hardened son Aethelbald found it easy to gain the support of the Witan in pushing his father off the throne of Wessex. On his return, Aethelwulf did not start a civil war (so much a feature of other Saxon and Frankish kingdoms at that time) but wisely accepted the new division of power and simply took over again the rule of the south eastern counties from his loyal son Aethelberht.

The little boy Alfred had already experienced so much. Before his seventh birthday he had not only lost his mother but had twice travelled right across Europe to visit Rome. As we have seen, on his first visit, when he was only three, he had been sent by his father to see the Pope, who had confirmed him and shown some interest in him. Rome itself, as well as the cities en-route, must have been eye-openers for a child used to the simple ways and wooden buildings of ninth-century Wessex. After a few months back at home, Alfred had returned to Rome, this time with his father King Aethelwulf, and found the old Pope dead and a dispute over the succession in full swing, one candidate supported by the Emperor Lothar. After spending nearly a year visiting the churches and ancient monuments of Rome, the King and his son returned to England, stopping on the way at the Court of the Emperor's brother, Charles the Bald, where the fifty year old Aethelwulf married the thirteen year old Princess Judith. Bizarre as this seems to us, this political marriage represented an important alliance between the still rather obscure house of Wessex and the royal line of Charlemagne. Again, it showed Aethelwulf's broad continental outlook which must have made an impression upon Alfred, himself only a few years younger than his new stepmother and queen.

Two years after his return to Wessex, King Aethelwulf died and was followed to his grave in 860 by his ungrateful son Aethelbald. If Aethelwulf had held hopes of reorganising Wessex along Carolingian lines, he had failed to do so. The Kingdom of Wessex was now inherited and reunified by the faithful Aethelberht, who himself died in 865 leaving the kingdom to Alfred's only surviving brother Aethelred who, probably due to wounds inflicted by the Vikings, died in 871, passing the whole kingdom to the twenty one year old Alfred. Alfred had related well with Aethelred, the youngest of his brothers, and indeed had been his favourite. Thus the potentially troublesome issue of inheritance had been worked out amicably in the presence of the princes' councillors, the Witan, and in the face of the growing Viking threat the Wessex nobles had wisely agreed to reunite their kingdom under one ruler. Alfred's sister Aethelswith was married to the king of Mercia and, in 868, this important political alliance was further cemented by Alfred's marriage to the Mercian noblewoman Ealswith. At his wedding feast, however, Alfred was smitten with the onset of an unidentified illness that would continue to afflict him for the remainder of his life. The main symptom was sudden and severe abdominal pain. Some doctors have suggested this was Crohn's disease, or maybe it was a stress-related condition. Certainly it encouraged Alfred's lifelong interest in medicine.

Alfred had looked up to his brothers and now suddenly found himself alone, without parents, brothers or wise advisers such as Swithun with whom he had consulted as a child. He fought and narrowly lost a battle at Wilton against the Vikings' Great Heathen Army and then paid off the enemy while the Vikings attacked and conquered Mercia, forcing its king into exile. Alfred was now the only Saxon king who was not a Viking puppet. Instead of using the next four years of peace to fortify his kingdom, however, Alfred seems not to have realised his vulnerability, nor the new determination of the Vikings to conquer rather than merely to pillage. Suddenly, in 875, the Viking leader Guthrum marched out of East Anglia, right across Wessex, and occupied the Saxon south coast port of Wareham, to await reinforcements from a large Viking fleet of 120 warships anchored in nearby Poole harbour.

For the first time in his short reign Alfred showed some military initiative. He successfully prevented the Viking fleet from joining up with Guthrum and then forced Guthrum to negotiate, making him swear to his terms not on the usual Christian relics but to the Norse gods. This was a clever innovation, but Guthrum, perhaps anticipating his subsequent conversion to Christianity, and showing no apparent respect for his own gods Thor or Odin, broke his treaty, left Wareham at dead of night and marched his army to Exeter, aiming to join up there with his fleet before overwhelming Alfred in pitched battle. Young King Alfred was only saved by the destruction of the Viking fleet in a freak storm off Swanage a few days later, on its way west to join Guthrum. Perhaps Thor, the Norse god of thunder, had had his revenge! Guthrum, now outnumbered by Saxons, was duly forced to withdraw from Exeter and march north. He was far from beaten, however, and, in early 878, he suddenly occupied Chippenham, taking over effective control of the whole of Wessex. Almost certainly Alfred had been betrayed by some of his own Saxon followers, most probably church leaders such as Aethelred, Archbishop of Canterbury, angered by having to yield land and treasure to Alfred in order to buy off Guthrum. This coup d'etat had probably been in the planning for several years. If Alfred, at this stage, had escaped to exile on the continent (as the ex king of Mercia had just done) then the whole of England would now have become a Scandinavian nation. But he did not do this.

Achievements

After Alfred had been ousted by Guthrum what did he achieve? Reduced to hiding in the marshes at Athelney with a handful of men, after several defeats, Alfred secretly drew his supporters together again, surprised and defeated the large Viking army at Edington, unexpectedly and compassionately persuaded Guthrum and his nobles to convert to Christianity, through skilful diplomacy made them agree to occupy only East Anglia, while he regained control over a considerably enlarged Wessex, took over and rebuilt much of London, established numerous fortified burghs across the South of England, reorganised the English navy, accepted the voluntary fealty of Wales and Northumbria, drew together scholars from all over Europe to recodify and publish laws, translated into English a number of classic texts, formed alliances with continental kings and successfully put down further Viking incursions while, at the same time, overseeing a renaissance in the arts, and encouraging poetry and philosophy. Alfred educated his children and grandchildren so well in the crafts of kingship that his son King Edward went on to reconquer East Anglia, his daughter Aethelflaed ruled Mercia wisely, and his grandson Athelstan (who, as a child, would have known Alfred) was acclaimed as the first king of all England in 927.

What can we conclude about the psychological origins of Alfred's remarkable achievements? The first observation is that, like many other outstanding men and women, Alfred had lost his mother when he was only a child. This most tragic of events can psychologically destroy some people, but in a few cases (see Horatio Nelson and Adolf Hitler, for example) it plays a part in producing a determination to succeed. Just as Nelson's memory of his mother as an admirer of the Navy and a despiser of the French probably influenced the direction of his career, so with Alfred, his memory of his mother's love of learning may have had a determining effect – Alfred went on to revolutionise his country's educational standards.

Secondly, like other great statesmen of later years, such as Presidents Franklin D. Roosevelt and John F. Kennedy, for example, Alfred's career was almost certainly affected by his chronic painful illness, which gave him both a determination to overcome adversity and a sympathy for the suffering of others.

Victorian scholars, probably quite rightly, saw Alfred as a remarkable all-rounder. He developed skills to react successfully to all eventualities. As William Hunt put it:

> *In a reign of singular alternatives of overthrow and success, he is never castdown by ill luck or puffed up by good. In any case of war or of peace, of good luck or bad, he is ready to act with a single mind, as the needs of the moment most call upon him to act.* (WH 153).

While skilfully fighting off, in the early years of his reign, major raids by large Viking armies attacking by sea, land and from the Thames estuary, and by defeating these armies so thoroughly that the Vikings for many years gave up their assaults, Alfred became the most redoubtable European military ruler of the period. In addition to this he was the educator of his nation, a law giver, a visionary and a statesman. Personally he was modest and merciful, on several occasions making lasting treaties with Viking leaders based upon his generosity and kindness to his prisoners. (Only one act of harshness is recorded against him, which was when he hanged the crews of several captured Danish ships after their repeated breakings of treaties and their bloody attacks upon Saxons.) He ruled wisely with the consent of his Witan and, by the end of his reign the people of Wales, Wessex and Mercia looked upon themselves as one nation – the prototype of the later England. By the time of his death, his Court was filled with outstanding scholars and lawyers from all over Europe. Alfred had been England's Charlemagne but without the latter's ruthlessness.

If we consider Alfred's early life we can see that his two childhood trips to Rome must have opened his eyes to some of the wonders of the world of that era. They probably gave him a vision of how his own benighted country could be improved. This early experience widened his whole outlook. Initially, however, he may have been seen by his colleagues as being, like his father perhaps, out of touch with the serious military situation in Wessex. Such behaviour may have provoked his early betrayal, yet it was his close relationship with his slightly ineffectual but far-sighted father, that created Alfred's wider vision. Aethelwulf had always looked over the horizon to France and Italy, to the past glories of Charlemagne and Rome, and he shared this fascination with his son Alfred.

The great emperor Charlemagne, who had unified Europe and died only thirty five years before Alfred was born, must have been his principal model. As his father's youngest and favourite, Alfred was, perhaps, supposed to have become the sophisticated prince rather than the hardened warrior. It was only the early deaths of his four military brothers that projected Alfred unexpectedly onto the throne of Wessex. When he got there he probably resembled more a scholar than a soldier. Quickly, however, Alfred had learned to become an effective war leader.

One must conclude that Alfred's undoubted greatness was in part due to the extraordinary education he experienced as a boy, seeing the sights of the past Carolingian and Roman empires, meeting the most powerful and learned men of the age, many of whom could remember the great emperor, learning all about their remarkable achievements, witnessing on the Continent and at close quarters, the effects of diplomacy, scholarship, treachery, incompetence and warfare. These experiences, surely, shared as they were with his father, gave Alfred his vision of civilisation and his determination to emulate the example of Charlemagne, thus putting into effect his father's unfulfilled mission.

So King Alfred's life itself illustrates not only the beneficial effects of a good education, through first-hand experience of the world, but also the driving influence of a loved parent's unrealised ambition upon the life of the child. The latter is a dynamic of great importance and one that is to be found in several of our case studies.

THE FAMILY TREE OF ALFRED

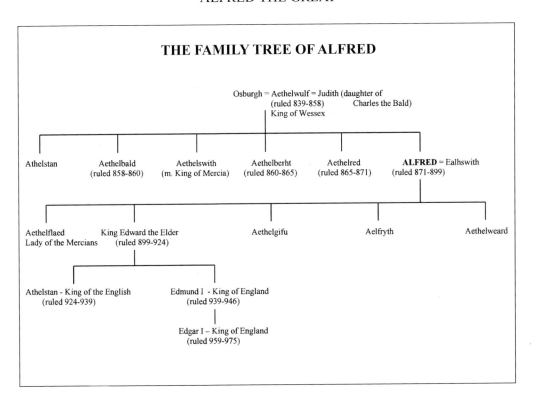

Osburgh = Aethelwulf = Judith (daughter of
(ruled 839-858)   Charles the Bald)
King of Wessex

Athelstan

Aethelbald
(ruled 858-860)

Aethelswith
(m. King of Mercia)

Aethelberht
(ruled 860-865)

Aethelred
(ruled 865-871)

ALFRED = Ealhswith
(ruled 871-899)

Aethelflaed
Lady of the Mercians

King Edward the Elder
(ruled 899-924)

Aethelgifu

Aelfryth

Aethelweard

Athelstan - King of the English
(ruled 924-939)

Edmund I - King of England
(ruled 939-946)

Edgar I – King of England
(ruled 959-975)

SOURCES:

T. Spencer Baynes: *Alfred*, The Imperial Dictionary of Universal Biography, William MacKenzie, 1863.

William Hunt: *Aelfred*. The Dictionary of National Biography, 1908, London.

Justin Pollard: *Alfred the Great: the Man who made England*, John Murray, 2005.

15

QUEEN VICTORIA (1819 –1901)

Monarch

Princess Victoria was a stubborn and wilful child who was determined to get her own way. If frustrated, she would stamp her little feet and burst into tears. Once, in a tantrum, she hurled a pair of scissors at her governess. She could also be alarmingly truthful. When her mother rebuked her, saying that her tantrums had upset both of them, the little girl corrected her – "No, Mama, not me, not myself, but *you*!" Indeed, her mother found her 'unmanageable'. Yet, on the positive side, the princess was lively and intelligent, and progressed well at her studies.

Victoria, 'plump as a partridge', had been born at Kensington Palace on 24 May 1819. Her mother, the widowed Princess Victoire of Coburg, had married the fifty four year old Duke of Kent (one of King George IV's younger brothers) twelve months earlier in an unseemly family race to produce an heir to the British throne. The marriage itself had been a success and the Duke and Duchess of Kent, together with their baby Victoria, had moved into a small house at Sidmouth in Devon on Christmas Day 1819. The following month, the Duke had caught a cold and, after ferociously cruel treatment from his doctors, had died. Two men now came to the aid of the doubly widowed duchess, her brother Prince Leopold, still living in England after the death in childbirth of his own spouse Princess Charlotte, and Sir John Conroy, the late Duke of Kent's equerry.

The Role of Sir John Conroy

Conroy was a dark and handsome Anglo-Irishman who was cheerful and efficient. When asked some years later whether Conroy was the Duchess of Kent's lover, the Duke of Wellington would reply that he "supposed so". The poor duchess took Conroy's advice in most things and, particularly, as regards the management of her difficult child Victoria. Under Conroy's direction an elaborate system of discipline was established at Kensington Palace to protect and direct the headstrong little princess. This so-called Kensington System aimed to shield the child from outside influences while encouraging her education. Conroy wanted Victoria to be constantly protected by her mother, and never to be alone. She even had to share her bedroom with her mother. Conroy desired Victoria to become, he said, 'the People's Queen'. I have been unable to discover exactly what he meant by this or what sorts of danger he feared. Were they threats to Victoria's character, her virginity or her life? Was Conroy driven by liberal political tendencies? These questions remain unanswered.

Historians have almost unanimously taken against Sir John Conroy, seeing his behaviour as an unscrupulous attempt to gain control of the future monarchy for himself. Yet it is possible to see his behaviour in an altogether different light. He had rescued his late employer's widow from an impossible situation. She was surrounded by hostile, eccentric and often dissipated remnants of the old royal family, some of them intensely jealous of the young princess's claim to the throne. Certainly, there were not many at the courts of King George IV, or of his brother King William IV, who could provide wise counsel on how to bring up a wayward child. Their own offspring, many illegitimate, demonstrated this by their wild and sometimes dangerous behaviours. It was the age of Lord Byron and of aristocratic elopements, adulteries and early deaths. Conroy was no prude but he could see that the little princess, with her vivacious love of partying, was highly vulnerable to bad influences. If she was to grow up with a seriousness and sense of duty appropriate to a Queen, then somebody had to take control of her. Clearly the feather-headed Duchess of Kent, on her own, could not manage this, and Victoria's uncle Prince Leopold was far too ponderous and, at that time, too deferential to the court of St James, to do so.

In fact there were three good reasons why the little Victoria risked becoming completely unruly. First, she was an only child: a classic situation in which the child is pampered by those around her, and untempered by having to share parental attention with others or by being brought down to earth by abrasive siblings. Secondly, she had no father, and it is, traditionally, the father who imposes structure and discipline upon the child. Thirdly, she was royal and, like nearly all royal children, she was surrounded by artificial deference that encouraged a sense of self-importance and entitlement. Given the innate liveliness of this particular child, all this was a highly combustible mixture. Any psychologist today could see the potential for an uncontrolled princess Victoria running off the rails. Victoria may also have inherited the bipolar genes of her grandfather and, if so, these might have given her an additional potential for disturbed behaviour. Furthermore, she was unusually physically small for her age, and was extremely sensitive about this in a way that tended sometimes to encourage her to compensate by bumptiously and assertively putting herself forward. She could so easily have become a spoiled brat, or a delinquent little monster. That she did not grow up quite like this was, I would suggest, due largely to the Kensington System and its creator, Sir John Conroy.

I would submit that whatever his other failings, Conroy may have tried to do what was right for the little princess by imposing limits and controls upon her demanding behaviour. He was, however, a soldier and not an expert in childcare. He did his best but sometimes made mistakes. By standing up to the strong will of the child for many years he certainly made himself extremely unpopular with Victoria, and by the age of twelve, she clearly hated him. To make matters worse there were several members of the nursery staff, led by Baroness Lehzen, who pandered to the princess, constantly and deliberately undermining Conroy's authority and turning her against him. Other courtiers disliked Conroy merely because of his less than aristocratic background.

Nevertheless, the young Victoria grew up remarkably well despite all these difficulties. She was variously described as comely, intelligent, polite, graceful, 'either very serious or all smiles', merry, self-possessed, composed, brave, accomplished, 'full of girlish glee', and an uninhibited laugher. By her early twenties the high-spirited girl had matured, according to Sir Robert Peel, into a woman who showed 'great kindness and consideration' and 'a scrupulous and most punctual discharge of every public duty and an exact understanding of the relation of a constitutional sovereign to her advisers'. Moreover, she showed great concern about the conditions of the poor, about women in factories and about cruelty to animals. She had turned out remarkably well. Why was this? Despite her irritation with Conroy and her mother, both of whom she ordered away from her presence as soon as she became Queen, were they not, in fact, responsible for most of Victoria's good qualities?

Some historians have suggested that Conroy's excessive involvement in Victoria's care was because he was her natural father. It is certainly true that the Duke of Kent, who had many mistresses, is not known to have had any child except Victoria. It is also strange that three of Victoria's own children had haemophilia, whereas none of her royal forebears is known to have been a sufferer of this condition. So had Victoria's mother, if she suspected that her husband the Duke of Kent was infertile, taken a lover in order to enhance her chances of pregnancy, thus providing the heir to the throne? One fact argues strongly against this theory and that is that Victoria's facial features resembled those of George III – receding chin, prominent nose and, above all, the large and slightly bulging Hanoverian blue eyes. On the other hand Conroy also managed to look like his late employer the Duke of Kent. So did he secretly imagine that he was related to the royals in some way? Was he, in fact, Kent's son?

This does not rule out, however, the chance that Conroy had indeed been an early lover of the Duchess while *not* being Victoria's father. He could nevertheless have *believed* he was her father. While this could explain his obsession with Victoria's upbringing it could not account, however, for her haemophiliac gene. That must have been a new mutation, however statistically unlikely this is.

After her ascension to the throne in 1837, her coronation in 1838, and her marriage to Albert six months later, it was all over for Conroy, who retired from court, although still maintaining his friendship with Victoria's mother.

Victoria's childhood had been a lonely one. Rarely did she meet other children, and then only when chaperoned by governesses and other staff. She grew up in an adult world. Victoria had always yearned to have a father and throughout her early adult life she formed special and dependant relationships with older men. Because of her position this often meant that they were her Prime Ministers, the first of whom was Lord Melbourne. Her love for him was reciprocated and clearly had an unexpressed sexual component. Later, after marriage – and after Victoria had discovered how to enjoy her own strong libido, the flirtatious father-daughter relationships continued, but on a less erotic level, with ex or current Prime Ministers Peel, Wellington and Disraeli.

Conroy's plan for Victoria's education had gone far beyond the Kensington System. Quite rightly afraid that the little girl could become cut off from the real world, he arranged several tours of the country for her, where Victoria stayed in the great houses of members of the (mostly Whig) aristocracy, passing through villages and industrial towns, glimpsing at least, some of the poverty of her people. Aged thirteen she toured the Midlands, Wales, Cheshire, Derbyshire, Lancashire, Oxfordshire, Hampshire, Dorset and Devon. The following year, against opposition from the King, she visited Lincolnshire, Nottinghamshire, Yorkshire, Rutland and Leicestershire. Conroy at least had ensured that the princess had seen some of the country over which she was about to reign.

Marriage

In 1839 the young Queen proposed to and married her cousin, the serious but good-looking Prince Albert of Saxe-Coburg-Gotha. She adored him, and much of this feeling was sexual. It was soon quite obvious that the Queen was a highly sexed young woman. Nearly all of her recorded descriptions of Albert at this time are about his physical sex-appeal – she eulogised his 'beautiful figure', 'fine waist', 'delicate' moustache, 'pretty' mouth and 'exquisite' nose. He was 'perfection', and quite quickly the Queen was expecting her first child. Victoria went on to have nine children and was seriously depressed after the birth of each of them. She loved sex but disliked babies. Apparently the prince made little effort to avoid making his wife pregnant – an indication either of his selfishness (as the Queen later believed) or of his confused and neurotic attitudes about sex. Albert was both a misogynist and a prude. He had many good qualities, but his hang-ups about sex (and his sadism in blood sports) arguably were to pervert British culture, and the culture of the royal family in particular, for well over a hundred years. These issues arose because his own unhappy childhood had been ruined by his profligate father and the elopement of his mother when he was five. He never saw her again. He grew up melancholic and searching for love and loyalty. His conscientious exterior no doubt concealed his anger with women in general, with whom he was rarely at ease. Some of this anger was vented onto the wild animals whom he slaughtered mercilessly, and through the strict corporal punishment he occasionally administered to his children. The stress he endured through the constant control of these deep impulses, and his stoic maintenance of a civilised and rational exterior, were probably the reasons why he seemed to weary of life around his fortieth birthday, surrendering all too easily to death when stricken by illness a year or so later. Under family pressure he had let himself in for a marriage that, in many ways, went against the grain of his personality – to a dominant little extrovert who bestowed upon him some of *her* wealth and *her* status and not, as was far more usual in matrimony, the other way around.

Widowhood

When Albert died, apparently of typhoid fever, in December 1861, the Queen was devastated and, for many years, withdrew from public life. Melancholy, and surrounded by busts, clothing, and other memorabilia of her beloved husband, she revelled in her loss. This reaction went well beyond the normal bounds of bereavement, lasting until the end of her own life, forty years later, in 1901. She even directed that his dressing-gown must share her coffin with her. It seems to me that there are at least eight partial explanations for this extraordinary behaviour, and several or all of them may have been true simultaneously.

The first explanation is that the Queen was an unstable and histrionic person who reacted melodramatically. Second, is that her highly ritualised post-mortem obsession with Albert was a way of continuing the happy marriage it-self; she was thinking of him almost continuously. Third, her preoccupation with him after his death was what he himself had covertly or overtly ordered. Fourth, it was an attention-seeking or love-demanding performance by Victoria, as if she was saying – "look how miserable I am… please help me". Fifth, it was self-punitive, punishing herself for her rows with Albert, and reflected guilt about the various little squabbles over household (and state) powers she had had with him. Sixth, it was an excuse she employed to avoid or lessen the oner-ous burdens of state and other duties that had been imposed on her. Seventh, it was a superstitious ritual that helped her to assuage her fears about the future – as long as she continued to worship Albert's memory, everything would be al-right. Eighth, she was wallowing in self-pity – itself a self-admitted source of comfort to her.

With a live subject we could test the varying strengths of these and other fac-tors. With Queen Victoria we cannot do this, so all these hypotheses must re-main as possibilities. Personally, I suspect that all played a part and the most important of them is that her elaborate bereavement behaviour was an appeal for love. It was not particularly adventurous nor successful. After three years normal mourning a widow in her mid-forties today would probably find a new partner. We do not know, of course, when Victoria's menopause occurred and this could have complicated matters. Her royalty also made it hard to take lovers discreetly. Victoria's pronounced disapproval of women who remarried in their forties was, however, a clear indication that part of her would have liked to do precisely this. It was not just the sex she missed, of course, but, far more importantly, it was the 'care', as she put it. She repeatedly said that she needed 'support' and to 'feel safe'.

What is sometimes forgotten is that Victoria's somewhat rejected but always doting mother had also died in 1861, shortly before Albert. So Victoria's huge and prolonged performance of mourning was really for both of them. She talked far less of mother than husband but in her treatment of the former may have originated much of her undoubted guilt. Yet Victoria had always needed a *man* rather than a woman to love her. It was, once again, her obsession with the father she had never known. Conscious or unconscious memories of her first ten years may have surfaced. Other than her rather slow Uncle Leopold, and the dreaded Conroy, what men had there been in her life at that time? Ac-tually, not much is known about these early years. There may have been un-recorded events in her childhood that had caused her to feel physically unsafe or insecure. Either it was such an unrecorded trauma, or the anxious and over-protective behaviour of her mother, that made her feel so insecure, or both these things. Now, in middle-age, more than at any time since she had become

Queen, she felt she needed a male guardian and protector – a rock to shield and support her. Her childhood anxieties had re-appeared – as they sometimes do in middle age. Her negative qualities, such as her peremptory hauteur, her self-centred obstinacy and her pert stubbornness were obvious. But there was a hidden side that was quite opposite to these traits: fears of failure, weakness and physical collapse.

For twenty years after Albert's death Victoria tried to avoid all public events, fearing that she might faint at them. If she did attend, her legs would sometimes tremble with fear. Did these symptoms indicate real anxiety or did they have an ulterior (perhaps unconscious) motive, namely, an attempt to attract support? Or both? She had certainly lost the apparent self-confidence she had shown as a teenager, and now involuntarily revealed her need for human care. It was dominant-dependent behaviour: like some who have driven themselves for years to be dominant and dutiful, she now wanted to flop back passively into babyhood. (Nelson showed the same tendency in the last few months of his life.)

So after the loss of Albert, Victoria regressed to her childhood, avoiding the heavy burden of her royal duties, revealing signs of depressed mood and anxiety when at Windsor, but, while in Scotland, indulging in wild Highland balls at Balmoral. Scotland became, for her, an escape from the pressures of royalty which she always felt in London. Furthermore, she had discovered in her favourite Highland servant, John Brown, a strong man who would protect her. At Balmoral, she was regressing back to before the days of the Kensington System and its inculcation of 'dullness' and a sense of royal duty, to her childhood longing for carefree and rowdy behaviour, alternating with her need for being looked after.

Unconsciously, no doubt, she was physically attracted to Brown, who was a handsome man, but it was his sheer physical presence that made her feel protected. Seven years older than the Queen and Prince Albert, he had been selected by Albert to watch over Victoria's safety, and this was the role he now continued to play. Albert had sanctioned it. The same three words frequently recur in her descriptions of Brown – 'protection', 'care' and 'comfort'. Unlike almost everyone else, Brown showed no fear of the Queen and so she dropped her grumpy carapace when in his presence. He addressed her unceremoniously as 'woman', showed her total loyalty, whisked her off on incognito trips through the Highlands, laced her tea with whiskey and organised boozy ghillies' balls that shook the palace late into the night. Often the better for drink himself, Brown would brusquely keep visitors, relatives and senior officials at bay. 'God knows how much I want to be taken care of' the Queen wrote in a letter dated 1865, and Brown filled this role as her 'straight forward' and 'devoted friend'. This was the strong and protective male presence that Victoria had always wanted. 'He protected me so – that I felt safe!' she wrote after his death in 1883.

Personality

Much of Victoria's grumpiness in the last decades of her life seems to have been built upon a sense of self-pity. She felt cross that life had somehow treated her unfairly. The loss of her father when she was a baby, her loneliness as a child, the strictness of the Kensington System, the fussiness of her mother, the awfulness of Sir John Conroy, the tiresomeness of her children, the death of her beloved Albert, the onerousness of her royal duties, the demise of her devoted protector John Brown, the outrageous prejudice against her Indian favourite Abdul Karim ('the Munchi') and, generally, the lack of what she felt was the veneration due to her as Queen. She was obsessed by the past and by its failings. She wallowed in self-pity, demanding sympathy. She was also angry with Albert for not having had 'the pluck' to stay alive. She felt, she said, like 'a deserted child'. (H.291). Like her father, Albert had, indeed, deserted her.

Yet Victoria remained a contradictory personality. Much seemed to depend upon her mood, and sometimes her severe demeanour would break down and she would burst into uncontrollable girlish laughter. The story was told at table, for example, of how her physician William Jenner had been squashed very intimately into sharing a ski-lift chair with the stout and formidable Fräulein Bauer, because some official mistakenly took them for man and wife. (H.474) Everyone tried not to laugh at first until the nineteen year old Princess Louise burst into giggles. This set off the Queen who laughed uproariously. She did so again when an old admiral, who was deaf, and had bored her with his long description of salvaging a ship off the south coast, responded to the Queen's question about his sister, by replying: 'Well, Ma'am, I am going to have her turned over, take a good look at her bottom and have it scraped'. All this rather suggests that the formality at court, imposed by the Queen herself, was something of a charade. There was still, beneath the old lady's lace and buttons, the mischievous young girl trying to escape. Both these examples of hilarity clearly have sexual connotations and the Queen, who had undoubtedly been an enthusiast in this field, may have been affected by her long self-enforced chastity over the last forty years of her life. Her reasons for this self-denial were possibly not so much for the sake of morality or even decorum, as her assumption that sex after forty, for a woman, just did not happen. Besides, in her own case, after nine children, her plump little body had grown as wide as it was long. Judging by her interest in portrayals of the nude in art, and especially sculpture, she was extremely aware of the erotic importance of physical beauty. It was her awareness of her own lack of this commodity after middle-age that probably ruled out, in her mind, the possibility of taking a lover. Her own vanity about her figure, at least, would make it impossible. I suspect, however, and unlike in some women after menopause, that the desire was still very much present in her case. Again, this may have been a further reason for her frequent grumpiness in her later years. Consciously or otherwise, her lack of sexual satisfaction was, for her, another of life's unfairnesses. Of course, she also kept the memory of Albert so alive that it was in some ways as if she was still married to him. So any dalliance with a living male might well have seemed to her, like adultery.

There were other contradictory qualities. As Christopher Hibbert writes:

'Inconsiderate as she so often was, she was also capable of great kindness and understanding sympathy. In the same contradictory way, she was alternately almost painfully honest and capable of the most devious machinations, prudish and tolerant, hard-headed and sentimental, artless and acute, combining sound common sense with outlandish prejudices, real and pretended'.

She was also a strict enforcer of status among guests and servants, while loudly lamenting the very existence of social class. As regards religion, too, she could be both devout and irreverent. So she was almost provocatively inconsistent. Because of this inconsistency those around her must have been uncertain what they should say or as to how to show their loyalty. No doubt Victoria enjoyed their consequent discomposure.

What else is there to say about Victoria? We can see that she constantly overreacted to death, ordering mourning clothes and other ritual observances for the whole court at the deaths even of distant relations. She was reminding everyone how she had suffered through the loss of both her father and her husband. For many years after his death servants had to lay out Albert's bed clothes on his bed each evening, and she went to sleep clutching items of his clothing, rather as a child clutches a teddy bear. During mourning, even small children had to wear black or purple and show no gaiety. When Victoria's mother died in March 1861 Victoria had cried for days. 'I do not want to feel better' she said to her eldest daughter – 'I love to dwell on her' (H.266), asserting that 'the constant crying was a comfort and relief'. (H.266) Perversely, Victoria basked in her grief and, by her own extraordinary admission, enjoyed it. These great bereavements of her middle age set the pattern for the remainder of her life, which became one huge grumpy sulk – as if she was demanding sympathy for all the unrecognised pains of her life. She wanted people to acknowledge the sacrifices and achievements of her youth, when she had bravely taken the crown at the age of just 18. That was why her friend and therapist Benjamin Disraeli was so clever to have realised that the Queen needed to be praised and thanked for what she had done. Instead of advising her, he habitually asked for *her* advice on matters of state, affecting to defer to her greater experience and wisdom. During the 1870s he partially succeeded in coaxing her back into public life by making her an Empress – a novel form of anti-depressive treatment!

Children

As a mother, Victoria had always behaved like a tyrant and her children were often afraid of her. Yet, as the years went by, she began to cling to them, attempting to delay or abort their marriages so that they would stay at home and 'care' for her. The parent-child roles were beginning to be reversed. At times she behaved like an abandoned child and several of her daughters, especially Alice and Helena, tried to step up to the mark to mother her. When Alice, however, tried to persuade Victoria to come out of her self-imposed seclusion, Victoria snapped back at her: 'I require to shape my own life and ways'. In her regression to childhood, Victoria was sounding like the fifteen-year-old girl, telling her mother and Conroy to get off her back. She wanted the 'care' and 'protection', but not the control.

With her sons, however, she was ever more controlling and managerial. She tried to stop them having sexual relations with women and overreacted when first Bertie (the future Edward VII) and then Alfred, did so. She became extremely censorious towards both boys. She bossed them about, so *they* bossed the servants about – something their mother detested. Servants had to be treated with 'friendliness' she said. Little Prince Arthur was a model child and her favourite, but even he had a tendency to be 'stiff' with the servants. Like her eldest (Bertie), her youngest, Leopold, was not to her liking. He was 'ugly', 'common looking' and 'difficult'. He was also haemophiliac and, after the Queen realised this, she became increasingly protective towards him. Leopold, together with his sculptor sister Louise, became the family rebels, along with Bertie, of course. After Prince Albert's death the Queen tried to gather her two youngest children (Leopold and Beatrice) around her as a mutually supportive team – 'the three inseparables', but it did not turn out well. Leopold resented her 'tyrannical' and possessive behaviour and, at eighteen, managed to escape to Oxford. (He died in 1884, after an accidental fall in Cannes. Victoria was, of course, 'utterly crushed' and went into deep mourning again, as usual). Beatrice, however, responded better than her brother to her mother's yearning for care and support, and became like a 'sister' to Victoria. Even when she married in 1885, much against her mother's wishes initially, Beatrice and her husband agreed to take up permanent residence at Windsor in order to be near Victoria.

Why was Victoria such a prude about her children's sex lives? In part it was out of a respect for her late husband's sexual problems. Because of his childhood experiences he had feared sex. But in Victoria's case it was more than this. Quite simply, she envied her children's sexual freedoms just as she envied their successes and the attentions they received generally. She had become a control freak as far as her poor children were concerned. Rarely has a mother been as jealous of her children as Victoria was. Her children, and especially Bertie, rebelled by indulging in the pleasures that she, too, longed to enjoy – sex, parties and alcohol.

As the years went by Victoria mellowed and she began to show considerable affection towards her thirty-eight grand-children, the eldest of whom, the future Kaiser Wilhelm II of Germany (see chapter 11), would one day become so jealous of his Uncle Edward VII of England that he would make little attempt to stop the Great War of 1914, despite being in a position to do so. As with all children, the Queen tended to feel 'shy' or ill at ease with them. She was only at ease with her dogs and ponies. She found it difficult to understand children in general and, instead of developing true insights into their behaviour, tended instead to lecture them, and their parents, on how they *should* behave and on what was good for them – fresh air, low temperatures, avoiding fast company and so on. She also had a tendency to interrogate children, question after question, and to lose her temper with them if they appeared to be stupid.

Dynamics

In later life Victoria continued to shrink from public appearances. She hated them; they made her feel 'nervous'. All she wanted, she said, was 'quietness' and 'protection'. Arguably, there were sound reasons for such attitudes: during her reign at least seven public attempts had been made upon her life, none of them as part of a conspiracy, all by solitary males, four of whom were well below normal height and all of whom were deemed to be insane. (None of these attackers were executed and all were, by today's standards, treated extraordinarily leniently). So, in this sense, her fear of public events seems to have been entirely rational. Yet it also speaks of a far deeper insecurity within Victoria going back, I would suggest, to her own childhood, when her lonely life was dominated by the fussing of her mother on one hand and the ideas of Sir John Conroy on the other. I believe that the parents of spoiled children can behave in five different pathogenic ways – they can pamper, flatter, over-control, over-indulge or over-protect. In the first case, *pampering*, the child is given things (toys, food etc) which are often substitutes for real love and understanding (anorexia can ensue). In the second case, parental *flattery* can give the child a vastly inflated view of their own importance, whereas *over-controlling* frustrates the child and makes her angry, while *over-indulgence* makes her feel all-powerful and intolerant of any other views than her own. Finally, *over-protection*, paradoxically, can make a child feel unsafe and fearful, as well as angry and frustrated. The Duchess of Kent's and, later, Baroness Lehzen's, fussing of their historically precious child Victoria, had elements of all these five forms of pressure but it was the *over-indulgence* and the *over-protection* that stood out, making the little Victoria appear headstrong, angry and yet, paradoxically, afraid. After Albert's demise, it was these characteristics that re-emerged to dominate Victoria's middle and later years, and their very inconsistency encouraged all the other contradictions and ambivalences in her behaviour.

As for Sir John Conroy and his Kensington System: this had been a belated attempt, surely, to control the effects of the Duchess' earlier spoiling, and that of the two Baronesses Lehzen and Späth, which had made little Victoria become, by puberty, so dangerously wilful. Conroy's attempt at discipline and structure was only partly successful, perhaps because it was actively sabotaged by Lehzen. It succeeded initially in enhancing Victoria's self-oppressive sense of her royal duties, but it also made her almost permanently angry. She expected others to praise her for being, contrary to her truly self-indulgent nature, so dutiful!

Victoria's last few decades saw a long struggle between the Queen and her ministers about her need to publicly observe her royal duties. Often, obstinately and childishly, she refused to comply. This was Victoria repeating her childhood struggle with Conroy and her mother. Unconsciously, Victoria wanted exciting parties and some 'beautiful' men to care for her. She needed both a father and a lover. She did *not* really want to comply with her boring and frightening royal duties. The passive-aggressive tactics that she adopted, continued to the end of her days. She used her childlike grumpiness and petulance to frighten away the adults while she tried to live in the past, remembering and exaggerating the happy times she had had with Albert. Hubris gripped her.

Two further factors need to be borne in mind. Little Victoria's surroundings – the royal palaces of London in the early 1830s – were far from their calm ordinariness of today. First, the big characters in the palaces were often bizarre in the extreme. Victoria encountered two 'Uncle Kings' – George IV, a rouged and bewigged monster, and William IV, a peppery old admiral. Neither had liked her father, their brother, and both were outrageously rude to her mother. Then there were her four other royal uncles, all eccentric and one, the sinister scar-faced Ernest, Duke of Cumberland, who was widely rumoured to have murdered his own valet and fathered his sister's child. He was next in line to the throne after Victoria. So, like half a dozen other royals, all of whom no doubt seemed, to the Duchess of Kent, equally debauched and unscrupulous, Cumberland had a genuine motive for wishing that Victoria did not exist. The Duchess had grown up on the continent during the French Revolution and could easily believe that such men were capable of kidnap or murder. The country was awash with fierce and unemployed veterans of the Napoleonic wars, battle-hardened and desperate men looking for work. Furthermore, their once commander-in-chief, the Duke of Wellington, was now Prime Minister. Who could be trusted? The second factor was that many people believed at this time that England itself was on the edge of revolution. In the year of Victoria's birth radical reformers had been killed by troops in the so-called Peterloo Massacre in Manchester. When she was a year old, in 1820, half the cabinet had nearly been murdered over dinner by insurgents based in Cato Street. Now, in 1830, parliamentary reform was the issue, with huge rallies in British cities, rioters attacking the houses of anti-reformers, and narrow votes for and against reform in Parliament. In the countryside the Captain Swing rioters broke farm machinery, burned barns and were brutally suppressed. Scores of rioters were also killed by troops in Bristol and elsewhere but, in 1832, the Great Reform Act was eventually passed. One of its most fanatical supporters, John Lambton, Earl of Durham, regularly advised the Duchess of Kent. Clearly there were good reasons for 'distancing' the young Victoria from the unpopular Royal Family at this time. If there was going to be a revolution then it would be better for the child not to be found with the reactionary royals, but touring the shires, staying with reform-minded Whig grandees and being acclaimed by the general people.

Manipulations

It may well be that the common view of Conroy is the correct one. But, as a psycho-biographer, one must try to keep an open mind. All possible explanations of human behaviour should be considered and eliminated one by one according to the available evidence. Human behaviour is not always as it seems to be. This is especially true in over-heated and dysfunctional family situations such as those existing at Windsor Castle and Kensington Palace in the early 1830s. So I will try to put the positive view of Conroy. Clearly, feelings were running high and manipulations were in full swing. But who was the principal manipulator? Was it John Conroy, as the historians have asserted, or was it somebody else? Possible candidates range from King William IV and Queen Adelaide on the one side to Conroy and the Duchess of Kent on the other, while somewhere in the middle are the two childless German spinsters, the nursery Baronesses Späth and Lehzen, and in the background, Victoria's uncle Leopold, head of the Coburg family and, now, King of the Belgians. And what was the real issue? Was it whether the young Princess Victoria should appear more often at Court (this was King William's understanding of the problem), whether the Duchess of Kent should be paid more money and treated with a lot more respect by the King (as the Duchess of Kent saw it), whether the Princess could be made to marry a Coburg and not one of Leopold's enemies (as King Leopold perceived matters), or whether the poor little Princess should be more indulged and mothered (as the two German Baronesses understood the situation). I don't know what the 'sympathetic and cheerful' Conroy (P.58) saw as the main issue at stake because I have seen no convincing primary evidence. Did he really feel, as Queen Adelaide and the historians have claimed, that this was his chance to make himself the power behind the throne when Victoria became Queen, (admittedly, he did try to persuade Victoria to appoint him as her Private Secretary), or was he merely trying to ensure that Victoria received a proper education and upbringing away from the intrigues and battyness at Court? He was surrounded, as Victoria was, by the emotions, manipulations, and eccentricities of a very odd family. Yet, somehow Victoria *did* receive an excellent education, both from her tutor Dr George Davys and from other teachers. But one has to remember that this regime was arranged and overseen by Conroy himself and the Duchess of Kent. Furthermore, the little girl was formally examined (at Conroy and the Duchess' suggestion) by three bishops who gave her an excellent school report, finding her knowledge of History – 'remarkable in so young a person' (P.94). She had a good knowledge of Scripture, they said, and of Geography, Arithmetic and Latin, and could speak some French and German. She could also draw rather well. As Victoria grew older Conroy not only ensured that she travelled around England and Wales meeting ordinary people but that she often attended concerts, operas, ballets and plays. These she enjoyed immensely. As there was a shortage of children in Kensington Palace, Conroy and the Duchess included in such excursions not only Conroy's children but also various cousins from Germany. Several outside experts were also invited to give lectures at the Palace including, for example, two scientists who spoke about Chemistry (in industry, concerning heat, experimentation and solvents) and the properties of matter (particles, cohesion, capillary action and magnetism). Conroy was definitely a moderniser. If he was the half-mad egomaniac that is usually portrayed, would he have organised such a balanced and progressive programme of education?

Conroy was all too aware that the knowledge that she was heir to the throne might go to little Victoria's head, and apparently it did so, when she was told by Lehzen. There are special problems in becoming a monarch in the middle of adolescent rebellion. This is when, probably, Conroy took further steps (with the Duchess) to try to contain the princess's wilful overconfidence. Immediately, he found himself up against the two nursery Baronesses – Lehzen and Späth. They both adored the little Victoria – 'the poor fatherless child' – and quite simple, spoiled her. They had also spoiled Victoria's half-sister (from her mother's first marriage), Princess Feodore, until the elderly George IV began to show a, possibly unhealthy, interest in her, and she had to be sent abroad. Now that they had only one nursery charge – Victoria – these two powerful women set about spoiling her in a big way. Whatever she wanted she was given. Conroy's attempts to impose controls were undermined (AP 88). Eventually, Conroy managed to persuade the Duchess to dismiss Späth who went abroad to rejoin her (now married) other protégé, Princess Feodore. Lehzen, however remained at Kensington and, as we have seen, continued to poison Victoria's view not only of Conroy but of Victoria's own mother, the Duchess of Kent. It was a familiar relationship in aristocratic and royal circles – the rivalry between two mothers – the natural mother and the governess, and Lehzen was destined to win it hands down. It was all done with supreme cleverness, with Lehzen outwardly protesting her loyalty to the Duchess while devastatingly destroying her child's confidence in her mother when alone with Victoria. I suspect it was Lehzen, and not Conroy, who was the great manipulator.

Conroy and the Duchess fought back for several years, supported by the King's sister, Princess Sophie. Living at Kensington Palace, Sophie, almost alone among the senior royals, was in a position to see what was really going on, and could discern Lehzen's subtle tyranny. But Victoria could not – and never did understand how she was being misled. In consequence, she grew up always the spoiled and wilful child, and after Albert's death, dissipated the sense of duty that had been earlier instilled into her, while wallowing in her self-pity and self-importance, and causing difficulties for many of those around her.

Lehzen's influence continued supreme until after Victoria's marriage. By then, Lehzen may have been also acting as a political agent for the interests of the scheming Coburg family. King Leopold sent Baron Stockmar as his official representative to the royals in London while Lehzen was, in effect, his secret agent keeping an eye on Victoria. So Conroy had to contend not only with a hostile governess and a spoiled child, but also with political pressures coming from two directions – from King William on one hand and King Leopold on the other. He did not stand a chance. He had no formal position, hence his attempts to become Victoria's secretary. Indeed, the more I read the evidence the more I suspect that it was Lehzen and the Coburgs, and not Conroy, who were the manipulators. (Victoria eventually married into their family). They simply used Conroy as a scapegoat. Instead of being thanked for helping to bring up Victoria reasonably successfully, he was blamed for anything that went wrong and was, eventually, got rid of. The Coburgs (and their agent, Lehzen) had won. It was left to Albert, several years later, to reveal Lehzen's jealous duplicities, and to dispose of her. After he had done so, the Duchess of Kent was reinstated at court and her relationship with her daughter improved spontaneously.

Whatever the truth about Conroy, in the 1860s Victoria reverted to her old childhood ways. Much of the time she could still be polite and charming, but by pretending her seclusion was all due to her inconsolable feelings of bereavement, she had found a good excuse for avoiding much of the exhausting work of being royal. In Scotland she could get away with a little more high spirits but in London she became, for much of the time, a domestic tyrant draped histrionically in widow's weeds.

Long after Conroy's death in 1854, Victoria developed a remarkably bad relationship with her Prime Minister William Gladstone. Almost everyone was puzzled by this including her children, subsequent historians and even Gladstone himself. There was something irrational about her personal dislike of Gladstone. Surely this was because she was being reminded of Conroy and was transferring her old feelings for him onto Gladstone. Both men were tall and dark, both were radical and modern, and neither flattered her. She believed that both of them hectored and lectured her, and showed insufficient respect. Victoria was as unreasonable about Gladstone as she had been about Conroy.

Conclusions

There had been four public sides to the young Victoria. First, the dutiful, well-educated and poised princess. Second, the genuinely compassionate Victoria who cared about poverty, the plight of gypsies and the welfare of animals. Third, the tireless party-goer who loved meeting beautiful men. Finally there was, and always remained, the headstrong little tyrant, who was often passively, and obstinately, aggressive. The first two elements of Victoria's personality must have been encouraged by her mother, George Davys, Lehzen and Conroy between them. The tyrant, however, had been there since infancy, and nobody had tamed it. Indeed, as far as I know, only the Duchess and Conroy had ever tried to tame it and both were effectively banished as soon as the princess became Queen. Only Victoria's passion for Albert saved him from a similar fate and the little tyrant was, for a few years, concealed. Then, after his death, the Queen regressed to her adolescence, put herself into seclusion, placed her royal duties on the back burner and re-emerged as a petulant child. She had returned to being what she had always been.

THE FAMILY TREE OF QUEEN VICTORIA (1819-1901)

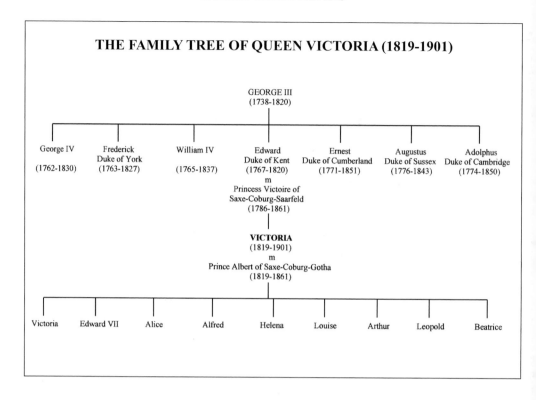

SOURCES:

Christopher Hibbert, *Queen Victoria: a Personal History*, Harper Collins, 2000.

Elizabeth Longford, *Queen Victoria*, The History Press, 1999.

Alison Plowden, *The Young Victoria*, The History Press, 1998.

A N Wilson: *Victoria: a Life*, Atlantic Books, 2014.

16

SIGMUND FREUD (1856 – 1939)

Psychoanalyst

Ironically, although he pioneered the concern for the importance of infantile experiences in the adult lives of his patients, Sigmund Freud, in his so-called *An Autobiographical Study*, published in 1927, scarcely mentions his own life before he went to college. His autobiography concentrates not upon his early relationships with his parents and siblings, nor with his emotions generally, but with the development of the ideas and practice of psychoanalysis itself. This technique started formally in 1896, shortly before his fortieth birthday. So in his autobiography, we are left almost in the dark by Sigmund himself as to what, from his early years, really influenced the development of his own personality. Furthermore, as the originator of the then highly controversial ideas that sexual drives and the unconscious are both crucial to the understanding of every human being, Sigmund's autobiography never mentions either of these in relation to himself.

Clearly, Sigmund Freud desired to defend his own privacy. As Lionel Trilling points out (J. Preface), Sigmund "expressed himself strongly against being made the subject of a biographical study". Indeed, in 1885 he bragged to his bride to be, Martha — "Let the biographers chafe; we won't make it too easy for them...even now I enjoy the thought of how they will go astray." His first biographer, Ernest Jones, who worked with Sigmund, states that Sigmund twice destroyed all his correspondence, scientific notes, diaries and manuscripts relating to his earlier years, doing so in 1885 and 1907. "Everything that fell before the decisive break in my life, before our coming together and my choice of calling, I have put behind me" he wrote to Martha in 1885. That was certainly a crucial year for him in which he chose to take on the responsibilities of marriage and gave up scientific research in order to gain the steadier income of a medical practitioner. Yet Sigmund was quite prepared for future biographers to have access to his papers dating from 1907 onwards (the time when he began to become famous). From this date he carefully preserved his correspondence. No doubt he wanted his years of failure to be forgotten and his years of great achievement to be remembered.

Introduction
Sigmund was the eldest of seven surviving children of wool merchant Jakob Freud (1815 – 1896) and Amalia Nathansohn (1835 – 1930) and was born in Freiburg in what is now the Czech Republic, only eight months after their wedding. Jakob, who was twenty years older than his wife, had two sons by an earlier marriage. Sigmund was his mother's favourite child — her "golden Siggie", of whom she had high hopes. He was followed by five sisters (Anna, Rosa, Marie, Adolfine and Paula) and then by his brother Alexander, the youngest of the family. Another brother, Julius, died in infancy. A family photograph taken in about 1878 is rather dominated by the handsome Sigmund who stands in the centre of the back row, right behind his mother, his arm on the back of her chair. His father Jakob sits some distance from his wife. Nobody smiles and Emmanuel (Sigmund's older half-brother), has his back to Sigmund. All around Sigmund are his good looking sisters and other female relatives. His little brother Alexander, some fourteen years younger than Freud, sits upon the floor. Four of Sigmund's five sisters would eventually die in concentration camps and three of his nephews or nieces would commit suicide. Sigmund and his wife Martha would have six children, and eight grandchildren, their son Ernst having two sons, Lucian and Clement, who would live their lives in England. Sigmund's youngest daughter, Anna (1895-1982) was, in many ways, his favourite child and would, herself, become a distinguished psychoanalyst in London, to where Sigmund escaped from Hitler in 1939, shortly before he died.

When Sigmund was four, his father's work failed and the family moved to Vienna where Sigmund did well at school. He felt no special interest in medicine but joined the University as a medical student in 1873 where he encountered some anti-Semitic feeling. He did not take his medical doctorate until eight years later, in the interim doing some histology, and research into cerebral anatomy, aphasia, neuropathology and the effects of cocaine. In 1882, due to what he called his father's "improvidence", he was advised to give up these studies and became a junior hospital doctor. Nevertheless he continued to lecture on neurology, proudly recalling years later how "the fame of my diagnoses" brought him an influx of American students, although admitting that at this stage he "understood nothing about the neuroses". Appointed a lecturer in neuropathology in 1885 he then travelled to Paris on a scholarship to study with the celebrated Jean-Martin Charcot where he witnessed Charcot's use of hypnosis in the treatment of so-called hysterics. On his return to Vienna Sigmund married his long term sweetheart, Martha Bernays, in 1886, the first of their six children (Mathilde) being born in the following year. He also began to use hypnosis in his private treatment of neuroses, collaborating in this with his friend Josef Breuer who referred some of his patients to Sigmund. It was not, however, until ten years later that Sigmund began to discuss and publish his ideas. His *Interpretation of Dreams* appeared in 1900 when he was forty-four. It contained some of the basic concepts of psychoanalysis, but nevertheless received little attention at the time.

It is important to notice that, although Sigmund had been under some pressure from his parents to succeed, he achieved no great success until middle age. Few people had heard of him until after 1900. Yet he was clearly an ambitious man. Indeed, there is some evidence that Sigmund himself felt something of a failure throughout the first two decades of his professional life. Then, in what would today be called a mid-life crisis, he abandoned his emphasis upon science (which had been much encouraged by his admired professor, the physiologist Ernst Brücke) and began to freely express what he called his "philosophical" or "speculative" ideas. By this he seems to have meant his thoughts about the motivation of human behaviour.

Although Sigmund was anxious to stress that his ideas came from the careful observations of science, I believe that they were, in fact, nearly all based upon introspection into his own personality. Sigmund, instead of recording dispassionately the behaviours of all his patients, only selected those cases which tended to support his introspections. By giving the impression that his insights mostly came from the observation of his patients, however, he deflected from himself some of the criticisms which he, rightly, anticipated. In fact, most of his famous patients were treated years later. Sigmund's dilemma was that he genuinely respected science while realising that his introspections were not scientific at all. For example, they did not involve the examination of experimental data. He was, he admitted, an "adventurer" with ideas, and not a scientist. His ruthless candour when observing himself, however, and his fierce determination to understand his own motivations correctly, were the reasons why so many of his conclusions have proved to have the lasting ring of truth about them. Almost certainly, nearly all the content of *The Interpretation of Dreams* is autobiographical and introspective. This is not the place to examine his theories in detail but his claims concerning the huge role of the unconscious, the importance of the libido, the tripartite nature of the personality (id, ego, and superego), the defences of repression, displacement, projection and resistance, as well as the significance of the Oedipus Complex itself, were all, in my opinion, based upon his observations of himself. To an extent, he saw himself as a warrior fighting the forces of Viennese bourgeois convention. Perhaps he despised the Viennese culture precisely because it was so far removed from psychological realities.

As a proud but unreligious Jew he felt he could see through the defences forced upon his (often female Roman Catholic) patients, which obliged them to deny their angry and sexual feelings which they often felt for their suppressive parents. Like Hannibal (his childhood hero) Sigmund saw himself as attacking all the bogus superstitions of Rome — a city that fascinated him all his life but which he could not bring himself to visit until 1901. The word 'Roman' itself had many conflicting connotations for him. As a small child he had endured an overbearing Roman Catholic nursemaid who had tried to teach him the ways of Roman Catholicism, taking him to church services. (See paragraph 4 below.)

While pondering about himself and his inner workings, he recalled his childhood sexual fascination with his slim and beautiful mother, realised that young children have their own strong sexual feelings, and tried to face up to the fact that he had felt great anger and rivalry towards his father. It is hardly surprising that it was only after his father's death in 1896 that Sigmund dared to start to reveal his theories. Much of his suppressed contempt for his father was because of Jakob's financial failures. The family had often been short of money. Worse than this, his father's brother was accused of fraud and Jakob became caught up in the ensuing scandal. I think, at this juncture, Sigmund felt that his father had let his mother down. (See paragraph 9 below.)

Throughout his life Sigmund sought the support of wise male supporters. Two were outstanding in his middle years — Josef Breuer and Wilhelm Fliess. He also had a circle of younger male admirers. As long as these men behaved as sons or younger brothers with him, Sigmund tolerated their minor differences. But as soon as any of them assumed that their familiarity with him allowed them to behave in any way that appeared authoritative or dominant, Sigmund fell out with them, sometimes bitterly. This was true of both Breuer and Fliess, and of at least four of his disciples (Stekel, Jung, Adler and, eventually, even the rather childlike and unstable Ferenczi). Ostensibly, the doctrinal differences that caused these ruptures were of two principal types: (i) criticism of Freud's almost exclusive emphasis upon sex as motivation, and (ii) Freud's tendency to overgeneralise from the particular to the universal. If Freud had not been so intolerant of criticism, the alternative theories of some of his ex-followers (e.g. Adler) might have been useful additions to his own theory. The more eclectic approach, adopted today by many therapists, reflects this.

For many psychologists the strict interpretation of the Oedipus Complex as described by Sigmund Freud — that the son unconsciously wants to have sexual relations with his mother — has remained controversial. Personally, I believe that for most sons it is the *attention* and *love* of the mother that is longed for rather than *sexual intercourse*, (a point later partially conceded by Sigmund (F49)). Yet for Sigmund himself the Oedipus Complex certainly had an erotic tinge. Not only is this illustrated by the *matrem nudam* memory (even Sigmund had to use Latin to describe this) but also, so I believe, by his memory of himself urinating in his parents' bedroom and in their presence. (See paragraph 8 below.) It was certainly a remarkable lapse for the usually exemplary golden boy. Sigmund later linked scientific curiosity in general, and his own "greed for knowledge", with sexual curiosity. He said he was inspired to take up medicine not to help reduce the suffering of others (which he dismissed anyway as no more than an attempt by the medical professionals to smother their own innate sadism), but because he was inspired "by Goethe's beautiful essay 'On Nature'" — an essay that, interestingly, eroticises Nature and portrays her as the 'mother'.

Sigmund undoubtedly showed remarkable, indeed rebellious, courage in facing up to the sexual origins of much of his own behaviour. Unlike his father he would be brave and defiant in his search for truth. Like the allegedly Semitic Hannibal he would challenge the 'establishment'. He had been shocked by a story his father had told him of how he had been insulted by an anti-Semitic lout — instead of standing up to the challenge, Jakob had meekly stood aside. (See paragraph 10 below.) The young Sigmund had vowed to take a more defiant and aggressive attitude in life, and this may partly account for the audacity of Sigmund's new theory of psychoanalysis. Hannibal had been a bold general, steadfast and strategically creative, as he fought against superior Roman armies for fifteen years in a foreign country. It is easy to see why the adult Sigmund still identified with him.

The History of Psychoanalysis
To suggest to the late nineteenth century middle classes that much of their behaviour was motivated by sex, and incestuous sex at that, was an act of outrageous provocation, and, of course, the respectable Viennese bourgeoisie responded accordingly. Sigmund writes, almost proudly, that:

...after my separation from Breuer (circa 1896) I had no followers. I was completely isolated. In Vienna I was shunned, abroad no notice was taken

of me. My Interpretation of Dreams, *published 1900, was scarcely re-viewed in the technical journals* (F67).

The reason for this lack of acclaim was largely Sigmund's emphasis on sex. In Europe, he said, he felt despised. Only after 1906 did he begin to receive support from a few pupils in Vienna and from Eugen Bleuler and Carl Jung in Zurich. Then, in 1909, he was invited to America where his theory began to receive popular support. In retrospect, Sigmund divided the history of psychoanalysis into two phases:-

In the first of these I stood alone and had to do all the work myself: this was from 1895 – 1896 until 1906 or 1907. In the second phase, lasting from then until the present time (circa 1925), the contributions of my pupils and collaborators have been more and more important. (F78)

Taking an even longer view one can see that four watershed years stand out as far as the history of psychoanalysis is concerned:-

(1) **1885/6** Sigmund visits Charcot in Paris and has an insight into dreaming. He gives up a strictly scientific career and takes up private practice dealing with nervous disorders. In the same year, he marries his long betrothed sweetheart Martha Bernays, and begins his introspective self-analysis. Being married probably gave Sigmund that extra sense of security he needed to do this.
(2) **1896** Sigmund's father dies. Sigmund starts to discuss his self-analysis more openly, and 'discovers' the Oedipus analogy. His wife's sister, Minna Bernays, moves in with Sigmund and Martha and, possibly, has an affair with Sigmund.
(3) **1900** Sigmund quarrels with Breuer and begins to grow closer to Fliess. Sigmund publishes his great work *The Interpretation of Dreams*.
(4) **1906/7** Supporters such as Karl Abraham, Carl Jung, Arthur Schnitzler, Max Eitingon, Alfred Adler and Otto Rank step forward in support of psychoanalysis.
(Most of the famous clinical cases Sigmund quoted, occurred later; for example, the Rat Man case in 1909, the Dora case of 1905 and the Wolf Man case of 1914. Only Breuer's Anna O case was earlier - in 1882.)

Clearly, the high expectations for him held by both his parents, and especially by his mother, in some ways typical of Jewish family culture of the late nineteenth century, endowed him with massive ambition. In order to achieve self-satisfaction he had to become a celebrity. Eventually he did so. Sigmund's uncertainty was how to fulfil this high ambition — would it be as a general like his boyhood heroes Oliver Cromwell or Hannibal, as a scientist like his hero Charles Darwin, or as a writer such as Goethe or Shakespeare? (See paragraph 11 below.) It was only in about 1885 that circumstances forced him to realise that his road to fame and greatness would be to utilise his piercing understanding of himself and other human beings. His quest to discover the truth about human nature required some of the virtues of all of his heroes — their courage, perseverance, honesty, defiance of convention, and unswervingly rigorous powers of observation.

By facing up to the pervasiveness and power of sex, Sigmund both shocked and liberated many subsequent generations. But was he so honest and perspicacious when it came to feelings of anger? Did he really recognise the extent of his own anger towards his father as his Oedipal rival, towards his siblings and even towards his mother, not only for producing a long string of new sibling rivals but for stimulating both his libido and his ambition without helping to satisfy either of these yearnings? He displaced much of this nameless anger into his battles with errant disciples and other critics and only fully incorporated anger into psychoanalysis towards the end of his life, dramatically and unconvincingly, in the form of the *death wish*. As some of his contemporaries said, Sigmund narcissistically over-generalised his ideas. What were often excellent insights into his own behaviour he insisted on applying to the whole of humanity. This not only made his ideas seem more important but was also a screen behind which he could partly conceal his own pathology. The death wish, for example, is not universal. Furthermore, Sigmund failed to recognise that it only became a part of his own psyche towards the end of his long life, after many family bereavements and his own, ultimately fatal, cancer had made him chronically depressed.

Like nearly all highly creative people, Freud experienced spontaneous swings in mood, evolving new ideas when his mood was elevated, and organising and cogently expressing them when he was moderately depressed.

The Adult Sigmund Freud

In his young adulthood, Sigmund was a neat and handsome little man (only 5'7" or 5'8") and not the towering and glowering figure suggested by the often reproduced photographs taken in his old age. He usually appeared calm and quiet. Only his dark searching eyes betrayed the keenly analytical mind within. Jones remarks that there was something feminine about him. From the 1880s he was addicted to cigars. He was also fascinated by sculpture, archaeology, mushrooms and books.

Sigmund saw himself as rather lazy, intolerant of competition and intellectually under-endowed. But he was also bold like his enduring hero Hannibal, and, as we have seen, he described himself as an "adventurer" with ideas and not a scientist. Like a scientist, however, he had "a veritable passion to understand" and a fearless integrity. He only published his revolutionary ideas when he was sure of their accuracy. As an ethnic Jew, Sigmund deeply resented Roman Catholicism and anti-Semitism, both powerful cultural features of the Vienna of this period.

As we have seen, the great skill that Sigmund possessed, and which distinguished him from others, was his power of introspection. He had felt a searing need to understand himself and others since his confusing experiences in infancy (J. Preface). As an aspiring scientist, however, he was wary of any subjective approach and, as we have noticed, for years had kept in check what he rather contemptuously described as his own "speculative" and "philosophical" tendencies. Sigmund viewed the study of Nature, scientific curiosity, as an evolved or sublimated form of sexual curiosity, probably because his own sexual curiosity in early childhood had been especially strong and because he deeply associated Nature with his mother, whom he admired sexually. Furthermore, some of his confusion in infancy was about his mother's sexuality itself — about how it functioned. In his older years Sigmund appeared kind, dignified and controlled. He lived a life of faithful and loving monogamy, and he rarely hinted at any other (adult) sexual interests. Indeed, he seemed almost puritanical, Jones commented, in his attitude to sex.

His grandson Clement Freud described Sigmund as "a warm and kindly grandfather who was fond of the children and his dog" (*Personal Communication*), and in later life, he grew immensely fond of his dogs — "One can love an animal like Topsy (or my Jo-fi) so deeply", he wrote to Marie Bonaparte in 1937 - "affection without any ambivalence, the simplicity of life free from the conflicts of civilisation...a feeling of close relationship, of undeniably belonging together" (J509). When his dogs died, Sigmund mourned them deeply.

Sigmund's Mother, Amalia (1835 – 1930)

Born Amalia Nathansohn, she married Jakob Freud in Vienna in 1855 when he was aged forty and she was twenty. Jones recalled her "lively personality" and says "when young she was slender and pretty and she retained to her last her gaiety, alertness and sharp-witted intelligence". There was a "close attachment" between herself and her "golden Siggie". She had borne him, her first born, when she was only twenty-one. Sigmund said he had inherited from his mother his "sentimentality" (Jones suggests this ambiguous term, in German, covers "temperament" and "passionate emotions". (J405)) One of Sigmund's sons, Martin, recalled that his grandmother had "a lively temper and was impatient, self-willed, sharp-witted and highly intelligent" (G504). It seems she was also vain, egotistical and used to getting her own way. Sigmund's niece Judith said of her — "she had a sense of humour, being able to laugh at, and at times even ridicule, herself" (G505) and that she worshipped Sigmund. He recognised the importance of his relationship with his mother, and of his Oedipal attachment to her, but never fully analysed this. One may note that Sigmund's wife, Martha, was not like his mother at all, being altogether quieter and more submissive.

Sigmund's Father, Jakob Freud (1815 – 1896)

Jakob was born in Freiburg where he became an impecunious wool merchant. Amalia was his third wife. He abandoned virtually all Jewish religious observances but always remained proud of his Jewish origins. Sigmund later described his father as "an interesting human being, inwardly very happy" (G88). His death moved Sigmund deeply, triggering childhood memories. Sigmund paid tribute to Jakob's "deep wisdom and fantastic lightheartedness" (G88), but many questions have been raised about Sigmund's unconscious Oedipal feelings for his kindly father, such as rivalry, contempt over his failure to make money for the family, and anger for his weakness against anti-Semitism. He was, said Jones, slightly taller than Sigmund, of a gentle disposition and well loved by all his family (J4). Sigmund said he inherited from his father his sense of humour, love of Jewish anecdotes, scepticism, liberalism and, perhaps, his uxoriousness. Jakob was, said Sigmund "always hopefully expecting something to turn up" (J4).

Childhood Experiences

We know of only a handful of early experiences that may have affected the developing personality of Sigmund Freud. I have tried to arrange these in their approximate chronological order. All of them involve memories recalled by Sigmund during his self-analysis, mainly through the interpretation of his own dreams. With supreme integrity Sigmund revealed what was usually concealed — a typical child's mental world of fantasised lust and violence.

1) His Mother's Esteem

As we have seen, Sigmund was his mother's first born and was treated as her "golden boy". Throughout his life, until she died in 1930 when he was aged seventy-four, this gave Sigmund, in Ernest Jones' opinion, his lifelong self-confidence. Sigmund was certainly made to feel "special" by his mother, and destined for greatness. "A man" Sigmund wrote later, "who has been the indisputable favourite of his mother keeps for life the feeling of a conqueror, that confidence of success that often induces real success". Note his use of the word 'conqueror' – again a reference to his heroes Hannibal and Cromwell.

2) Death of Brother Julius

When Sigmund was nearly two years old, his younger brother Julius died aged seven months. Sigmund, as he said, welcomed this death with "malevolent wishes and genuine childish jealousy". Julius had been born when Sigmund was only seventeen months. Years later, Sigmund wrote of the reactions of a baby girl to the birth of a sibling:-

It feels dethroned, despoiled, damaged in its rights, throws a jealous hatred upon the little sibling and develops a grudge against the faithless mother...the child's claims for love are immoderate. (G507)

As Gay has said, this sounds like a self-portrait. Sigmund himself attributed his later fainting attacks in the presence of a male rival (e.g. Jung) to this early experience (J380), and in Jones' opinion "he never ceased to reproach himself for being, through his hostile wishes, responsible for the intruder's early death" (J381).

3) Nephew John: Tyrant and Friend

Baby Sigmund found himself often in the company of a nephew, John, who was more than a year older than him. John Freud was the son of Sigmund's half-brother Emmanuel, who lived nearby. Jones says that "there is every reason to think that the most important person in Freud's early childhood was, next to his parents, his nephew John...affection and hostility between them alternated...at least on Sigmund's side, the feelings aroused were much more intense than is usual" (J8).

Years later, Sigmund speculated that his own "martial ideal" stemmed from

...my alternately friendly and hostile relations with a boy a year older than myself...my nephew John has since then had many incarnations which have revived first one and then another aspect of a character that is ineradicably fixed in my unconscious memory. At times he must have treated me very badly, and I must have opposed my tyrant courageously...

In Sigmund's opinion "this childish relation has determined all my later feelings in my intercourse with persons of my own age" (F8). More than this, Julius and John "now determine what is neurotic, but also what is intense in all my friendships" (G11).

These are strong words. They help to explain the adult Sigmund's (a) firmness when facing adversity generally, (b) his childhood admiration of soldiers such as Hannibal and Cromwell, (c) his tendency to fall out with males of about his own age — for example his close male friends and followers such as Josef Breuer, Wilhelm Fliess, Alfred Adler and Carl Jung, and (d) his understanding of ambivalence. Sigmund said: "an intimate friend and a hated enemy have always been indispensable to my emotional life; I have always been able to create them anew..." So he understood the active role he played in this.

John was also part of the unusually complicated family of which Sigmund found himself to be part. Having an *older* nephew was itself unusual. In consequence, from a very early age, Sigmund strove to understand relationships. Ernest Jones has also suggested that John was a figure onto which Sigmund *displaced* the hostility really intended for his father (J10). Sigmund once described John as his "companion in my misdeeds". One of these delinquencies was when John and Sigmund (aged about three) fell upon John's little sister Pauline in a meadow where they were picking flowers and roughly snatched away her bunch. Later, Sigmund attributed eroticism to this encounter.

4) Roman Catholic Nanny
Jones records:

> In the household there was also a Nannie, old and ugly, with the nurse's normal mixture of affection for children and severity toward their transgressions; she was capable and efficient. Freud several times refers in his writings to what he called 'that prehistoric old woman.'

(The word 'prehistoric' here may not only refer to his early childhood but be also associated with Sigmund's collection of archaeological artefacts which, in turn, were associated with important but unconscious psychological issues that had to be 'excavated' in order to become conscious.) Jones continues:

> He was fond of her and used to give her all his pennies, and he refers to the memory of the latter fact as a screen memory; perhaps it got connected with her dismissal for theft later on when he was two and a half years old. She was Czech and they conversed in that language, although Freud forgot it afterwards. More important, she was a Catholic and used to take the young boy to attend church services, implanting in him the ideas of Heaven and Hell, and probably also those of salvation and resurrection. After returning from church the boy used to "preach a sermon at home and expound God's doings. (J6-7).

Arguably, the whole idea of the psychoanalytic process – the release of guilt-laden material to the listening psychoanalyst – is analogous to the Catholic confessional.

Sigmund told Fliess in 1897 that the "primary originator" of his neurosis was this "ugly, elderly but clever woman who told me a great deal about God and hell, and gave me a high opinion of my own capacities". (MB 148)

5) Half-Brother Philipp: Confuser

When Sigmund was born in 1856, Philipp was already twenty, more or less the same age as Sigmund's mother Amalia (1835 – 1930). He was the second son of Jakob (Sigmund's father) by his first marriage. Ernest Jones suggests that Philipp became the butt of baby Sigmund's anger on two counts. First for being close to Amalia (Sigmund's mother) and secondly for being perceived as responsible for the sudden disappearance of Sigmund's nanny when he was aged two and a half. In fact, what had happened was that the nanny, later recalled as a feisty older woman, a strong Roman Catholic and the imparter of sexual knowledge to Sigmund (see 4 above), had been found to have stolen money and toys from the family. She was arrested, tried and imprisoned. When Sigmund asked Philipp where she had gone, Philipp had replied that she was *eingekastelt* — or "boxed in". This confused Sigmund into worrying that his mother (absent expecting the birth of her next child, Anna) had also been boxed in. He began desperately searching for her, howling. Philipp had then opened a cupboard (*kasten* in Austrian) to show that she was not in there. Years later, Sigmund realised he had perceived Philipp not only as a rival for his mother's attention but in some way the cause of the arrival of his next sibling, Anna. So Philipp was seen as responsible for simultaneously removing both maternal figures (mother and nanny), for introducing a new baby rival, and for generally confusing him. Maybe some of the confusing was done deliberately by Philipp as a form of teasing. Were Philipp and his mother having some kind of affair? Anyway, little Sigmund was already confused: his mother was the same age as his half-brothers, mother-figures could suddenly disappear, babies arrived mysteriously, his father was much older than his mother and slept with her, while his nephew who was older than him was simultaneously his best friend and worst enemy. One outcome of all this was that Sigmund became a dedicated searcher after truth. Another was that he never liked his sister Anna. (Yet he was to call his favourite child by the same name).

6) Moving Home: Family Decline

When Sigmund was three his father's shortage of money forced the family to move first to Leipzig and then to Vienna. Sigmund said he never liked Vienna, but found it oppressive and "disgusting". He was heartbroken and indignant when his two older half-brothers, together with John and Pauline, all emigrated to Manchester. England subsequently became, in his eyes, a utopia of justice and social wellbeing which he longed to visit. Now, in quick succession, between 1860 and 1866, four more sisters were born — Rosa, Marie, Adolfine and Pauline, followed by his only full brother, Alexander. Each birth challenged his position as the centre of his mother's attention and then began to empower it as the oldest child — having greater strength, knowledge and responsibilities. Sigmund mourned the lovely countryside of Freiburg where he had been the solitary apple of his beautiful young mother's eye. Now in Vienna, with a rapidly expanding family and a shortage of funds, he felt the insecurity of threatened poverty. He still remained, however, the golden boy of the family, with his own unshared bedroom.

7) Matrem Nudam

At the age of four, on a train journey from Leipzig to Vienna, Sigmund saw his mother naked. We do not know under what circumstances she was naked but this event had a powerful erotic impact upon the little Sigmund. Years later, when he recalled it, Sigmund could only write of it in Latin. He told his friend Wilhelm Fliess that his "libido towards matrem had awakened" (G11). For many people the Oedipus Complex lacks this genuine erotic quality but for Sigmund it was there. But then, for most heterosexual males of any age, the sight of a naked woman who happens to be slim, beautiful and aged only twenty-five, is likely to be arousing.

8) Urination in his Parents' Presence

Another embarrassing childhood event was recalled by Sigmund during his self-analysis in the 1890s. When he was six or seven years of age Sigmund had urinated in his parents' bedroom, in their presence (G23). Exasperated, his father told him he would never amount to anything. This memory haunted Sigmund for years and became "a terrible blow to my ambition". Whenever he recalled it in later years he would quickly recite his achievements, as though to show his father that he had, after all, amounted to something.

Surprisingly, this act of urination has been interpreted as itself a symbolic act of ambition or as the effect of excitement due to the invasion of his parents' bedroom out of sexual curiosity. I see it as, possibly, more Oedipal. Boys of seven in the 1860s may well have been mystified by the details of the sexual act, confusing the two penile functions of ejaculation and urination. So this action may have been a reckless and confused attempt to demonstrate his sexual potency — as a tribute to his beloved mother and a challenge to his rival father.

9) Family Scandal

When Sigmund was nine a scandal hit the family. His father's brother, Uncle Josef, was convicted and imprisoned for trading in counterfeit roubles (G8). Sigmund recalled that his father's hair turned grey with grief and anxiety over the course of a few days. Anxiety because he and his two eldest sons, now safely in England, had been implicated.

10) His Father's Weakness

When Sigmund was twelve, his father told him that he (Jakob) had once been challenged by an anti-Semitic thug who had knocked off his new hat into the gutter, shouting "Jew, get off the pavement". When Sigmund had asked what Jakob had done next, his father calmly replied: "I stepped into the gutter and picked up my hat". Jones says that Jakob never regained the place he had previously held in his son's esteem — "submission was not in his nature". Indeed, Sigmund began, in fantasy, to identify himself with the defiant Hannibal (J19).

11) Childhood Heroes

From childhood into his teenage years, Sigmund, clearly not satisfied with his father, identified with various heroic male figures from history. First were the *conquerors* such as Hannibal and Oliver Cromwell. Both of these were rebels and brilliant tacticians who had fought their way to the top. They were, to an extent, outsiders who overthrew their unjust rulers. Hannibal was a successful general for fifteen years in a foreign country (Italy) and Cromwell had cut off his king's head. (Kings and fathers were often symbolically equivalent in Sigmund's opinion.) Sigmund, a Jew living in a Roman Catholic city, resented the overbearing presence of its cathedral and churches, and may have seen some parallels between his own feelings and Cromwell's dislike of Roman Catholicism and Hannibal's defeat of the Romans. Sigmund had been hostile towards Roman Catholicism since infancy and seems to have had a complex ambivalence about the words 'Rome' and 'Roman'. He had a lifelong fascination with the city of Rome itself although he was strangely reluctant to visit it. Sigmund's thwarted career as a scientist may have been inspired partly by another of his heroes, Charles Darwin, whose revolutionary theories — "held out hopes of an extraordinary advance in our understanding of the world" (J19). This was the young Sigmund speaking — the *explorer* of ideas with "his veritable passion to understand" (J22). Darwin, too, had upset the church. Finally, there were the great writers such as Shakespeare and Goethe who inspired him. We have seen the impact on himself of an essay by the latter (perhaps wrongly attributed) which eroticised Nature and spoke of her as "mother". Most of Sigmund's heroes challenged orthodoxy, prejudice and religion, rather as he did.

12) Sigmund's Criticism of Some Jews

Sigmund, like his father, was not religious, but both men were proud of their Jewish origins. Jews from Eastern Europe were, however, flooding into Austria at this time, stirring up ever stronger anti-Semitism. When he was sixteen, on the train from Freiburg to Vienna, Sigmund encountered an immigrant Jewish family and described its son, apparently influenced by the father, in the following terms:-

> *He was the kind of wood from which fate carves the swindler when the time is ripe: crafty, mendacious, encouraged by his dear relatives in the belief that he has talent, but without principles or a view of life.* (G19)

Could Sigmund possibly be condemning something he *might* have become under his father's influence? Was he, at this formative time in his life, defining himself in the opposite terms?

Some writers have suggested that Freud fraudulently distorted his theory. Robert Oxlade, for example, speculates that Sigmund's equivocation on the subject of incest – where he revised his original suggestion that actual incest often occurred, to saying that such reports were merely *fantasies* on the part of the child – might have been a deliberate falsehood in order to conceal some of Sigmund's own sexual misdemeanours of childhood – with his mother for example. (Oxlade. Personal communication. Oct 2014). If this was the case, however, how is it that on most other occasions Sigmund was so frank on the subject of sex? (At one stage Sigmund even suspected his father of having sexually abused his (Sigmund's) siblings). It seems to me that he may have been less candid in describing his own *anger*. Oxlade suggests that Sigmund may have employed "deception in the interests of expanding his importance and grandiosity". Well, I do not find much deception in Freud. Rather the contrary. I find ruthless candour. Yet, I accept that he was certainly anxious to prove his own importance. This was in order to realise and live up to his mother's (and nanny's) very high opinions of him. Since infancy he had been burdened with these demanding expectations – 'Siggie as a genius', one might call them. In order to reduce the painful cognitive dissonance between these demands and the reality of his drab life until the age of 40, he had to become successful. His ambition was overwhelming.

Freud's Neuroses

Although outwardly apparently calm and controlled, Sigmund suffered turbulence within. The remarkably ordered life he led, of faithful monogamy and courteous good humour, was itself a usually successful defence against the eruption of his internal feelings. These did, however, become visible at several times in his life, most notably at the time of his self-analysis. This formally began, according to Jones, in the July of 1897 when Sigmund was forty-one. For the next three years, until mid 1900, Sigmund was clearly neurotic. Which came first, the neurosis or the analysis, is uncertain. Did he undertake his rigorous self-analysis in order to face up to and deal with his 'mid-life' neurotic problems, or did his courageous recall of his childhood cause his emotions to boil to the surface? Or both? At this same time he wrote his first great book, *The Interpretation of Dreams*, and transferred and acted out his early family feelings into a tempestuous termination of his intimate friendship with Wilhelm Fliess. Indeed, Fliess can be seen as the unwitting 'analyst' who had to receive Sigmund's confused and angry feelings engendered by his recall of infantile relationships within his family, and especially with his father and nephew John. (See items 3, 4, 6, 7 and 8 above.) Poor Fliess could hardly cope with this. He was ill-prepared with insight or skin thick enough to endure Sigmund's fury. The existence of the process of *transference*, by which is meant the transference of childhood feelings onto persons in the here and now, had yet to be recognised by Sigmund. Their friendship came to an end around 1900 with Fliess accusing Sigmund of making a violent attack upon him. He then accused Sigmund of plagiarism by stealing his idea that all human beings have a bisexual constitution (J200-206).

One could make a Freudian comment here about the unconsciously homo-erotic nature of the Freud/Fliess friendship. In fact, their friendship had always been somewhat ambivalent as both constantly sought the approval of the other. Neither really understood or had time for each other's theories. Fliess increasingly became obsessed with numerology. As with Carl Jung years later, Sigmund ultimately rejected all such forms of irrationality, keeping his feet firmly on the ground, however delicate his extraordinary powers of insight. Sigmund remained the aspiring biological scientist who was prepared to boldly explore the fundamental biological drive of sex, but not to countenance the occult or bizarre.

What, then, were Sigmund's neurotic symptoms? The answer is that they were manifestations of anxiety and disturbances of mood. The anxiety showed as a fear of travel (as we have seen, Sigmund had had some searing childhood experiences on trains such as seeing his mother naked), and a dread of dying. He complained of marked heart symptoms, pains and arrhythmias. His moods swung, as Jones says "between periods of elation, excitement, and self-confidence on the one hand and periods of severe depression, doubt, and inhibition on the other...in depressed moods he could neither write nor concentrate..."(J199). When he could write he continued to record the analysis of his own dreams for his book, and dealt with his discovery of the Oedipus complex in 1897 — a few months after the death of his father made all this psychologically possible. The late 1890s were a wonderfully creative period for Sigmund. When he was elated (Sigmund himself uses the word *hypomanic* to describe himself) the written insights pour forth. Freud, always the aspiring scientist, but without the availability in the 1890s of appropriate tranquilisers or anti-depressant medications (although eagerly foreseeing their discovery), self-prescribed cocaine and nicotine. Both produced temporary improvements in his condition, but greater long-term problems emerged, including Sigmund's lifelong addiction to cigars (around twenty a day) which would eventually kill him with cancer.

Jones notes that, while depressed, Sigmund would sometimes study maps of Pompeii or gaze upon his remarkable collection of archaeological artefacts. Sigmund himself could see the analogy between archaeology and the psychological excavations of psycho-analysis. But the analogy between his fascination with the volcanic wreckage of Pompeii and his own volcanic eruptions of the 1890s may have escaped him.

The most dramatic of Sigmund's signs of anxiety were the few recorded instances of fainting when in the presence of a gifted male rival. The best known of these is when he fainted in the presence of Carl Jung in November 1912 (again a highly creative period for Sigmund). Their relationship was already in disarray (J376) as Jung and his Swiss followers were rejecting Sigmund's emphasis upon the importance of sex. Jones said they met for lunch at the Park Hotel in Munich where Sigmund reproached Jung for writing articles about psychoanalysis without mentioning his (Freud's) name. "I remember thinking he was taking the matter rather personally" says Jones. "Suddenly, to our consternation, he fell on the floor in a dead faint." The sturdy Jung carried Sigmund to a couch where he recovered. Sigmund subsequently told Jones he had suffered two similar attacks in the same room four and six years previously when in the presence of Fliess. "There is some piece of unruly homosexual feeling at the root of the matter", Sigmund concluded (J207), with his usual courageous candour. Others have suggested that these faints were associated with Sigmund's dissention with powerful male rivals, his tactical victories over them, and his fear of harming them (as appeared to happen to Julius). Fainting reveals his anxiety about his anger and competitive feelings. Rather than admit to this Sigmund produced a sexual interpretation as a distraction. (Sigmund never postulated the possibility that both fainting and symbolic homosexual submission could be subtle unconscious tactics for defusing an attack from an aggressive male).

Conclusions

The whole world has been transformed by the ideas of Sigmund Freud. Without always realising it, our attitudes towards human behaviour have been revolutionised by him. I have suggested that this revolution has stemmed from Sigmund Freud's fearless introspections into his own personality, where he found all the principal components of his theory. Biographers have, in general, underemphasised the influence of childhood military heroes on Sigmund's outlook, his opposition to Roman Catholicism, the origins of his rivalry with other males and his need to live up to the high expectations of his parents. All these features gave his theories and his life their characteristically combative quality, opening the minds of millions to a more frank appraisal of human behaviour. We live at a time, in the early twenty-first century, however, when there are signs that Freud's wise insights into the sexual instinct, are beginning to be forgotten.

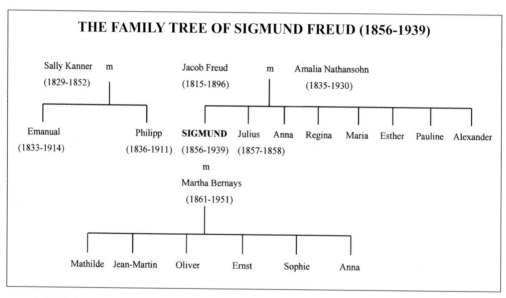

THE FAMILY TREE OF SIGMUND FREUD (1856-1939)

Sally Kanner m Jacob Freud m Amalia Nathansohn
(1829-1852) (1815-1896) (1835-1930)

Emanual Philipp **SIGMUND** Julius Anna Regina Maria Esther Pauline Alexander
(1833-1914) (1836-1911) (1856-1939) (1857-1858)

m

Martha Bernays
(1861-1951)

Mathilde Jean-Martin Oliver Ernst Sophie Anna

SOURCES

Marie Balmary: *Psychoanalysing Psychoanalysis*, translated by Ned Lukacher, John Hopkins University Press, 1982.

Ernst Freud (Editor): *Letters of Sigmund Freud*, Basic Books, 1960

Sigmund Freud: *The Autobiography of Sigmund Freud* (translated by James Strachey), Read Books, 2013

Peter Gay: *Freud: A Life for Our Time*, W.W. Norton, 1988

Ernest Jones: *The Life and Work of Sigmund Freud* (1953) (Ed. Lionel Trilling and Steven Marcus), Basic Books, 1961

Richard Wollheim: *Freud*, Fontana, 1971

17

HORATIO NELSON (1758 – 1805)

Warrior

Horatio Nelson is one of the best examples of how a person's whole life can be irrationally influenced by events in early childhood. In Horatio's case, I believe, he was driven to join the Navy and to recklessly defeat the French by his unconscious desire to impress his long dead mother and to win her love. By doing so he repeatedly trounced the French ships and prevented Napoleon's invasion of Britain. It was because of his deeply felt but unconscious motives that he showed such unusual levels of courage and sense of duty.

Early life

Horatio was born on 29 September 1758, the fourth surviving child of the Reverend Edmund Nelson, Rector of Burnham Thorpe in Norfolk and his wife Catherine (née Suckling), a great niece of Sir Robert Walpole, England's first Prime Minister. Four more siblings followed him. Horatio was thus right in the middle of a large family all of whom, so we can surmise, had to compete for their parents' attention. A middle child in such circumstances is often at a disadvantage, the eldest most often feeling valued by being given 'adult' responsibilities by the parents, and the youngest commanding the greatest cosseting. Nevertheless, Horatio found a means of securing his mother's attention. According to family folklore he became recklessly adventurous, or 'game' as they then said, raiding a neighbour's garden for fruit at night, for example, undertaking a dangerous journey through heavy snow, and climbing trees for birds' eggs. Horatio had found a way to stand out from his brothers, all of whom were rather unexciting. Horatio was, according to at least one modern biographer, Colin White, probably his mother's favourite.

Edmund and Catherine Nelson had eleven children of whom three (including a previous Horatio) had died in infancy. Three more died in early adulthood. Horatio was emotionally closest to his boorish older brother William, destined to become the first Earl Nelson in 1805, and to his lively sister Catherine who was the youngest in the family.

As a baby, Horatio was considered a physically weak child, and was baptised early in case of his demise. But he was given a Walpole godfather and the favourite Walpole first name of Horatio. His early childhood was unremarkable for a child of a Norfolk clergyman in the middle of the eighteenth century. He grew up in a quiet and, as he said, 'lonesome' village three or so miles inland from the sea, surrounded by salt flats, sand hills and marshland. Later, he and his brother William would be sent to be educated in the grammar school in Norwich and, later still, to one in North Walsham. Colin White has described the young Horatio as 'a bright, engaging little boy who constantly sought attention and approval from adults and was naturally impulsive, especially in his affections'.

Tragedy struck the family at Christmas 1767 when Horatio was nine. On a bitterly cold Boxing Day Horatio's mother died, quite suddenly, aged only forty-two. Ten days later Ann, his maternal grandmother, who had been staying in the village, also died.

The family

Catherine, Horatio's mother, was rather plain in appearance and little is known for certain about her personality, but she was probably forthright and feisty. She would have had little time for fussing her children with so many of them, so her love and approval probably had to be earned. Nevertheless, she was clearly a good wife and mother, and quite a forceful and practical woman. She may also have been vivacious, rather as two of her children also were – her namesake, little Catherine, and Horatio himself. The daughter of a Norfolk rector, Horatio's mother had aristocratic connections, her mother Ann being the daughter of Sir Charles Turner and Mary Walpole of Houghton Hall. So Catherine could count among her relations the celebrated agricultural pioneer Viscount 'Turnip' Townsend, Baron Horatio Walpole of Wolterton and Sir Robert Walpole himself; hers was a family of famous achievers. Her father, the Reverend Dr Suckling, had died when she was only five, and at twenty-four she had married the Reverend Edmund Nelson, then a young curate, in 1749. She seems to have had most of the family's brains and energy, as well as their class connections.

Edmund Nelson was not so well born as his wife but was a modest, kind and devout person. In later years he described himself as 'an odd whimsical old man, who knows nothing of the present time and very little of any other' and as having 'a weak and sickly constitution'. Edmund was not exactly a capable organiser nor a tower of strength; he expected his wife to do almost everything for the family and she, or her relatives, secured him his living as a rector. After his wife's death, left with eight children to look after, he struggled incompetently to care for them, but he never married again, remaining strongly loyal to his wife's memory. Horatio was not particularly close to his father, probably seeing him as rather inadequate and far duller than the members of his mother's family.

Horatio

Horatio would, he once admitted, continue to think of his mother all his life. Although dead, she was always, psychologically speaking, with him, and his awareness of her presence was heavily laden with emotion. In a letter written in the year before he died, Horatio confessed: 'The thought of former days brings all my mother into my heart, which shows itself in my eyes.'

Horatio was aware that his mother had married beneath herself. Perhaps his lifelong quest for glory was partly an attempt to regain for his mother her true social standing, by himself achieving titles and acclaim. Social class was a matter of huge importance at the time and he may have felt this was her birthright as well as his. By giving him the Walpole name of Horatio his mother had, as it were, singled him out as one of her own family. Maybe she had even indicated to him that she hoped he would honour the Walpole history of outstanding achievement. So, such achievement would be the best sort of present that a little boy, desperate to regain her love and approval, could give to the mother who had deserted him by dying. It seems that he fantasised that such achievement could, somehow, bring her back. Furthermore, if he died in the attempt, he might, after all, see her again in heaven. Such half-conscious and entirely irrational fantasies can be very powerful.

It was Horatio's mother's younger brother, Captain Maurice Suckling, that she had admired so much. He too, in 1770, was in mourning (he had recently lost his wife – a Walpole cousin), and it was to this upper class and childless uncle that the forlorn Horatio turned in his hour of need. Clearly, if his dead mother's approval was to be won back then he should emulate the one male figure she had obviously admired and adored – her dashing naval brother with Walpole connections. Besides, Suckling must have reminded him of his mother. Deciding to contact him for help was itself a sign of Horatio's continuing maternal fixation. The young and bereaved Horatio initiated the approach to his uncle, asking to join the Navy. Captain Suckling was surprised that it was Horatio rather than one of his more physically robust nephews who was applying to be provided for in this way, blithely remarking, 'What has poor Horatio done, who is so weak, that he, above all the rest, should be sent to rough it out at sea? But let him come, and the first time we go into action a cannon-ball may knock off his head, and provide for him at once!' So, in April 1771 Horatio was duly admitted as a midshipman on board his uncle's ship *HMS Raisonable*. Both uncle and nephew were to do well; the former becoming Comptroller of the Navy before dying in 1778.

The young Horatio always had a sense of his own importance. He felt he was a man of destiny. Even as a junior officer he did not hesitate to write letters to those in command and, when an admiral, he sought and obtained quite frequent meetings with the high and mighty, even with William Pitt the Prime Minister. Later, he lapped up the praises lavished upon him by Emma Hamilton, posed repeatedly for portraits, ensured that his brave exploits were widely reported in the press, and wallowed in the applause of the British public.

Like many highly successful and famous people, Horatio had access to surprising reserves of energy, both physical and mental. Under stress, or the excitement of the occasion, he would glitter, becoming the magnetic centre of attention. As we shall see, Adolf Hitler had this trait too. Instead of being subdued by events both had the capacity to switch on a mental turbo-charger. This *hypomanic* potential is largely genetic in origin. Horatio was certainly not without fear in battle. Far from it. But he had this capacity to rise above it by experiencing 'a sudden glow' of almost ecstatic courage, believing he would die only in God's good time. His impulsive enthusiasm, informality, boyish energy and his 'wonderful mind' were often remarked upon by contemporaries, and all are parts of this temperament. Such hypomanic capacity is probably the secret ingredient in the lives of many outstanding people, providing surges of extra drive when required, as well as the star-dust of their charisma.

An outline of Horatio's career
In 1797 Horatio distinguished himself at the Battle of Cape St Vincent, was knighted and promoted to Rear-Admiral. After the battle he ensured that his exceptionally daring exploits would be widely reported in England by sending accounts of them to his old comrade William Locker, urging that he get them published. In 1798 Horatio was appointed to command a squadron in the Mediterranean, and proceeded to destroy the French fleet almost totally at the Battle of the Nile, where he received a shrapnel wound to the head. He returned to Naples to be nursed by Emma Lady Hamilton, the wife of the British ambassador, and in April 1801, Emma gave birth to his daughter Horatia shortly before he sailed to the Baltic, where his guile and determination won the Battle of Copenhagen. From the end of that October until May 1803 Horatio was

based, together with the Hamiltons, at his newly purchased home at Merton Place in Surrey.

But what was it that drove him on? Where did his extraordinary courage, patriotism and sense of duty originate? How did he inspire such loyalty and devotion in his men? Did all these traits link, somehow, with the devastating loss of his mother at Christmas 1767?

Some Contradictions

Many aspects of Horatio Nelson's personality have puzzled historians and his life was full of apparent contradictions. He was kind and sensitive, yet he was also brave to the point of foolhardiness and, on one occasion, ruthlessly put down acts of sedition and disloyalty in Naples. Although Horatio adored honours and royalty he never lacked the common touch, unusually for the times shaking the hands of ordinary sailors. Despite his love of titles, he was quite unsnobbish for an Englishman of his era; the informality and empathy he showed to all ranks often surprised people. Horatio was a careful planner but could also be impulsive and reckless. He longed for peace yet, untypically for the era, sought the utter destruction of his enemy's ships. In victory he insisted on magnanimity and gentleness, and yet in battle he personally led boarding parties and took flagrant risks that were unnecessary for an officer of his seniority. He was conservative politically yet introduced novel forms of management and fairly unusual battle-tactics, creating a feeling of trust and enthusiasm among his men and fellow officers, explaining his battle plans to the latter in advance over dinner. He was conventional in social outlook and yet lived openly in an extraordinary and adulterous ménage à trois with the Hamiltons, defying the norms of the polite society to which he aspired. He loved his celebrity and yet, by the time he had settled at Merton with Emma, he was described as being quiet and unobtrusive. How can we begin to explain such paradoxes in the character of one of Britain's most famous heroes? In particular, what were the causes of Horatio's extravagant courage, extraordinary charisma and excessive sense of patriotic duty?

To understand someone fully, one has to consider nature as well as nurture. Horatio's sensitivity and empathy for others were, surely, partly genetically determined. Whereas other, more robust, sailors may have reacted to hardship by becoming hardened, the young Horatio did not. Instead, he became permanently sensitised to the sufferings of others and to cruelty – a trait that was to endear him to his men in future years. He detested, for example, the cruelty of a bull fight he saw in Cadiz in June 1793. Indeed, stories abound as to his kindness. When an officer's son was arrested for rowdy behaviour by foreign authorities Horatio secretly paid the fine to have the boy released; when a sailor was distressed to have missed posting a letter home by mail boat, Nelson ordered that the boat return specially for this one letter; a nephew said in later years that Horatio 'was anxious to give pleasure to everyone about him, distinguishing each in turn by some act of kindness and chiefly to those who seemed to require it most'.

Psychodynamics

Horatio once said that he constantly thought of his mother, yet in adulthood he could recall few details of her. This was probably a defence, as it may have been too painful for him to do so. Two points about her he did recall, however: that she had hated the French and loved the Navy. He must have concluded that these clues indicated the way to her heart. Certainly, it was the way he was to follow with sublime success. As a child he had seen his relations preparing for a French invasion of his native East Anglia in the 1760s. By fighting off the French it was as if, unconsciously, he could rescue his patriotic mother from such a fate. Indeed, Horatio's own outstanding patriotism can partly be explained in this way. When his naval uncle Maurice died some years later Horatio imagined Maurice murmuring on his deathbed that he would "Leave Horatio to his country" – saying "serve her well, and she'll never desert, but will ultimately reward you." These are significantly strange words but ones that Horatio described as being no less than 'the inward monitor of my heart upon every difficult occasion'. Note the feminisation of country and the mention of desertion. Country and mother unconsciously became associated in Horatio's mind, rather as they would do for Adolf Hitler. Even the famous signal at Trafalgar – 'England expects that every man will do his duty' – can be seen in this light. Horatio was obsessed by patriotic duty and detested disloyalty; these may have been attitudes that his mother had shown, but they were, at the same time, expressions of his continuing but unconscious loyalty and sense of duty to *her*. His last words, as he lay dying on HMS *Victory* were, repeatedly, 'Thank God I have done my duty'. His constant references to duty, 'bequeathing' and death were noticed by his contemporaries but their significance – as signs of his largely unconscious obsession with his dead mother – was missed.

Maybe, as bereaved children often do, Horatio even felt unconsciously responsible in some way for his mother's death. If so, then he also had to expiate this guilt. Robert Oxlade suggests that he may have felt unconsciously that he was contagiously lethal to others. This, too, sometimes happens in bereaved children. If so, then it might be that Horatio's exceptional and constant kindness was an attempt to counteract this perceived lethality. Somewhere in Horatio's mind 'country' meant 'mother', and 'duty' meant 'protection of mother'. Deep down he probably believed that if only he had protected her in 1767 she would not have died. Oxlade has pointed out that the egocentricity of bereaved children not only leads then to feel responsible for a parent's death but may make them believe that 'being good is a way to fend off further disasters'. I very much agree with this and I think this could be a further reason for Horatio's constant desire to be successful and to win praise. Horatio was always highly motivated to be 'a good boy', as his father used to say.

It cannot be seriously disputed that Horatio was often perceived by his contemporaries as being 'little', 'sickly' and 'weak'. These are the words they used to describe him and they surely reveal the effect that Horatio had upon the men and women whom he met. The important point, psychologically, is that such words often indicate that the speaker's protective and affectionate feelings towards Horatio had been activated.

Horatio was widely seen as an heroic little daredevil and he unwittingly used such perceptions to his advantage. If he had been physically big and reckless many would have written him off as foolhardy or buffoonish. But being physically little and reckless he inspired admiration and provoked a remarkable degree of protectiveness among his men. They were, he later said, 'a band of brothers'. Physically bigger brothers naturally feel protective towards smaller brothers, and so it was in Horatio's case, not only with his actual brother William, but with his fighting men. Big burly seamen were sometimes reduced to tears of affection in his presence. Seeing their little brother rashly leading attacks upon the enemy their instinct was to follow and protect him. On several occasions Horatio's life was saved by his 'brothers' in this way. And the more he was wounded the more he provoked these feelings of affection and protectiveness. It was this extraordinary charisma that was Britain's secret weapon. By its means he inspired his men to acts of exceptional daring and determination that transformed mere naval efficiency into near invincibility. Of course, Horatio's leadership qualities did not just consist of his manic charm and his outstanding bravery as a little man leading from the front, but on a number of other factors too. He cared for his men, ensuring they were well fed, entertained and given proper medical treatment. As Nicholas Rodger points out, after the Battle of St Vincent in 1797 Horatio was also gaining the reputation for being a winning fighter. Increasingly, men began trusting in his military judgement. Rodger has explained that all these factors, when combined with the Royal Navy's traditional emphases upon training and strict discipline, produced deadly results. In battle, Horatio's men would keep their nerve under fire, holding back their own salvoes until they would be fully effective. They would still operate efficiently, just as they had been trained, even when they were afraid. The combination of this discipline and their devotion to Horatio proved to be devastating for Britain's enemies.

As a naval tactician Horatio was fairly orthodox and eclectic. He was, however, outstandingly flexible and able to seize opportunities as they arose. Not only did he discuss his plans with his captains in advance and over good food, but he gave them far more encouragement and praise than censure. This was rather unusual for the times. Officers, used to fearing their admirals, were deeply moved by his trust in them. He would discuss various alternative courses of action and gave them the confidence to act flexibly in battle, on their own initiatives and judgement. Today it would be said that Horatio 'empowered' his men.

Horatio's extreme sense of patriotic duty

If Horatio was a patient of mine today I would want to explore his possible feelings of guilt and anger over his mother's death. Was getting himself wounded not only an unconscious attempt to win his mother's love but also a means to punish himself for what he felt was his responsibility for her demise? These sorts of feelings may appear very strange and irrational to some readers but they are surprisingly common among bereaved children, and could have been present in Horatio's case, as both Oxlade and Hession have confirmed.

As a psychologist, one becomes used to discovering the exact opposite to what is first presented. Horatio presents us with his extreme patriotism. He throws all this in our face, constantly. I have already speculated that England and his mother became connected in his mind and that patriotism, therefore, unconsciously represented his love for his mother. But why did he so often emphasise all this? Could it all be a defence – a concealment even from himself – of exactly the opposite sorts of feelings: of rebellious anger against his mother? Was his exaggerated sense of duty towards her a way of concealing his unconscious fury with her for deserting him by dying? It seems that Horatio protests his duty far too much!

Conclusions

It seems to me that Horatio never really grew up. He was always the little boy bereaved. He was always stuck at Christmas 1767, looking for someone to care for him. In his wife, except for a few months when, significantly, she had *nursed* him after he lost his arm in 1797, he had failed to find the mother he yearned for. It was to Emma Hamilton and her billowy embrace that he finally and rapturously came home emotionally, falling in love, equally significantly, as she *nursed* him after he had been wounded at the Battle of the Nile in the following year. Nursing, as an emblem of maternal affection, was what Horatio had always needed, and he needed it especially at that time when he was showing marked signs of what today might be called post-traumatic stress disorder after the shattering battle of the Nile. Emma gave him motherly love in buck-etfuls and intuitively responded to his hunger for approval by heaping praises upon him, often to an absurd degree, and putting up portraits of him everywhere she could, both in Naples and later at Merton. Besides, Horatio had, literally, rescued Emma from the French advance in 1798, just as he had probably fan-tasised he would rescue his real mother. He had thus earned and won her love. He felt redeemed. The contented ménage à trois with Sir William Hamilton merely served to reinforce this parental ambience, and to such an extent that Sir William not only provided the aristocratic feeling that was associated with his mother, but also treated Horatio affectionately as the son he had never had. (Sir William was twenty eight years older than Horatio, who was only seven years older than Emma.)

The whole of his career can be seen as a desperate attempt by Horatio to re-play the family experiences of his childhood so that, instead of with the tragedy of his mother's death, it would all end happily the second time around. And for Horatio it did – when he had repeatedly defeated the French, he fell in love with the seductive yet motherly Emma Hamilton and died before that relation-ship itself could turn sour. Emma resembled his mother in several ways: she was, for example, physically strong; indeed, both women have been described as being 'statuesque'. She was certainly physically larger than Horatio. More importantly, both were good practical organisers and Emma had hugely im-pressed him by sensibly and calmly organising the panicky Sicilian royals dur-ing their escape by sea to Palermo in December 1798, in one of the fiercest storms Horatio had ever known. Emma was what psychologists sometimes call 'the good mother': she flattered, nursed and idolised Horatio. Her love was unconditional. Fanny, Horatio's wife, on the other hand, had failed to realise that he needed this mothering. She did not see his baby side and was, herself, looking for paternal love (which she found, to an extent, in Nelson's father). Even worse, Fanny could not understand Horatio's need for fame and flattery. So she had inadvertently starved him of these emotional essentials. He had also felt an outsider as regards the 'establishment'. Emma was, above all, a booster of his fragile self-esteem, a 'rewarder of his exploits', as White puts it, just as his mother might have been. Like many love-starved children Horatio had fantasised an 'ideal family' and the ménage à trois appeared to re-create this perfection. This is one reason why Horatio ignored the disapproval of polite society and brazenly flaunted the ménage: he saw it not as a scandalous sexual arrangement but as his happy family, at last reunited.

Some final thoughts

As with Adolf Hitler, Christmas time was often a problem for Horatio. His mother had died at Christmas in 1767. After that he tended, so it seems to me, to be ill or to behave oddly or significantly at Christmasses generally. John Sugden noted that Horatio's father was also affected at this season; at Christmas 1797, for instance – thirty years after his wife Catherine's death – he was still mourning her and blaming himself, all too accurately, for being an inadequate parent. It was at Christmas 1798 that Horatio rescued the Hamiltons and the Sicilian royals and took them to Palermo, beginning to fall in love with Emma at that time. Their sexual liaison probably started at Christmas 1799, a year later. It was also at Christmas – in 1800 – that Horatio abruptly separated from his wife Fanny and went to Torquay, via Fonthill, where he had 'such a spasm of the heart' that he thought he would die. Sugden also indicates that there was a further childhood precedent for this timing – at Christmas 1770 his father had left his unhappy children in the cold Norfolk rectory while he selfishly went off to Bath for a holiday. This was only three years after they lost their mother, and this feeling of lack of strong support from his father is almost certainly one reason why Horatio was covertly angry with him.

It was in Sir William Hamilton that he eventually found an altogether more psychologically satisfactory parent: worldly-wise and, above all, aristocratic. Sir William seems to have impressed Horatio just as much as did Emma when first they met. Indeed, I will go further and suggest that it was Sir William who actually changed Horatio and gave him a wholly new outlook on life. Horatio, like most naval officers at the time, had hardly had a proper education – except in gunnery, discipline and nautical knots. Sir William was cultured, extremely knowledgeable about art and a pioneer vulcanologist. When they went on tours together Sir William would show Horatio the grand houses, the paintings and the countryside, and take him to the theatres. All these were new experiences for Horatio. His improved performance as an admiral and administrator after 1800, to which Colin White has drawn our attention, can, I believe, be put down largely to Sir William's influence. He provided Horatio with a far wider and more progressive perspective culturally, historically, politically and morally. Furthermore, he gave Horatio some confidence in his own intellectual powers. The ménage was, indeed, Horatio's ideal family.

Just an aside about Sir William: Some people find it extraordinary that such a distinguished man could have tolerated the ménage à trois with Emma and Horatio. I would give three principal reasons for this. First, the culture of the time and the circumstances of his marriage to Emma: Sir William was a broad-minded eighteenth century aristocrat and an elderly man of the world. He understood women and their needs, and adored them for their beauty and accomplishments. He had acquired Emma as an ex-mistress off his young nephew and had trained her to become his skilled diplomatic assistant among the elite of Naples. His relationship with Emma was no longer, if it ever had been, primarily sexual. She was his protégé, and almost a daughter to him.

Secondly, the last thing Sir William would have wanted to happen was to lose such a capable and caring wife in his old age. Emma had had several lovers in her early years and jealous scenes on his part could have precipitated her separation from him. She could always find another man. Sir William handled the ménage with supreme tact and skill; he was, after all, a diplomat!

Thirdly, and perhaps most importantly, Sir William genuinely adored Horatio, and his fatherly love was reciprocated. Horatio was the son he had never had. And what a son! Horatio was, by 1801, perhaps the second most famous man in the world after Napoleon. Sir William, a life-long politician, could see Horatio's historic importance even before his government did so back home. Sir William had been badly neglected by his old friend George III, as had Horatio, and together the Hamiltons and Horatio could form a rebellious team, fêted in their journey across Europe, in defiance of the disapproval back in England. All this suited Emma very well. She just loved the excitement and attention. But she was also a kindly soul and enjoyed looking after both her boys.

Sex may have been an important part of the arrangement as far as Horatio was concerned. Like many sailors on long patrols at sea, he had not had much of it over the years. Even more important for him, however, was Emma's strong, capable and motherly qualities. She was in so many psychological ways the mother he had lost as a child. By courageously beating the enemy and, literally rescuing her from the French, he had indeed won her heart, just as he had always fantasised he would do with his dead mother. The fantasy had now come true.

But Sir William also provided the aristocratic component that Horatio never received from his dull old father in Norfolk. Sir William, a relation of the premier peer of Scotland (the Duke of Hamilton), provided that affirmation of nobility that Horatio had always craved. Horatio had been the son of an aristocratic mother and a middle class father, and so aristocracy, besides flattering his ego, made Horatio feel close to his mother again. Moreover, the broadminded and down to earth attitude towards sex was itself aristocratic – it was that time-honoured and half secret link between British aristocracy and the working class that contemptuously ignored the prudery of the middle-classes. Here Emma, the stunningly lovely ex-working class courtesan, could provide what was wanted.

So the ménage worked for all of them, and often at a deep level. Emma had her men, William had a son and Horatio had both father and mother. All three adored fame and, working together as a team, that fame was multiplied. Furthermore, William enjoyed helping Horatio to catch up on his neglected education – he had educated both of his 'children', Horatio and Emma. Both, no doubt, made clear that their loyalty to the old man was deeper than mere sexual fidelity: he was eventually to die in Emma's arms, as Horatio held his hand. William knew that he could trust Horatio as a loyal friend; deep loyalty was, after all, Horatio's trademark. Horatio's relationship with Sir William, an older man, was also a little like his boyhood relationship with the other William – his older brother; a relationship that was repeated with several of his captains. In these relationships, Horatio played the leader while the older or larger man was the 'back up'. I do not see such relationships as latently homosexual. Their instinctive basis, if there is one, is in the male instinct for military bonding.

As far as fame is concerned, we can see Horatio, in some ways, as being the first modern celebrity. There had never before been such spontaneous crowds of admirers. They followed his coach, cheered his arrival at important functions and sang songs of adulation in the streets. A monarch could attract crowds but not such ecstatic ones. Horatio was applauded in the theatres and other public places he visited. Ballads and eulogies were printed, and prints of his portraits were sold by the hundred.

In the last few idyllic weeks before Trafalgar, now living with Emma and their daughter, Horatio seemed to have changed. His whole career had been a quest for maternal love and approval. That quest was now achieved and he longed for retirement and childlike dependence on Emma. Lord Minto, visiting at this time, concluded, 'he is in many points a really great man, in others a baby'. Friends thought he had put on weight and a nephew described his kindly uncle as now being 'quiet, sedate and unobtrusive'. What a change indeed! Game little Horatio had got his mother back at last.

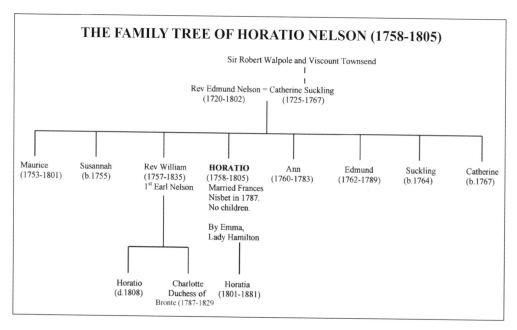

THE FAMILY TREE OF HORATIO NELSON (1758-1805)

Sir Robert Walpole and Viscount Townsend

Rev Edmund Nelson = Catherine Suckling
(1720-1802)　　　　(1725-1767)

Maurice	Susannah	Rev William	**HORATIO**	Ann	Edmund	Suckling	Catherine
(1753-1801)	(b.1755)	(1757-1835) 1st Earl Nelson	(1758-1805) Married Frances Nisbet in 1787. No children.	(1760-1783)	(1762-1789)	(b.1764)	(b.1767)

By Emma,
Lady Hamilton

Horatio	Charlotte	Horatia
(d.1808)	Duchess of Bronte (1787-1829	(1801-1881)

SOURCES:

Coleman, Terry, *Nelson: The Man and the Legend* (Bloomsbury, 2001)

Hession, Michael, Personal Communication, April 2005

Oman, Carola, *Nelson* (Hodder & Stoughton, 1947)

Oxlade, Robert, Significant Dates Replay Nelson's Traumatic Childhood Bereavement, *Trafalgar Chronicle,* 14. 2004

Rodger, N.A.M., Personal communication, December 2007

Ryder, Richard D., The Character of Horatio Nelson: A Note, *Trafalgar Chronicle,* 14. 2004

Ryder, Richard D., Nelson's character: A Further Note, *Trafalgar Chronicle,* 15. 2004

White, Colin *The Nelson Encyclopedia* (Chatham, 2002)

18

THE DUKE OF WELLINGTON (1769-1852)

Warrior

Few men have been more written about than Wellington, yet surprisingly little has been said about his first twenty years – the period in which personalities are mostly formed. In particular, there is a remarkable lack of information in the usual biographies about his relationships in childhood with the other members of his family. We need to find answers for the following questions: what made him become a soldier in the first place, where did his outstanding qualities of prudence, planning and judgement originate, and, in short, what made him one of the greatest generals of all time?

The Wellesleys (or Wesleys) had come from Somerset in England in the twelfth century and settled in Ireland where they became part of the Anglo-Irish Protestant ruling class. Arthur spent his early years in or around Dublin and Trim but always regarded himself as English. In later years (like Napoleon) he showed some sensitivity on the subject of his island origins. Arthur was the fourth of six children of Garret Wesley (Earl of Mornington) and his wife Anne Hill. Garret's father had died leaving the family short of money and when Garret himself died in 1781, Arthur being eleven, the financial problems worsened, forcing the family gradually to sell up their estates in Ireland and to move to London. Arthur's eldest brother Richard (now Lord Mornington) took over the running of the family's affairs as best he could. Unlike his two older brothers, Richard and William, Arthur did not excel at school and, because of the family's financial problems, was removed from Eton to make way for his younger brothers Gerald and Henry. Arthur's only distinction at this period was his ability to play the violin like his father. Maybe this talent was inherited, or perhaps it was an attempt to gain the attention and approval of his parents.

Wellington the Man

Arthur was in many ways a typical middle child. He was the least noticed and least loved of a brood of children who were largely unwanted by their parents. It seems that his parents had been happy enough together, as his father (who was said to 'lack judgement') pursued his career as Professor of Music at Trinity College, Dublin, but they had regarded their offspring rather as an unfortunate by-product. Anne, Lady Mornington, has variously been described as 'stern', 'rather gauche' and of 'commonplace character'. Together with her husband, both parents were dismissed by their eldest child Richard as 'frivolous and careless personages'.

The reaction of the children to their financial difficulties and to the death of their father was quite remarkable. Instead of falling apart, the six siblings clung together under Richard's leadership. Anne quite quickly married rather well and the five boys began their successful and productive lives, Richard eventually becoming Foreign Secretary and a Marquess, William an Earl, Gerald a prebendary, and Henry a Baron. As with many such successful families (the contemporary Austens being a case in point) the boys helped each other with their careers and also, occasionally, competed with one another. All, except Arthur, made good starts at school and Richard then got some promising jobs in government. Arthur looked like he might become the failure in the family. Thanks to Richard, however, Arthur ended up with a commission in the Army – often regarded at that time as the last resort for the lost sheep of upper class families. He was, concluded his mother, 'food for powder and nothing more'.

What do we know about Arthur as a child? Christopher Hibbert describes him as 'a shy, indolent and dreamy little boy who was often to be seen standing silently alone under a walnut tree while the other children played their rowdy games'. (CH4) Andrew Roberts quotes (AR5) Lord Holland's contemporary description of Arthur as 'a good humoured, insignificant youth' and Richard Holmes describes him as a 'shy', 'awkward' and 'idle' boy, while Elizabeth Longford sees Arthur as 'lonely and withdrawn'. (EL16) The solitary and shy boy would mature, however, into a wild and drunken youth before becoming, in his later twenties, the cool and prudent soldier of history.

One story about Arthur is very well known, and that is the one about Kitty Pakenham and Arthur's violin. Early in 1793 Arthur proposed to the pretty Kitty and was refused on her behalf by her brother, the bumptious new Lord

Longford, apparently on the grounds that he was not going to allow his sister to be thrown away to an impecunious and untitled drifter like Arthur. This rebuff must have been made even more painful by the fact that Longford was five years younger than the twenty-four year old Arthur. It may have brought home to him that the elite world at that time was regarding the Wellesleys with growing disdain – as a pack of unruly boys with few jobs, little money and no prospects. Their father had left them with debts and they had been selling their assets in Ireland. They appeared to be on the way down generally. To make matters worse, Arthur's attempts to overcome his adolescent shyness had led to several years of drunkenness, gambling and rowdyism. His grandmother, Lady Dungannon, had been arrested for debt in 1788 and Arthur himself had been fined by the magistrates for fighting a Frenchman in a Dublin pub a few years later. (EL23) While some of the more racy ladies found the witty and spirited young man rather attractive, respectable people were inclined to avoid this dysfunctional young aristocrat.

Arthur's reaction to Longford's rejection of his proposal to marry his sister Kitty was extreme. He went home and burnt his violins. Maybe Longford had said something scathing about the pennilessness of musicians generally, or that Arthur was clearly following in the footsteps of his wastrel father. Anyway, this was undoubtedly a watershed. Defiantly, as Arthur flung himself into military service, he publically vowed that his offer to Kitty was not withdrawn. He wrote to her that 'my mind will still remain the same'. (EL 29) (It would turn out to be a rash promise. On his return from India, twelve years after this rebuff, he married the neurotic Kitty, found her irritating and kept away from her for most of her life while he pursued his political career in London.)

Whether or not his rejection by Longford was the cause or not, this bombshell of a rebuff coincided with other changes in Arthur's life. He began to reign back on his pseudo-extraversion, eased up on the heavy drinking, began to educate himself by reading books on philosophy and economics, started lobbying the authorities for military advancements and commenced his long study of how to become a successful soldier. Certainly, after 1793, Arthur showed a lifelong determination to prove himself. Above all he started to transform himself into the cool, careful, prudent military planner who would one day defeat Napoleon. Why did such qualities appeal to Arthur? I suspect that the answer is that they were the exact opposites of traits displayed by his parents. He was rejecting the parents who had rejected him. They had narcissistically indulged themselves in music and frivolity and the results were financial ruin and the threatened downfall of the family. His parents had been careless, unreliable, ostentatious and emotionally incontinent. He would be the opposite. Just as his parents had ignored detail and planning, so Arthur applied himself to studying all aspects of military finance, administration and logistics. Never would his armies be short of proper clothing, good food, or the best weapons. In India, he studied carefully the battle tactics of Alexander and Hannibal and, as a military commander, deployed an effective mixture of impregnable defence and sudden unorthodox attack; of stubborn resistance and tactical retreat; of deft manoeuvre and the concentrations of power. Above all, he decided that everything had to remain under cool and planned control throughout a campaign. Yet flexibility must be total. His was the ultimately rational approach. Among an officer corps well populated by fops, blockheads, ditherers and drunkards, Arthur Wellesley began to stand out, and by the age of thirty Arthur had developed total confidence in his own judgement.

One aspect of his battle-craft was his unsurpassed understanding of how to use the lie of the land to his own troops' advantage. As he rode or drove around the countryside of India, Belgium or Portugal he would constantly be appraising the landscape as to how it could be used for purposes of defence or attack. He would play a game with his travel companions of guessing what the countryside would look like 'on the other side of the hill', and famously he would often guess correctly. Where did this faculty originate? I believe it, too, may have come from his childhood when as a shy and dreamy school boy at Eton he had played games by himself, jumping over and over a broad black ditch at the bottom of the garden belonging to his boarding house. (EL16). No doubt his childhood fantasies were about using the micro contours of the garden for the purposes of warfare. By the time he actually entered the Army he seemed already to understand intimately even the slightest undulations of the terrain. At Waterloo it may have been the effect of two slight ridges that made the difference between defeat and victory. Arthur had an empathy with the countryside that made him the poet of battlefield tacticians.

So, after 1793, Arthur seems to have rejected his father's fascination with music and to have dedicated himself to a life of solid achievement. He rejected, too, his mother's social affectations and frivolity. All his adult life subsequently he would be drawn only to women of seriousness and intelligence. His wife told the story of how his mother had once forced the youthful Arthur to walk all the way home rather than ride in her carriage after he has refused to divulge to her one of his brother Richard's secrets (probably about a girlfriend). In consequence he felt a lasting and 'painful sense of his mother's tyranny and injustice'. (CH7n). At the end of his life he once said that no woman had ever loved him. He might perhaps have added that no woman had ever loved the solitary musician, the *real* Arthur. Anyway, in the 1790s, the Wellesley brothers proceeded to form an ambitious clique under Richard's leadership. Arthur went through a phase of worshipping Richard, although later on Richard felt jealous of Arthur's success. When they fell out Arthur would use his younger brother Henry as their go-between.

Another formative experience for Arthur was when at sixteen he was sent to a finishing school in Angers in France to learn the military and manly arts. For Arthur the experience was hugely significant because it was here that he first met with powerful paternal approval. It came from the Academy's director Marcel de Pignerole. He was 'the first to detect the signs of brilliance which had been invisible to Arthur's countrymen' (E.L.19). Pignerole described Arthur as a boy 'of great promise'. This made a huge impression on Arthur who suddenly grew taller and handsomer to such a degree that, on his return to England, his mother could hardly recognise him. There is no record of any continuing contact between Arthur and Pignerole but it must have hurt Arthur deeply when, three years later, the French Revolution broke out and the Royalist Pignerole was arrested and, eventually, executed. Pignerole had taught Arthur a love and respect for the Bourbon Kings of France that would stay with him for years. No doubt such attitudes were at the root of Arthur's lifelong respect not only for Royalty but for gentlemanly qualities in general. The only older man ever to show him fatherly approval, Pignerole, had been a gentleman who had been murdered by revolutionaries. Here, also, surely, is the origin of Arthur's permanent fear of the mob, of his determination to keep his own troops under control and prevent them from rape, pillage and murder. Here, too, are the origins of Arthur's contempt for Napoleon who not only allowed his troops to run amok but who, in ungentlemanly fashion, connived at the murder of Royalist prisoners. Arthur would later be called a snob because of his dependence upon a gentlemanly officer corps. But I think this attitude ran deep, and was one of his few irrationalities. He believed that the mob was murderous and cruel because his psychological father – Pignerole – perhaps the only adult ever to have shown him affection and interest as a teenager – had been killed by them.

So, how far have we got with understanding the personality of Arthur, Duke of Wellington? Basically, he was an unwanted and unloved child. He grew up as a loner, shy and sensitive. He thought deeply, played the violin, admired his eldest brother and made friends with the landscape. When he gained some confidence as a teenager he went through a phase of heavy drinking and chasing girls. He was handsome and charming and probably had sufficient money to go to bed with quite a few of them. But when he proposed marriage to Kitty Pakenham he was brashly turned down by her brother. Arthur's family was hard up and in apparent decline, and he had no particular prospects for a career. As we have seen Arthur felt humiliated,burned his violin, took to reading serious books, momentarily became a Member of the Irish Parliament, and then got a commission in the Army. He became determined to prove himself. It seems he felt some shame that his parents and grandparents had frittered away the family fortunes. He had little patience with those who were preoccupied with the inessentials of life. As his experience of warfare grew he had no time for fripperies, for his mother's pettiness or for his wife's fussing over trivia. He dedicated his life to facts and to his duty to serve the state. He kept his emotions brilliantly under control, never panicking in battle but always remaining cool and rational. Yet after a battle and at funerals he was melancholy and would often weep at the loss of friends. Never was there such a soldier who hated war so much. (Perhaps he always maintained his musician's sensitivity). He had good male comrades and adored many women both as companions and as lovers. As a politician he supported some reforms such as Catholic Emancipation and the creation of the Police, but resisted Parliamentary Reform, apparently basing this resistance on his belief that it would open the floodgates of revolution. That the opposite might be true never seemed to impress him. (The loss of de Pignerole had, perhaps, distorted his usually reliable judgement here.) Yet he was always a genuinely kindly and compassionate man, providing accommodation for various orphans and for the bereaved widower of one of his lady friends. Above all he always thought things out for himself and then trusted absolutely in his own judgement. He had, in consequence, little time for the advice of colleagues or for the role of seconds in command. He remained basically a loner, who, as he himself once said, preferred to walk by himself. As a child he had probably been inundated with well-meaning but ill-informed and irrational advice. He wanted no more of it. Once he had established the facts he would make his own decisions based upon common sense.

Wellington is usually seen as a reactionary and as the founder of a long British tradition that continues to this day. He created or recreated the British stereotype of the man of understatement, of clipped speech, stoic endurance, stiff upper lip, down to earth practicality, humility, integrity, fairness and basic kindness. He was also a prudent planner, and a searcher after truth. 'All the business of war' he once said 'and indeed all the business of life is to endeavour to find out what you do not know by what you do; that is what I called "guessing what was at the other side of the hill"'. (EL496)

The Battle of Waterloo, June 15th 1815

Arthur Wellesley, Duke of Wellington, is so different from most of our other cases. He appears thoroughly normal, lacking their quirks and vanities. He was obviously a man of strong intelligence and good judgement and he defeated Napoleon at Waterloo, despite having the lesser army. Why was this? Quite simply because he knew what he was doing and what had to be done. He was the expert. He galloped from crisis to crisis on the battlefield giving timely, clear and successful orders. He appeared calm and purposeful throughout the battle. It was a magnificent display of man-management and leadership. Today, Arthur could be a successful Chief Executive. The only plausible reason for Napoleon being out-generalled on that day was that he was not very well, although it has often been suggested that his greatest mistake was to underestimate Wellington, despite warnings from several of his generals who had already been defeated by him. But is this true?

On June 18th 1815 Wellington was at the top of his game. He had to be. He knew what was at stake – the future of Europe and the world. His army, however, was a rapidly cobbled together collection of soldiers of six or seven different nationalities, some with little training or frontline experience. There were language difficulties and differences in weaponry and traditions. The French Army totalled some 73 thousand men and Wellington's combined forces were 69 thousand, of which only 28 per cent were British. (Both sides had further troops separated from their main forces who did not fight at Waterloo that day.) Napoleon's artillery consisted of 246 guns to Wellington's meagre 156. The French opened fire at around 11.30am and launched repeated cavalry and infantry attacks throughout the day. All failed to break through Wellington's carefully prepared defensive positions.

Around seven o'clock in the evening, just as Blücher's Prussian soldiers joined the fray in force on Wellington's extreme left flank, Napoleon launched his final desperate assault on Wellington's centre, using his elite Imperial Guard. These veterans were then deceived and decimated by Wellington's forces hidden behind the central ridge and, (allegedly) for the first time ever in their history, were forced to retreat. This French retreat turned into a rout. What might have been merely another battle won by Wellington became, thanks to the timely arrival of the Prussian Army, a total victory for the allies and to the capture of Napoleon himself a few days later.

Wellington had shown his skill as the master of defensive warfare. He had applied two key principles. The first was that a well-positioned defensive force can withstand attack from far stronger forces. Second, that fire from an extended line across the enemy's front can destroy attacks by massed columns, even when these are composed of some of the best troops in the world.

In retrospect, we can see that over the previous 30 years Wellington had had the perfect training for such a day:

• In 1786 he had attended the French Military college at Angers where he learned about traditional French military tactics, and to speak the language.

- In 1794 he had his first experience of war in Flanders under the incompetent command of the Duke of York. He saw for himself the full range of mistakes that can be made by military commanders, and their consequences. "At least I learned what not to do," he said later.

- In 1797, in India, he was rapidly promoted by his older brother Richard (who was Governor General) and learned a) how to train and cooperate with troops of other cultural backgrounds and b) how to win battles against far larger opposing forces, some of them French trained. He was given total command young enough to learn and to apply his judgement.

- From 1808 to 1812 he was in command in the Iberian Peninsula where these skills were perfected, when a maximum of 70,000 British troops repeatedly defeated a French Army of over 300,000, under Napoleon's best generals, although never under Napoleon himself. Arthur trained local Portuguese troops and integrated them into the regimental lines fighting shoulder to shoulder with British soldiers.

By June 1815 Arthur was said to have been in command at some 23 major battles and to have lost none of them. His opponent, Napoleon, had survived some 70 battles but had lost ten of these. Both men were brilliant in attack but Wellington was also a winning defender. Neither had met in battle previously. Arthur's cool rationality had led him to reject the irrational military prejudices, common at the time, against tactical retreats and skilful defensive warfare. Napoleon, however, was a natural attacker who failed to understand Wellington's more subtle genius. Arthur was seeking not glory but results. By midnight on June 18th 1815 he had achieved both.

Wellington's carefulness meant that he made very few mistakes, whereas Napoleon's impatience created errors. At Waterloo Napoleon made at least three big mistakes while Wellington made none. Napoleon's mistakes were as follows:

- He failed to recall Marshall Grouchy and his 33,000 men whom he had despatched to search for and impede the approaching Prussian Army under Marshall Blücher.

- He attacked Wellington head on in his carefully prepared defensive positions instead of attacking from the South West, on Wellington's right flank. (Wellington had stationed 15,000 men here to foil such an attack. They, too, like Grouchy's men, never fired a shot at Waterloo).

• He should have used his artillery far more in attacking Wellington's infantry squares.

Waterloo was a battle that Napoleon should have won, but he lost it. This was not simply a victory of Northern efficiency over Southern flair, it was due to Wellington's carefully prepared defensive plans. Unlike Napoleon he understood that defensive battles, properly conducted, were not merely preludes to defeat but means to victory. Wellington knew that lesser armies in defence could actually defeat bigger and better armies attacking them even where there was a ratio of two to one. Wellington succeeded in doing this for some seven reasons:

• He had reconnoitred the lie of the land around Waterloo a year in advance, so he knew what to expect and utilise. He had chosen this location for the battle.

• The site allowed Wellington to hide several thousand of his soldiers behind its central ridge where the French could not see them and where they were partly protected from French artillery.

• He forced Napoleon to fight on an unusually narrow front (only 3 miles wide – about half the average width of a front for this type of battle) bounded by roads, hamlets and woods on either side. This caused the French formations to become congested and unable to take advantage of their greater size and efficiency.

• The site contained formidable stumbling blocks hampering Napoleon's advance, in the form of two fortifiable farm houses just ahead of Wellington's main lines, which were held by Wellington's troops.

• The site permitted Wellington to fire upon advancing French columns from a long thin line of infantry at right-angles to the attackers, thus maximising his fire-power.

• When charged five times by massed French cavalry Wellington's infantry formed some twenty squares which effectively held off these attacks. Wellington had forced the French repeatedly and exhaustingly, to attack up hill.

• Wellington believed that Blücher's Prussian Army would arrive before nightfall to join in the battle against Napoleon.

In the event, all these factors worked well for Wellington. He ensured they did so by galloping incessantly all over the battlefield, showing calmness and confidence and raising morale. The execution of all these tactics was almost perfect: his troops hidden behind the ridge survived Napoleon's heavy artillery bombardments, the narrow front reduced the manoeuvrability of Napoleon's forces, the two fortified farm houses held out nearly all day, drawing in thousands of French troops and blocking French advances, none of the squares were broken, and the British line when it rose up unexpectedly from behind the ridge, firing repeated volleys into the French infantry, caused even Napoleon's most elite troops to turn and flee. That was shortly after 7.00pm.

Both sides had been affected by the heavy rains which preceded the battle. Napoleon found he could not effectively manoeuvre in the mud and so postponed his attack for some three hours, opening fire at about 11.30am. This allowed the Prussians to draw closer to the battlefield from their base 14 miles away, but they, too, found the mud a disadvantage and could not join the battle until around 5.00pm (according to Napoleon). Struggling through the muddy lanes they arrived piecemeal. Such battles usually lasted about six hours but it was not until after 7.00pm that Wellington ordered his general advance after the retreating French forces.

After the battle Napoleon blamed everyone and everything but himself for his total defeat. He did not mention his illness and hardly accorded any significance at all to the Prussians. But why was he on such bad form that day? Although he famously appeared to be dismissive of Wellington's extraordinary abilities, describing him contemptuously as 'a sepoy general', I believe he actually feared Wellington far more than has been realised. His apparent contempt was actually false bravado. *Secretly, he had become convinced that Wellington would beat him.* He was therefore in an anxiety state before the battle and it was this that caused his stomach pains, torpor, insomnia and other symptoms. He appeared irritable and untypically indecisive. He yelled at some of his generals. He paced up and down but hardly rode out into the battle itself. He gave orders that lacked clarity and devolved too much responsibility onto Marshall Ney, not one of his cleverest generals, almost as if providing himself with a scapegoat in advance. Another scapegoat became Marshall Grouchy – he was blamed for not returning to help Napoleon, yet all he had done was follow Napoleon's orders to the letter in searching for the Prussians.

Final Thoughts

Wellington, with his reduced need for sleep, his amazing energy on the battlefield, his high-speed speech, shows some of the familiar features of controlled raised mood. He spoke, rode and walked fast. A contemporary described him as being "lively, buoyant and quick tempered" (DNB1114), although the temper was usually under control. (One could say that whereas bad temper is often a sign of depressed mood, quick temper is frequently an indicator of raised mood.) Arthur controlled his feelings extraordinarily well, but inside he was a nuclear reactor. Only those who were particularly close to him, such as Harriet Arbuthnot, ever saw his explosions of delayed rage that he used to let out in the privacy of his apartments.

Arthur never should have married poor depressed Fanny on his return from India. He did so in order to reverse the rebuff he had received from her family years before, and it demonstrates how important this was for his whole career. While they had been apart she had led a life of utter boredom and triviality while Arthur had been fighting a dozen horrific battles. He had changed. Their life experiences had been entirely different. Now he became irritated by her incompetence and apparent stupidity. After seeing his comrades being disembowelled or having their heads shot off in battle, it probably annoyed Arthur that Fanny could become so upset by apparently minor difficulties regarding her household affairs. As with Agatha Christie and Daphne du Maurier more than a century later, Fanny could not fully comprehend what her husband had experienced in war. For years Arthur and Fanny could not get along. Besides, Fanny's seeming obsession with trivia no doubt reminded Arthur of his mother. He loved women but, for him, they had to be brisk, efficient and intelligent women who were able to understand what was really (in his view) important: war and peace; law and order; life and death.

Arthur admired Napoleon as a soldier but not as a character, rather as he admired his older brother Richard as a fixer but not as a pillar of rectitude. Between both there was an element of sibling rivalry and transference on Arthur's part. He never confused Napoleon entirely with his older brother, but it is surely not a coincidence that, after Waterloo, Arthur slept with at least two of Napoleon's old mistresses. For Arthur the contest had contained this personal element of rivalry.

We still know very little about Wellington's relationship with his father, but he seems to have grown to dislike his mother. She had constantly put him down. The day he first put on his red coat in 1787 his mother wrote "Anyone can see he has not the cut of a soldier". (EL (ii)184). Arthur rejected entirely what he saw as his mother's silly and petty advice, just as he would later reject his wife's "emotionalism". (EL(ii)106). As a reaction he became the exact opposite: he became pragmatic, sagacious, succinct, cool, precise and level-headed. He wanted no more advice from anyone, cultivated complete confidence in his own judgement, became secretive about his plans and decisions, and entirely self-reliant. Yet he continued to love women who showed these opposite qualities, particularly if they were intelligent, beautiful and much younger. They needed, however, to be serious and efficient in providing him either with friendship (such as Harriet Arbuthnot, Angela Burdett-Coutts, or the Hatton girls) or with sex (for example, Harriette Wilson, Charlotte Greville and the three ladies in Paris.) Ultimately he wanted to serve the State (individual monarchs could be tiresome, too, he discovered) in order to preserve law, order and peace. He had seen too much of war: After Waterloo he wrote to Lady Shelley:

> *It's bad thing to be always fighting. While in the thick of it, I am much too occupied to feel anything; but it is wretched just after. It is quite impossible to think of glory. Both mind and feelings are exhausted. I am wretched even at the moment of victory, and I always say that, next to a battle lost, the greatest misery is a battle gained. Not only do you lose those dear friends with whom you have been living, but you are forced to leave the wounded behind you…I never wish for anymore fighting.* (R.H. p254)

So perhaps Arthur's mother was right after all when she had said he lacked the typical military style. Beneath the dashing and sometimes clipped exterior Arthur had somehow remained the boy under the walnut tree – the loner, the introvert, the poet, the musician. In command he hardly ever wore a uniform but simply white breeches, boots, cocked hat and a civilian blue coat. Most of his closest friends were women. He loved art and countryside, as well as the conviviality of a good dinner party where, so Sir Walter Scott recorded, his conversation was remarkable for 'the sweetness and abandon with which it flowed' (EL 391). This is perhaps why he excelled: he had mastered the art of war as if he was not quite part of it, but an onlooker who could, like an artist, remain somewhat aloof, always seeing, and helping to create, the larger picture.

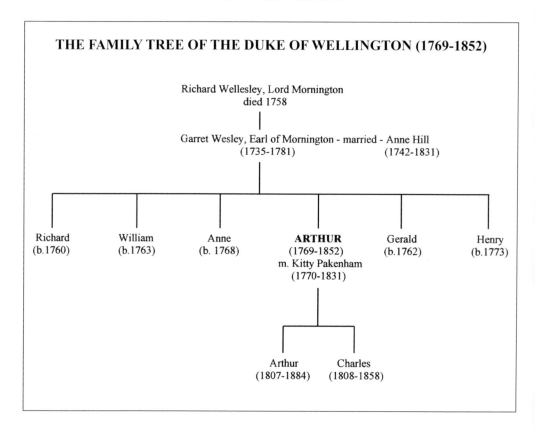

THE FAMILY TREE OF THE DUKE OF WELLINGTON (1769-1852)

Richard Wellesley, Lord Mornington
died 1758

Garret Wesley, Earl of Mornington - married - Anne Hill
(1735-1781)   (1742-1831)

Richard   William   Anne   **ARTHUR**   Gerald   Henry
(b.1760)   (b.1763)   (b. 1768)   (1769-1852)   (b.1762)   (b.1773)
                                      m. Kitty Pakenham
                                      (1770-1831)

Arthur   Charles
(1807-1884)   (1808-1858)

SOURCES

Christopher Hibbert: *Wellington: a Personal History*, Harper Collins, 1997

Richard Holmes: *Wellington: the Iron Duke*, Harper Collins, 2003

Elizabeth Longford: *Wellington: the Years of the Sword* and *Wellington: Pillar of State*, Weidenfeld & Nicholson, 1972

Andrew Roberts: *Napoleon and Wellington*, Weidenfeld & Nicholson, 2001

Peter Snow: *To War with Wellington*, John Murray, 2010.

CONCLUSIONS

First, let us consider what new insights we have gained in individual cases. Later, I will conclude by looking at some more general findings. If we start by looking at the five writers – Thomas Hardy, Jane Austen, Charles Dickens, Daphne du Maurier and Agatha Christie, I would say that with the two men some startling new discoveries have been made, or at least suggested. As a scientist I do not, of course, insist upon the absolute truth of any of my conclusions, but only put them forward as hypotheses, if possible to be tested over time.

With Thomas Hardy I have suggested that much of the melancholic content of his novels (but not his poetry) comes *not* from his own experiences at all but from those of his mother and his grandmothers. He is merely the mouthpiece for *their* tragedies. Furthermore, the very act of becoming an author and a celebrity was the 'acting out' of his mother's desire to re-climb the social ladder down which, so she felt, her own mother and she herself had fallen, chiefly through out-of-wedlock pregnancies. Thomas climbed back up the ladder on his mother's behalf. He was her proxy and her champion.

With Charles Dickens, the suggested revelation is even more shattering although far less certain. It seems possible to me that Charles' main motive in life was the same as Jimmy Saville's – the worship of teenage female bodies. His addiction to pretty young women went, I suspect, far further than his solitary, and rather recently discovered, young mistress, Nelly Ternan. Once he had secured his own financial position, his great acting and writing talents were, so I propose, chiefly deployed as a means to these erotic ends.

As regards Agatha Christie, Daphne du Maurier and Jane Austen, I have discovered no great psychological sensations. I have merely suggested that for Agatha the great medium in her human relationships was 'puzzle', and that this also became the chief content of her books. I believe that her muse was her sparkling sister Punkie. For Jane Austen, the main source of her ordinary satisfactions in life was her wonderful family – she wrote initially for them and, at the very end of her life, established herself in her own right as a novelist. For Jane, the subjects of her novels were the people outside her family. These, almost by definition, she often found to be somewhat inferior and, not a little funny. Daphne du Maurier, as is well known, lived in a remarkable world of fantasy. Like one other subject in this book I believe she is unusual in having had strong incestuous feelings for her parent of the opposite sex.

I have noted, in passing, that Agatha may have lost her first husband partly because she never seemed to appreciate the horrors of his wartime experiences.

She was not alone in this because her contemporary, Daphne du Maurier, similarly failed to understand or sympathise with her husband's Post Traumatic Stress Disorder. Perhaps this was also true of many pampered wives of the 1920s (and less so in the 1940s) who simply had no idea what their spouses had endured in the World Wars.

One or two other interesting features have emerged from our study of the five writers. First, three of them had at least one bookish parent who may also have been a frustrated writer. Hardy's mother and both of Christie's parents are examples and, in Jane Austen's case, it was not only her parents but at least two of her brothers who also wrote. With Daphne it was her grandfather, as well as her sister. This suggests the very common dynamic, already alluded to, in which the subject is driven by their, usually unconscious, desire to maintain or fulfil a thwarted parental or family ambition. We can see similar situations, with political ambitions, affecting King Alfred and Margaret Thatcher. Children try to complete their parents' foiled ambitions.

An unexpected common feature among the writers is that four out of five of them had felt, as children, that their social standing had been undermined or was threatened. Social class played a hugely important motivating role in the nineteenth century and was obviously powerful for Dickens and Hardy whose parents considered they were grander than their occupations and affluence suggested. In Austen's case, the high social class of her family, despite its lack of wealth, was of great importance to all of them. Although to a lesser extent, class was also of importance to Agatha Christie, where her foreign forebears further contributed, in a snobbish culture, to her feelings of insecurity. For Daphne too the family's social position was important. So all the writers were writing not merely to make money, but also to bolster their social standings. Not only most of the writers but several of our other celebrities too, seem to be inspired by far younger members of the opposite sex. So Dickens, Hardy, Christie, Wagner, Puccini and Hitler all show this marked tendency to be attracted to lovers (and sometimes spouses) who were ten, twenty or more years their junior. Wellington, too, was like this.

With the scientists, Newton, Einstein and Turing, I make less effort at profound analysis. But what I discover is that these three great intellectual adventurers showed one remarkable childhood dynamic in common: all three had been physically separated from their caring parents, abandoned geographically, and left to their own devices and to the protection of outsiders. In consequence, all three boys compensated for their loneliness by becoming deep thinkers. Far more than most children, they had developed their own comforting worlds of thought, undistracted by other people. They worked best on their own. *Their ideas had become their companions.* (Daphne du Maurier removed herself from her parents and similarly lived in her world of fantasy.) Becoming a searcher after truth, as these three boys were, is often a reaction to childhood confusion. Sigmund Freud is another example. The child attempts to make sense of the neurotic confusions and anxieties caused by puzzling family relationships, parental absences or ambivalences. This effort to understand then becomes a general life-strategy which they apply to many other issues in their lives. Surprisingly, perhaps, Wellington too was a lifelong searcher after truth.

As regards the composers, Richard Wagner, Giuseppe Verdi and Giacomo Puccini, I cannot, of course, throw light upon the mysterious issues of musical ability and inspiration, which are, surely, largely genetically determined. All three men came from musical or theatrical family subcultures (although less so in Verdi's case) and all three were narcissists. In other respects they were hugely different. I found Wagner to be a far more sympathetic person than I had expected, and Verdi to be far more grumpy. There is still a lack of information about the early life of Verdi which has made my job, in his case, extremely difficult. Whereas Verdi's opera music was driven by character studies, dramatic conflicts and emotion, and Puccini's chiefly by the love of love, Richard Wagner seems to have been motivated, musically, by ideas. Many philosophers influenced Wagner's *Ring* – Feuerbach, Schopenhauer and Nietzsche, for example – yet no coherent philosophy emerges from Richard Wagner's music. He was not seeking to produce a philosophical conclusion, but was using ideas as a framework around which he built his music. Unlike Puccini, or even Verdi, Wagner produced direct musical responses to ideas. (The use of *leitmotif* is a case in point.) Just as Wagner was synaesthetic, being able to link colours, textures and smells to ideas, so he could express ideas directly as music. So the hugely complicated philosophical structure of the *Ring* is merely the armature upon which Richard built his sound. The philosophical core of the *Ring*, if there is one, is about the death of religion and the emergence of a new order where "love and compassion are prized more than power and material possessions" (B.M. 98).

I have chosen an odd lot of politicians. Margaret Thatcher I found to be rather a dull subject and strangely overrated. She was certainly very lucky in her career. One could include King Alfred as a politician, and his glorious achievements reflect the importance of his closeness to his father, who gave him an extraordinary education and a sense of mission. Once again, Alfred illustrates the common dynamic among great achievers of trying to complete a parent's frustrated ambition. He succeeded. The two Germans, Kaiser Wilhelm II and Adolf Hitler, arguably two of the principal creators of the two World Wars of the twentieth century, both produce very rich and interesting psychological findings. Wilhelm is probably, in psychodynamic terms, the clearest case of all, and demonstrates all too obviously the simple psychological dynamics that helped to explain his behaviour – his damaged arm and his English mother's consequent rejection of him. Adolf is far more complex, but like many of us, and especially those of us with an artistic and fantasising turn of mind, like Daphne du Maurier, his whole life was irrationally affected by fantasy. In his case, the central theme was his fantasised struggle with his hated father in defence of his blue-eyed ('Aryan') mother. I am strongly of the opinion that this irrational, and largely unconscious, struggle was actually the essence of the Second World War. In both cases the world wars were unnecessary. So why did they happen? Wilhelm's and Adolf's idiosyncratic fantasies fill some of the explanatory gaps. Although psychodynamics provide a good explanation for Wilhelm's tiresome behaviour, he is also the only one of our subjects where brain damage (and ADHD) may also have played a part.

That an historic figure should be so motivated – by a fantasy that is both absurd and unconscious – is not unique. Horatio Nelson is the other case I have discovered. His whole life was governed by his unconscious and irrational quest to rediscover the love of his long dead mother. He succeeded in this quest by finding a mother–substitute and preventing Napoleon from invading England. My studies of Hitler, Nelson and the Kaiser leave little doubt in my mind that the psychology of famous people can considerably affect the course of history. Flippantly I might suggest that both unnecessary World Wars occurred only because of the odd personalities of just two men.

The aetiology of events is highly complex, and small incidents can sometimes trigger bigger ones in a cascade of happenings. Economic, political and cultural factors can all play a part but psychological issues, too, can sometimes provide key links in the causal chain. Alfred's enlightened personality, for example, clearly helped to cause some events, just as the accidents of Kaiser Wilhelm's birth turned him into a competitive tension builder who was essentially too weak to stop his own military machine. Psychology is not everything in history but it is, certainly, something. With Nelson and Hitler, indeed, their psychologies may account for most of what they are remembered for, including the protection of England from Napoleonic invasion and the causing of the unnecessary Second World War.

Sometimes things happen smoothly – gradual increases in x lead to gradual changes in y. But, at other times, events occur in sudden jerks, like earthquakes. The butterfly flaps her wings and catastrophes happen. Some of these little events that tip the balance are psychological in character. They clog the smooth running of the great impersonal causal processes, altering their outcomes. On other occasions the psychologies act as a background noise, an ambience, a context in which all other events are placed. Again, the character and the tone of all that happens can be affected in this way. So, psychology can fill in the gaps between the mighty forces of history, either like spanners in the works or as a background hum, either way affecting history's conclusions.

Queen Victoria and her supposed values dominated British culture for well over a hundred years, influencing all of us. Yet I have discovered that she was petulant rather than formidable and sulky rather than dignified. She was also very keen on sex! I also raise some questions about the role of her mother's friend, Sir John Conroy – and have suggested a completely alternative view to that adopted by most historians, seeing Conroy as an island of sanity in a sea of eccentricity and intrigue.

One of the advantages of Family Therapy with teenage patients has been that the beliefs held by family members about other members can be assessed by independent observers (such as psychiatrists and psychologists). I have noticed many families where family members view each other in distorted ways. They hold fixed ideas about each other that are not confirmed by the independent observers. When asked to support their distorted perceptions, individuals fail to produce realistic evidence. Yet it is difficult to change these beliefs. There is no question of schizophrenia in such cases but the distorted beliefs almost have the strength of delusions. I have called such belief systems Fixed Familial Misperceptions (FFMs). They are a form of *over-valued ideas*. Typically, FFMs are parents' opinions of their children and childrens' opinions of their parents. Common instances are of children accusing their parents of being oppressive autocrats, right-wing racists or cruel sadists, even when the parents are clearly none of these things. Just as common are FFMs where parents hold distorted views of their children, seeing them either as exaggeratedly brilliant or, more often, as wicked, devious or delinquent. If ever there was a clear historic example of an FFM parent then it is Queen Victoria. Seemingly almost at random, based sometimes merely upon the child's physical appearance, she would allocate her offspring to categories such as "dear, sweet child" or "vulgar and wicked", and would then stick with this simplistic and damaging opinion for years. Interestingly, such FFMs are common in some families and rare in others. Indeed, in some cases the same adult who holds distorted views of their child may also have had distorted views of their parents. Again, Victoria is a case in point. Not only did she cling to ridiculous and inaccurate opinions of her children but, as a young person herself, she seems to have been FFM about her mother (who really was not as awful as she made out), John Conroy and even Prince Albert (who was not quite as wonderful). Victoria just did not understand people at all well. We do not know why this was. She would also, so it seems, *transfer* her perceptions and feelings for one person onto others. This is probably why, for example, she had such a dim view of Prime Minister William Gladstone, seeing him as hectoring, radical and coercive, just as she had perceived John Conroy years earlier. Hardly surprisingly, Gladstone saw the Queen's animosity towards him as "something of a mystery, which I have not been able to fathom, and probably never shall". (ANW 511). I am not saying, of course, that such FFMs have no psychological significance for the individual who has them. Far from it. The further from the truth they are the more they indicate the holder's *need*. Victoria, for example, clearly needed to see her children as starkly good or bad, and her ministers as respectful or otherwise.

The Freuds seem to have been rather an FFM family and so were the Wellesleys. In both cases their most illustrious members (Sigmund and Arthur) reacted against such distorted thinking by searching after the '*truth*'. FFM is rather akin to the common adolescent phenomenon of finding parents intensely embarrassing. Mildly unconventional or 'uncool' behaviour on behalf of the parent can be deeply irritating to a teenager who is trying to be 'cool'. This is surely because the teenager closely identifies with the parent and so feels any uncoolness on the parent's part also brands themselves. (The desire to be cool is an almost universal adolescent trait to find acceptance among the esteemed peer group.) Charles Dickens found his parents rather embarrassing: his father flamboyant and his mother childish. Both Sigmund Freud and Arthur Wellesley found their fathers' behaviour improvident and irritating.

Finally, I analyse Sigmund Freud himself, and I gain some respect for his honesty and determination, as well as for his brilliance. I discover that his ideas came largely from his penetrating introspection into his own personality and not so much from his later studies of individual cases. What I had not previously realised is the importance of Freud's love of heroes, promoted by his rejection of his father as a role-model (largely for Oedipal reasons). Freud emulated throughout his life the rebel defiance of his three main childhood idols (two of whom were British) – namely, Cromwell, Darwin and Hannibal. He saw his life as a quest to defeat the status quo, just as they did. Freud is, of course, one of the many sources I have used to analyse not only Freud himself but all the other subjects in this book. Above all, my approach is based upon the belief that childhood and adolescent experiences shape the adult. I have been involved with several hundred cases professionally where I could see that this was the case. Of course, later experiences also affect the individual's behaviour, but these usually trigger what is already there. Admittedly, without particular political, environmental or other circumstances, things naturally would not have happened quite as they did. Nelson, for example, would not have been heard of today if there had been no Napoleonic wars. (Nor would Wellington.) But he survived all the fearful risks he took as a young man and, through a series of victories at sea, forced Napoleon to abandon his plans to invade England. Would any other British admiral have done the same? Others were equally good tacticians but did they inspire their men as Nelson did? Did they show that extraordinary motivation that drove Nelson to win the battle of Copenhagen rather than follow orders to retreat? Were they driven by the same determination utterly to destroy the enemy's ships that Nelson showed at the Nile? Would they have taken the tactical risks that Nelson took at the Battle of Cape St. Vincent and, finally, at Trafalgar? In every case the answer is probably a negative. In consequence, the morale of the French navy would not have been so utterly crushed as it was by Nelson. All these achievements were effects not of economics nor of training nor accident, but of the strange *psychology* of Horatio Nelson. What I am saying is that the psychology of the main players is a necessary key to understanding fully the history of important events.

Many, of course, sought fame and this drove them to contribute to the great happenings of their time. The natural search for fame which is, perhaps, in all of us, can become enflamed either by high parental expectations (as in the case of Freud, Dickens, Puccini, and Hitler, for example), or as a reaction against parental apathy (as in Churchill's, Wagner's and Wellington's cases), or as a combination of these two pressures. (Nelson, as it were, constantly had to show off and demonstrate how brave he was in order to hold the attention of his fantasised mother). This yearning for fame is very much a feature of today's world. Fame is a luxury that comes after life's basic requirements – food, shelter and security – are satisfied.

In psychotherapy the therapist has to pull together many events and memories in order to help the patient to see the connections. Sometimes the therapist will be cautiously jumping ahead of the firm evidence and speculating about what *might* have been. In this way, by using what is sometimes called her intuition, a good therapist can 'strike gold' and open up whole new avenues of understanding. Such interpretations should never be dogmatic nor directive, however, but only tentative. If the patient does not react with genuine recognition that a truth has been discovered then the therapist should drop the interpretation and allow the process of discovery to find other ways forward.

The psychobiographer, like the expert psychotherapist, sometimes has to lead. She is not waiting for all the evidence to come together into a conclusive cast-iron case before making every tentative interpretation. She is using her past experience. This is why writing psychobiography can be so difficult. What may be good insights can appear to outsiders to be without sufficient evidence and, of course, without a living patient there is no one to provide convincing confirmation.

Nevertheless, I think a psychobiographer who is experienced in psychotherapy should still be allowed to speculate. Hard evidence may be discovered at a later date, unread letters may be found, or biographies published in the future that cast new light. The experienced psychotherapist is, after all, drawing upon the dynamics she has found to operate in many other cases. Her apparently unsubstantiated hunches depend on much previous evidence and can still prove to be right. I have worked with many psychotherapists and this is often what distinguishes the talented therapist from the rest. Psychobiography, like psychotherapy, is an art rather than a science. Nevertheless it should be scientifically informed and should proceed by trying to disprove hypotheses in the scientific manner.

Selection is crucial. From hundreds of thousands of words of biography in each case, the psychobiographer, using her experience, must be able to select and condense into a few hundred words, what is psychologically important. She must give her reasons for her interpretations, but all remain speculative; none is certain.

I have several times mentioned the theories of Alfred Adler in which he postulates that attempts to compensate for handicaps may drive people on to achievement. Kaiser Bill's handicapped arm is the clearest example, but there is the general finding that many statesmen and dictators are men who are of smaller than average stature: Hitler was five foot eight inches tall, Churchill, Napoleon and Mussolini about five foot six inches, and Stalin only five foot four. In the lives of nearly all our celebrities we find some sort of childhood disadvantage which drives them on. Often these disadvantages are psychological but sometimes they are physical – not only a lack of stature in the men, but a self-perceived lack of beauty in the women – perhaps both Austen and Christie felt this. Sex of course is always important although the only generalisation one can make about sex is that, in general, few such generalisations are reliable.

Several of my subjects in this book were, indeed, superstar celebrities, and not least because their wounded childhoods had inflated their natural desire for fame into an obsession. Unlike Horatio Nelson and Charles Dickens, Adolf Hitler had always been assured of his mother's affection, and it was the outcome of the struggle with his *father* that was the uncertainty - thus the achieving and wielding of power was for him the overriding objective. For Adolf, power mattered more than fame.

Psychodynamics

So I go along in general with Adler's proposal that one of our chief motivations is a search for our own significance. This can take the form of a compensatory search for power (as with Hitler and Victoria), fame (as with most sports people and actors, as well as Wagner and Dickens), wealth (most self-made men and women), or fame through wisdom (Freud). For most people, more simply, we are driven by the search for happiness – being loved and loving. Freud himself said that happiness was about being able to love and to work. Yet we all like to feel that we have also contributed something to the world, and we can see most of our subjects in this book as massively ambitious, driving themselves on to *achieve*. Perhaps our most ambitious cases are Dickens, Wagner, Churchill, Thatcher, Nelson, Hitler and Freud.

Descriptions of historic figures are relatively easy but their *explanation* is much harder. I have tried to dig beneath the surfaces of my subjects in order to find out 'what really made them tick'. As I have said, it is usually their childhood experiences that are relevant, and we can see this most clearly where patterns of behaviour established in early life are repeatedly played back in later years, sometimes quite inappropriately. Hitler, for example, tended to see his generals as embodiments of his father. In consequence he mistrusted them, disliked them and over-ruled them – often with disastrous results for Germany. Freud himself showed such 'transference' when he repeatedly transferred his negative and competitive childhood feelings for his nephew John onto his peers such as Wilhelm Fliess and Josef Breuer, falling out with them quite unnecessarily.

We all carry the baggage of our childhood pasts with us, transferring to the people we meet in the here and now the feelings and expectations that we once had for the members of our families. Nowhere do we see the problems caused by such ill-fitting *transferences* more clearly than in marriage, where individuals transfer to their partners the feelings they once had for their parents and siblings. This causes endless trouble. With our celebrities, such transference helps to explain some of the behaviour of Hitler (for example, his quite different attitudes towards men and women), Puccini (his attachment to an unsuitable wife because she reminded him of his mother), Freud (his antagonisms towards his male colleagues) and Victoria (her constant repetition of her struggle with her mother and Conroy).

Let us look in more detail at the ways in which early relationships can affect the promotion of personality and behaviour later in life. There are the following outstanding factors:

The mother, by her presence or absence, is often the most powerful influencer. The desire to attract her love, the experience of Oedipal guilt, or the subject's anger at her lack of love, attention or approval, are the most usual effects. The subject can sometimes show some or all of these feelings simultaneously.

In our group of high achievers, it is the men more than the women who are obviously influenced by their mothers: Hardy, Puccini, Hitler, Freud and Nelson, had broadly positive relationships with their mothers, and one of the central motivations in their lives was to do what they imagined that their mothers wanted them to do or, at least, what would please their mothers and secure their love. Several of the men were, however, mostly angry with their mothers - Newton, Wellington, Wagner, Dickens, Wilhelm and, probably, Verdi also. Usually they were chronically angry because of their mothers' perceived rejection or lack of interest in them. Several lost their mothers when they were children (Newton, Einstein, Turing, Hitler (aged 18), Alfred and Nelson), either through death or geographical separation.

Mothers can, of course, do far more than love or withhold love, as we have seen in Victoria's case where her mother's possessive fussing made an already headstrong child even more cross and obstinate. Spoiling, in one way or another, can have just as big an effect as rejection. Churchill's relationship with his mother was most unusual, and the psychological puzzle it creates would be solved if it turned out that Jennie was indeed not his mother.

Fathers are sometimes even more important for daughters than for sons. Jane Austen, Daphne du Maurier, Agatha Christie and Margaret Thatcher were all strongly influenced by their fathers. The girls had happy times with their fathers and wanted to do what would please them. The absence of a father was very important for Victoria and many of her relationships reflected her yearning for a father figure. Newton and Puccini, too, had lost their fathers in infancy. Alfred, who lost his mother when a child, seems to have formed an unusually close relationship with his father and to have devoted his later life to fulfilling his father's thwarted vision of creating a secure and civilised Wessex. Churchill was driven throughout his life to prove that his father's low opinion of him was mistaken. Perhaps the most powerful paternal influence among our subjects, was that of Hitler's father whose ferocious bullying turned Hitler into the vengeful and belligerent man he was. The Second World War can probably be attributed to the violence and abuse of one man – Adolf Hitler's ogre of a father.

Usually, fathers also provide the main restraints and structures for a child. Where there is no father (or surrogate) then a child can grow up lazy, headstrong or wayward; just as the young Puccini and Victoria did.

Other childhood companions, whether blood relatives or not, can also be powerful influencers. Hardy's grandmothers, Austen's siblings, Puccini's and Christie's sisters, Wellington's brothers, Freud's nephew, Nelson's brother, Churchill's nanny, and Victoria's nursery carers, as well as her mother's friend John Conroy, all played their parts.

Siblings may become rivals, or warm friends and allies (e.g. with Austen and Puccini), although it is remarkable that, among our group, there is an absence of serious sibling rivalry. Daphne du Maurier is the only real exception. Out of fifteen men, ten were eldest sons and only the two warriors, Nelson and Wellington, were caught in the middle of a large family struggling to stand out from the others in order, in Nelson's case at least, to attract his mother's attention. Wilhelm, however, competed vigorously with his English cousins. Sometimes older sisters or brothers act as role-models (as in Agatha Christies' case) and parents, for better or worse, can do this too (Thatcher's, Churchill's and Alfred's fathers are examples). Human beings can also react against the example of others by doing the exact opposite. Wellington, I think, did this by rejecting his parents' frivolities and becoming intensely rational and pragmatic.

Whether through love or rejection, through emulation or rebellion, or by encouragement or restraint, those in a child's immediate environment are of great importance in influencing the later adult. As we have seen, the child adopts attitudes, values and habits of responding that continue into later life, and their perceptions of family members will often be transferred repeatedly to outsiders with whom they interact in later years. Children either go along with, and unconsciously copy, the behaviour of powerful people in their early lives, or they rebel against them and do the opposite. Sometimes, of course, they can do both, and such ambivalence can make the origins of human behaviour appear to be complex.

From the start, we should have remembered the famous quotation from Shakespeare's *Twelfth Night*:

> ...*some men are born great, some achieve greatness, and some have greatness thrust upon them.*

We can see that among our twenty 'great' characters from history, probably only three (the monarchs) were *born* great, whereas the remaining seventeen *achieved* greatness. In one case, Margaret Thatcher, there was an element of having greatness thrust upon her by her colleagues, and maybe Puccini, too, was lucky in having several powerful promoters (such as his publisher and his own mother) building his career for him in his earlier years. Thomas Hardy, also, was largely the creation of his mother. Without their accidents of royal birth Victoria and Wilhelm would have been nowhere in the celebrity stakes, whereas Alfred was so extraordinary he might well have been special anyway; although being born a member of the Wessex royal family certainly gave him the physical resources to put his specialness into effect.

Churchill, Nelson and Wellington, for example, were all driven to achieve greatness and all three succeeded in transforming themselves by sheer determination. In two of these cases they were assisted by external rebuffs –

Churchill's rebuffs from his father and Wellington's from the family of his fiancée. Their determination to prove that their detractors were wrong continued for years to provide them with powerful motivation to achieve.

I have argued that the behaviour of my subjects has often been influenced by unconscious motives and that these have frequently been irrational, where ideas and memories of relationships are linked through apparently tenuous associations. These associations take the form of both symbolism and contiguity, the two elementary mechanisms of magic, where one element is unconsciously associated with another either because of some shared attribute (e.g. authority in Victoria's case, nobility with Wellington, Englishness with Wilhelm, gender with Daphne, Rome with Sigmund Freud etc.) or because they have coincided in time or space (e.g. Puccini's Elvira with the death of his mother, Hitler's Geli and the death of his mother, and Freud's fear of trains and his seeing his mother naked on a train).

I suppose most of our high achievers can be described as narcissistic, although possibly Wellington, Jane Austen and Agatha Christie can be excluded from this category. Wellington concealed his narcissism behind studied humility. But I would say that only Adolf, and possibly Wilhelm, merit the label Narcissistic Personality Disorder. In my opinion there are two quite opposite causes of narcissism: parental (usually maternal) adulation (as with Freud and Hitler, for example) and parental apathy or rejection (as with Wagner and Wilhelm). In the first, the subject takes on his parent's high opinions of himself, whereas in the latter case he is forced to love himself because no one else does so. Narcissism is perhaps unique among psychological conditions in having these two quite opposite causes. Maybe both applied in Churchill's case because he had two quite different 'mothers'.

Raised Mood

We are left with the question: what causes great achievement generally? I feel one answer is *raised mood*. Mood is a big issue but frequently a neglected one, in biography. Admittedly, depression is often touted as an explanation for dark ideas and suicide (usually correctly) but not for its more subtle behavioural effects – indecisiveness, loss of interest, lack of drive, irritability, low self-esteem, rumination, loss of concentration, and failure generally. Such factors are probably relevant in explaining Hitler's years of degradation after his mother's death, the habit of deep thought in Einstein, Turing and Newton, the grumpiness of Verdi, and the self-seclusion of Victoria. Yet depression on its own rarely produces creative results. In high achievers there have to be occasional upturns in mood, as well, and the relevance of these is usually not recognised by biographers. Most of us have slight upturns of mood, revealed by our cheerfulness when something good has happened to us – we have had good news, rejoined an old friend, produced a child or won a prize, for example. Just as depression is so often precipitated by *loss*, so elevated mood can be provoked by *gain*. But many achievers experience 'highs' in mood that are either more extreme or more sustained than most peoples' and, sometimes, can occur out of the blue. In psychiatry, the most extreme highs are usually regarded as a form of mental disorder and are labelled *mania*. Mania is, in text book language, described as:

> *...elevation of mood, increased energy, over-activity, pressure of speech, reduced sleep, loss of normal social or sexual inhibitions... euphoria, anger... flamboyant dressing, unkempt (appearance)... flight of ideas... inflated views of his or her own importance and grandiose ideas... suspiciousness... delusions... (and) auditory or visual delusions.* (BKP 107)

When people alternately show both depression and manic episodes they are usually said to have Bipolar Disorder (or Manic Depression). Such conditions are readily treatable and I am not saying that any of the subjects in this book have been sufferers. But several have shown signs of *elevated moods* that do not progress to the extremes of mania. This is a more common condition, sometimes called *hypomania* (or lesser mania) by psychiatrists, and I suspect it is the secret ingredient in the lives of most, if not all, high achievers. At least half of the cases in this book are known to have had prolonged episodes of raised mood, especially when young. Many may choose to regard hypomania as merely an illness but I see it as the extreme end of the *elevation of normal mood*, so I propose to use the terms 'hypomania' and 'raised' or 'elevated mood' interchangeably.

The psychiatric textbook describes *hypomania* as:

- A distinct period of persistently elevated, expansive or irritable mood, lasting throughout at least 4 days, (with) at least three of the following...
- Inflated self-esteem or grandiosity
- Decreased need for sleep
- Pressure of talk
- Flight of ideas
- Distractibility
- Increased goal-driven activity
- Excessive involvement in pleasurable activities...e.g. buying sprees, sexual adventures or risky business undertakings.

(BKP 109)

In elevated mood (hypomania) there are clearly several features that predispose towards high achievement. First and foremost is the high level of *activity generally* (e.g. items 2,3,4,6 and 7 above). This provides the necessary levels of high drive to do whatever it is that the achiever does (write, compose, politics, science, business, warfare, etc.) The hypomanic, or person experiencing raised mood, requires less sleep than most people and never seems to tire. Also of interest are the *flights of ideas* and the *goal-directed behaviour* that are experienced in raised mood – these constitute the essence of creativity itself whether through writing, art, music, science or in other ways. The achiever channels all this intellectual energy into his or her chosen field of activity. He or she has harnessed all the raised energy that they are feeling within themselves and is putting it to good use. By 'flights of ideas' is meant an accelerated stream of thoughts in an active consciousness which is full of a wide range of concepts. The association of previously separated ideas is crucial to creativity. These associations can occur by noticing obscure but genuine connections or similarities, or through the characteristic use of clang associations (similarities in sound), alliteration, puns (double meanings) or other word plays. One idea leads on to another in quick succession and sometimes such flights of ideas are converted straight into words, providing 'pressure of talk'. I would say, however, that a feature of high achievers is that they can conceal their hypomania generally, and suppress their pressure of talk, converting their flights of ideas straight into the medium of their achievement, whether as science, business, art, or other outlet. The energy and intellectual arousal of raised mood is characteristically masked and controlled by the high achiever, but it is still there.

Let me stress again that I am not, in this context, using the word *hypomania* to describe mental illness but to indicate raised moods that a small but significant part of the human race can utilise in order to deal with stress and to achieve great things. Raised mood is an important but underestimated part of normal behaviour for a minority of individuals. I would put into this category at least ten out of the twenty high achievers described in this book.

At least four major biochemicals affect mood – serotonin, dopamine, noradrenaline and the endorphins – and all are connected with the work of the brain's Reticular Activating and Limbic systems. This is not the place to examine the engines of raised mood, however. I am merely postulating that a minority of people can react to stress by consistently raising their mood. As I have said, at least half of the high achievers dealt with in this book appear to me to be in this category. The lifetime experience of hypomania in the American population has been reckoned to be between 0.4 and 3.5 per cent. Whatever the real figure, it is likely that the creativity and achievement that come from sustained raised mood (hypomania) is quite rare in the general population. Sometimes such behaviour is wrongly attributed to drugs or drunkenness or hyper-thyroidism. So it is probably undercounted. Nevertheless, I would guess that no more than 5.0 per cent of all adults ever experience prolonged raised mood (or hypomania). The behaviour it provokes is, however, very much what the layman, in the past, would have called 'genius'. Sometimes, when it is publicly displayed, as in the case of Hitler's oratory, the profusion of ideas and the gen-eral arousal gives the overall impression of very high intelligence. The hypo-manic himself also believes he must be very intelligent. He feels so full of ideas compared with the slow-witted people around him that hypomania natu-rally leads to narcissism – the hypomanic feels intellectually superior. But al-though hypomania naturally encourages narcissism, narcissism does not always imply hypomania. Moreover, intelligence and hypomania, although correlated, are not the same. The volcanic eruption of ideas that is found in hypomania can throw up far more slag than gold. Unless the hypomanic shows self-disci-pline and judgement in filtering and testing his ideas against reason and reality, he will come a cropper. Ideally, the high achiever needs elevated moods that are moderately sustained if he is to harness them successfully.

Today, the effects of hypomania are mimicked by stimulants such as cocaine and amphetamine. Nevertheless, I believe that most high achievers have this rare natural elevated mood potential. Unlike with the hypomanic *patient*, pre-sented for treatment because of the unguardedness of their outbursts, or the ob-vious damage they have caused to themselves or to others, the high achiever uses his excess energy to good effect. He can remain outwardly calm and in control. Like a good driver he uses the power of his sports car's engine to get to predetermined places. Connecting many of the teeming ideas in his head he only publicly proclaims the connections that seem to really work. I suspect this was the case with Freud, Wellington, Dickens, Einstein, Turing, Newton, Nel-son and Hitler. In Churchill's case his flights of ideas would often erupt at Cab-inet meetings causing exasperation among some of his more staid colleagues. Usually by nightfall the ideas had been evaluated by officials and most, but not all, would have been discarded. I believe our subjects would never have become celebrities if they had not had access to this turbocharger of raised mood. Most probably the turbocharger has a genetic basis. Even Victoria's youthful high spirits seem to have been born into her, perhaps with her grandfather's (George III's) manic genes.

We must also note the motivating effect of rebuff. The three clearest cases are Churchill and Freud (who were both rebuffed by their fathers and told they would become wastrels) and Wellington (who was forbidden by Lord Longford to marry his sister). All three grew up determined to prove that their detractors were wrong. Dickens also felt terribly slighted by his sojourn in the blacking factory. Hitler, too, once service in the German army had helped him to overcome his depression, may well have had his urge to achieve further fuelled by the memory of his rejections by the Academy of Arts in Vienna, just as Verdi never forgot his rejection by the Milan Conservatory. Daphne du Maurier, too, was crucially rebuffed: her first lesbian lover (Ferdy) scoffed at her early short stories and said she could not see that Daphne would ever write anything worthwhile (MF 67).

Such rebuffs have unpredictable effects, of course. In some cases they can merely increase despondency and failure. Hypomanic resilience (as with all these male examples) is probably essential in generating a successful positive reaction.

One of the characteristics of hypomania (raised mood) is that it has an arousing effect on outsiders. In the presence of a hypomanic, people often feel excited by the hypomanic's so-called *charisma*. People felt like this in Wagner's presence and in Dickens', Nelson's and Hitler's. It is partly why Hitler's oratory was so arousing. People emerge from meetings with hypomanics feeling enthused and with their own mood elevated. Many composers manage to inject their hypomanic charisma directly into their music which, characteristically, also has this charismatic and uplifting quality.

The other characteristic of hypomania that is relevant to high achievers is their so-called '*goal-directed behaviour*'. This is, I would suggest, what happens when the hypomanic manages to *channel* his or her raised mental energies successfully. Goal directed behaviour not only includes art, music, politics, business and so on, but making friends, working hard at school, sexual activity, sporting endeavours, or anything else that involves the focussing of energy. Such a trait is found in most of our subjects, with the possible exception of Victoria in later life, by which time she had lost the high spirits of her youth. Hardly surprisingly, high achievers (and many celebrities in general) have this raised level of mood. It is their secret ingredient for success.

I hope I have managed to throw just a little light upon why some of our subjects did what they did, and revealed, in a few cases, why they became who they were.

SOURCES

Basant K. Puri: *Psychiatry*, W.B. Saunders, 2000.

Richard D. Ryder: *Nelson, Hitler and Diana: Studies in Trauma and Celebrity*, Imprint Academic, 2009.

Schultz, William Todd, editor, *Handbook of Psychobiography*, Oxford Univ. Press, 2005.

Index

INDEX